PENGUIN BOOKS
LEARNING HOW TO LEARN

Idries Shah was born in 1924 into a family that traces itself through the Prophet Mohammed and to the Sassanian Emperors of Persia and, beyond that, back to the year 122 B.C. – perhaps the oldest recorded lineage on earth. Shah is the author of many books, published throughout the world. Their subject matter ranges over travel, bibliography, literature, humour, philosophy and history, but their author is most prominent for his writings on Sufi thought as it applies to the cultures of both East and West. Despite the extraordinary success of these books, Shah refuses newspaper interviews and declines to play the role of a 'guru', preferring hard and silent work in his chosen *milieu* of thinkers and artists. He holds the Dictionary of International Biography's Certificate of Merit for Distinguished Service to Human Thought. In addition to *Learning How to Learn*, Penguin publish *Thinkers of the East* and *The Way of the Sufi*.

IDRIES SHAH

LEARNING
HOW TO LEARN

Psychology and Spirituality in the Sufi Way

With an introduction by Doris Lessing

Penguin Books

Penguin Books Ltd, Harmondsworth, Middlesex, England
Viking Penguin Inc., 40 West 23rd Street, New York, New York 10010, U.S.A.
Penguin Books Australia Ltd, Ringwood, Victoria, Australia
Penguin Books Canada Ltd, 2801 John Street, Markham, Ontario, Canada L3R 1B4
Penguin Books (N.Z.) Ltd, 182–190 Wairau Road, Auckland 10, New Zealand

First published by the Octagon Press, London, 1978
Published in the USA (with an introduction by Doris Lessing) by Harper & Row 1981
Published in Penguin Books 1985

Reproduced, printed and bound in Great Britain by
Hazell Watson & Viney Limited,
Member of the BPCC Group,
Aylesbury, Bucks
Typeset in Linotype Plantin

Take warning from the misfortunes of others, so that others need not have to take warning from your own.

– Saadi, *Rose Garden*
13th Century

When the camel of our efforts sinks into the mud, what matter whether the destination is near or far?

– Ustad Khalilullah Khalili,
Quatrains, 1975

The world has no being but an allegory:
From end to end its state is but a farce and play

– Shabistari, *Secret Garden*
13th Century

Contents

3

SUFI STUDY THEMES 91

Assumptions Behind Actions – Exercising Power through Kindness – Copying Virtue – Finding a Teacher – What is gained from Repetition – Robes and Apparatus of the Sufi – Why you are asked to Help – Laziness

4

THINGS OF THE WORLD

5

ACTION AND MEANING

8

SUFI STUDIES

Introduction

It was as recently as 1964 that Idries Shah's *The Sufis* appeared. It was evident that with this new classic on the subject, there had emerged the Exemplar who from time to time comes forward to offer the Sufi Way in new forms that fit modern needs. For Sufism is not the study of the past, or the worship of medieval saints; it is always, has ever been, evolutionary in spirit and action. The great Sufi classics of the Middle East, for instance, were once abrasively original, with new insights and information that shocked the hidebound.

Idries Shah has offered us many books, as many-faceted as Sufism has to be, from the re-issue of these classics, to jokes from the Nasrudin corpus, to printed university lectures, to traditional stories retold in fresh and sharpened language. *Learning How to Learn*, and others that Shah is writing now, in a modern format, pioneer where we, in our time, face the biggest challenges: human nature itself, how to understand our behaviour and our organisations and our cultures. Shah significantly calls anthropology and psychology the *infant* sciences; for he holds that we have hardly begun to use these tools.

It is now a commonplace that in the higher reaches of physics the same language and concepts as in traditional mysticism are used; but this common ground, this frontier, extends to include the new original thinking in psychology, anthropology, the religions, esotericism. Shah would like to aid this confluence. Specifically, he is offering the Sufic viewpoint, and – more than that – making available a stock of knowledge, of information. In our lifetime we shall see – are already beginning to see – our scientists, usually the younger ones, because of their greater flexibility, approaching Shah with the question: What do you have in your possession, as part of your tradition, that we modern researchers may use, that we may have overlooked or perhaps don't even suspect exists? I have seen this happen: a simple question opening up a new field.

Is it not worth our while to consider how it can have come about that what amounts to a treasure house of information, the results of centuries of research and skilled practice, can have existed so long without us being able to concede that it might be there? I am not talking about 'the secrets of the East', conceived of as something between Shamanism and tea-table spiritualism – what Shah dismissed as 'spills, thrills and chills'. There have always been travellers to the mystic East. 'Tell me, Master, what is the Secret?' 'Oh, you want a Secret, dear child, is that it? Well, stand on your head for a week, and chant this mantra . . .' But those of us who have tried to approach Sufism through what is offered to us in the West seem nearly always to have gone through something like that, and had to outgrow it: it is how we have been conditioned to think. What we find in the East is not the glamorous and the mystic but an approach to humanity, both as individuals and as an organic unity, that goes far beyond our own sciences, in conception and achievement – in sophistication.

How has this come about?

For one thing, perhaps the culture we inhabit is not the advanced, open-minded culture we believe it is. Outsiders, who have always been valuable in providing insights into societies, although they are always resisted at first, judge us differently.

We are judged as being fettered, and in many ways. We easily talk now of Western arrogance; we begin to know we are insular. But it is a slow business, for we have to contend, in the case of the Middle East and Central Asia, with the implanted results of hundreds of years of suspicion of the dreaded Saracen. This has had, still has, stultifying effects on our culture, from ignorance and bigotry about Islam, to something like this: that the symbols for the planets in astrology – Mars, Venus, Mercury and the rest – are no more than Arabic letters, easily recognisable as such to those who know Arabic. Yet we ascribe to them amazing origins. A tiny example, even an absurd one, of an enormous unmapped area. But why is it not being researched?

We may go on murmuring about Western complacency, but it is another thing actually to face it. Shah instances our belief that we in the West pioneered certain psychological ideas. But the 'discoveries' of Freud and Jung are to be found in Al Ghazzali and Ibn El Arabi, who died in the twelfth century, and in other great thinkers of the time. (Jung acknowledged his debt to the East. Is it not remarkable that his disciples are not curious about what else there might be?) Al Ghazzali wrote extensively about conditioning: then, as now, Sufi teachers were concerned about freeing people from social and religious indoctrinations. What happened to all that expertise? It was used. It became the property of doctors of the mind, of the soul, of the body; it has been built on, developed . . . But we, in the West, have been cut off from it – are still cut off from it, and will be until we are prepared to think hard about our own mental sets.

Another instance: we tell ourselves about our infinitely various and rich language. But the fact is that English is impoverished; it lacks words and concepts we need. Any writer who has tried to describe certain processes and experiences has come up against it: the absence of words. There are ways around it – analogy is one – but the problem remains. A handful of pitiful and worn terms – unconscious, soul, spirit, collective unconscious, super-mind, ego, super-ego, id, paranormal, ESP, super-nature – and suddenly, very soon, you've run into the sand. You cannot use these words for fresh experiences, new ideas, because each is loaded with unwanted associations. But other languages are not so barren; their words are not so overloaded. No, this is not an essay in disparagement of English, or in admiration of other tongues, for the sake of it, but a plea for recognition: if there is a desperate and urgent need for something, that need may be met. I hope so. Meanwhile, it is hard going. I am not a linguist, to put it mildly, but my tiniest acquaintance with Persian, for example, shows our own dreadful deprivation. But that is the language of a culture where certain kinds of spirituality were in active operation for hundreds of years. (The appearance of a manic bigot like Khomeini doesn't take that away.) Friends who study 'primitive' cultures and know the language of American Indians, or certain African societies, say that these, too, are well supplied with concepts that we lack. Our language is probably the best of tools for technical processes, as long as technical processes are still conceived of as being restricted to the mechanical, but when they impinge on the frontiers of the mind . . .

And there is another, Himalayan block, which we scarcely consider. It is that for 2,000 years the West has been under a most terrible tyranny, the Christian religion. (I am aware that at this point, readers are sighing, thinking vaguely, 'How very nineteenth century.') But it was, historically speaking, an extremely short time ago. I have met people who came into conflict with the churches, when all they wanted was to opt out of certainties and dogma into agnosticism. Wives and husbands left them, they lost jobs, were socially ostracised, were cast off from families – and went to the colonies. There I met them, as a child. Now the churches have a benevolent, harmless aspect, half social agency, half genial bully; they cajole people into thinking that they really have to be born again, or *belong* to something or other. But for 2,000 years we were kept in a mental straitjacket, and even the most limited rebellion was horribly punished. Luther's was limited. He said, I insist on the right to talk with God directly, without the mediation of the church. He did not say, For many thousands of years

9

there have been people in this world who have had the techniques, the information, to enable those with sufficient preparation to make use of these tools, to achieve states of mind, or of spirit, that the churches know nothing about. (But at this point I have to make it clear that Sufism respects all religions, saying that the Truth is at the core of each. It is the tyrant, benevolent or wicked, who has to be exposed.) What I would like to know is this: how is it that, undertanding that our culture has had two millennia of a certain kind of indoctrination, we, our scientists, are not researching the effects on our mental processes? For these effects are there; once you begin thinking on these lines, they are very evident. It is as if the ban, the ukase, the *no* of the churches into thinking about, for instance, what Jesus and his associates were really thinking (for the Sufis claim Jesus as one of the real Teachers of mankind, whose message has been obliterated by institutions) had been absorbed into the very stuff of our minds, making it impossible for us to look in certain directions.

And this *no* can operate in the minds of scientists as strongly as in anyone's.

What I am sketchily, inadequately, outlining here is a whole series of blocks and impediments that amount to a mental prison. Well, the Sufis say we live in such a prison, and it is their concern to give us the equipment to free ourselves. We are all *conditioned*, as we now claim so easily and trippingly; but perhaps being able to *say* that it is not enough to enable us to see how.

If we want to approach the Sufis, their ways of looking at life, at some point it is necessary to swallow the unpalatable fact that they think of us as backward, barbarian, ill-equipped, ill-informed, and primitive, with closed minds in areas where it is vital to our futures that we open them.

Meanwhile, Shah most patiently answers the questions he has been asked, waiting and hoping for questions that are more educated, more sophisticated, based on better information and self-understanding.

He gets thousands of letters from everywhere, for he is not a Western more than an Eastern figure, and people from Afghanistan to California ask about the Sufi Way. From these questions and answers he has compiled this book, which is so full of useful viewpoints and information that I cannot do more than draw attention to ideas that may be found profitable starting points.

Attention. Shah devotes a full section to it, so important does he consider it, and so indifferent are we to it. In our society we are not taught about attention as a need, as fundamental as food; and we go blundering about, seeking ways to assuage the craving, instead of learning how to provide ourselves with what we need, sensibly and calmly. We feed the hunger blindly, telling ourselvess we are seeking God or Love or Service; and we are not taught to recognise the drive in others, and how we are used and manipulated by them. Once the mechanism is brought to our attention and we begin to study it, it is as if a veil had been stripped off ordinary life, and we become freer in our actions, our choices.

Knowledge, 'God', as a commodity. Conditioned to the commercial, to having, wanting, trading, buying, selling, we treat everything in this way, including what Shah has to offer. But 'higher knowledge' is not a commodity, to be bought and sold.

The uses of literature. Here Shah is revolutionary. The Sufis know and use dozens of techniques, while we believe there is one. Our teaching in schools and colleges is based on simplistic ideas that take no account of the variations from hour to hour of the human mind. We Westerners demand a standardised product, says Shah: it is what we prize. But the standardised and mass-produced is not what interests him or his associates, who teach individuals, in individual ways.

The human group – its dynamics. Psychologists are indeed studying this subject, so vital to our society, and to all our associations. Shah has a good deal to contribute; the human group is what the Sufis work with, and their sophistication goes beyond anything we approach.

Emotionalism. Shah does not hesitate to make the claim, infuriating to religionists everywhere, that nearly all we claim as 'religion', as 'higher feelings', as 'mystical experience', is no more than emotionalism. We are taught that there are emotions and intellect, but not that there is something else possible, beyond both and not to be confused with either.

Exposing delusions.

Using religions, cults, sects, 'God', to satisfy power drives, the need for togetherness, to provide substitutes for the family, sex.

How to recognise false teachers and self-appointed Sufis. They proliferate, and delude unfortunate people who could be saved from them by the use of a little logical thought and some common sense.

Many words and concepts have fallen out of real use. Reading this book, we are forced to recognise that in our scientifically-oriented, materialistic culture, words like humility, pride, greed, love, idolatry, charity, tend to be disposed of into areas labelled 'religion' or 'ethics'. Shah rescues them, strips them of sentiment and vague emotion, and re-introduces them – as tools.

Abjure the *why* and seek the *how*, as one Sufi, the explorer Richard Burton, put it. Well, this book is about how we, individually and collectively, may learn to look at ourselves and our institutions differently. And if what we are being taught is unexpected and sometimes disconcerting, then that is in the great tradition too.

DORIS LESSING

'Beginning to Begin'

by Idries Shah

UNTIL only a few years ago, as literary people, psychologists and the increasing number of those engaged in studying human consciousness now so often remind us, Sufism was a closed book for the ordinary person. Its language, in the form found in its classical and technical writings, seemed almost impenetrable. Orientalists (now more correctly renamed Specialists in the Human Sciences in Asia and Africa) maintained a near-monopoly of information on the subject and yet could be found extensively disagreeing as to what Sufism was, how and where it started, and what its teachings meant. Some Islamic workers were against it: others claimed it as the true essence of Islam. Some non-Muslim observers were powerfully attracted to it, others found it too culture-bound for their liking.

The publication of Sufi stories stripped of didactic overlay and much verbiage, together with studies of Sufi psychological work and perhaps above all the observed analogies with current social and cultural concerns, has changed this picture quite dramatically. It is now generally accepted that Sufi research and experience during the past thousand years has been one of the most promising areas of development in the direction of understanding man and indicating his perceptions of extra-dimensional reality. But it was not until people, mainly in the West, began to note the congruence of religious and psychological, esoteric and cultural, thinking that a more holistic approach to the subject could develop.

Meanwhile, of course, laggards in science still regard Sufism as mysterious esotericism; cultists still want to preserve this aura; a few scholars wish to produce a monopoly by claiming that their interpretations alone are authoritative; the latter sometimes presenting a spectacle resembling that of the alchemist opposing chemistry because he does not understand it.

13

The work of displaying the many-sidedness and current relevance of Sufism has not been difficult, given two prerequisites: freedom to publish and a growing dissatisfaction, in many cultures, with hidebound and ignorant authority. All that has been needed has been to quote, from legitimate Sufi sources, including documents, teachings which show the scientific, as well as the religious, interest; to demonstrate, from the same sources, that the psychological insights of the Sufis have proved a source of continuing knowledge which is not inferior to the achievements of modern workers in the field of the mind. In addition, the 'discovery' of the Sufis by several such workers of undeniable importance, and the existence of a living Sufi tradition aside from repetitious cultism and the other deteriorated elements made it rapidly possible – within the span of a decade – for several workers to provide materials which have verified much of the true nature of the Sufi heritage and to confirm its continuing operation.

It has been objected, of course, that the 'popularisation' of Sufi materials might alienate many people from the ancient traditions and values which it is held by some to represent. In actual fact, the reverse has been true. In one publication after another, even traditionalist and formal scholars, as well as many others – in East and West – have eagerly accepted the recent reclaiming of the meaning of the materials: and the number of people interested has enormously increased. To disdain these newcomers because they are not always professional orientalists or cultists (still too many people are both) is to fail to observe that many of them are at least as intelligent, well-informed and potentially useful in human research as the 'specialists'. One of the saddest things, in fact, about the reaction in some quarters against the revelation of fresh insights into the essential Sufism has been the displaying of almost primitive and quite stupefying bigotry and small-mindedness in circles where these characteristics are prejudicial to the honour of the learned calling and dangerous to the likelihood that such people will continue to be taken seriously by those whose respect means so much to them.

In brief, Sufism has 'arrived' in the minds of people in the more flexible and increasingly interesting areas of contemporary thought. It has also become a part of the experience and interest of some of today's more distinguished people throughout the world. It is operating widely, in cross-disciplinary and general areas, as a factor whose value and contribution can neither be denied nor arrested. What has happened is that more people are prepared to study perennial truth apart from local manifestations and derivative sociological forms of mainly anthropological value.

Traditionally, Sufi understanding has relied heavily upon question-and-answer. The following pages, extracted to give a cross-section of materials elicited during hundreds of hours of talks, relate to many of the subjects which interest such a very large number of people today. The hundred conversations also represent answers to questions which have been asked again and again in a postbag of more than forty thousand letters, from all over the world.

In spite of the enormous demand for Sufi thought to be presented only in terms of familiar attitudes and local cultural expression, it would be unfair, both to the Sufis and those who might learn from them, to attempt putting this quart into a pint pot.

Sufi thought and action requires its own formats in which to manifest and operate: it is for this reason that it has always, in the past and in its several areas of expression, established and maintained its own institutions and teaching centres. But the modern Western atmosphere, however much it may have neglected to develop such formats for itself, is nowadays much more than formerly prepared to accept the hypothesis that there might be a form of learning which is presented, concentrated and disseminated through characteristic and specialised institutions. It is only where we get people imagining that the outward form of such institutions, suited to one place or age, is both suitable for here and now, and also representative of the thing itself, that the onus is on us to point out the fact that such opinions are limited and limiting. They disable those who hold them from understanding in the same way that the yokel in the Sufi tale could not benefit from his bowl of liquid soup because 'all soup has lumps in it'.

There was once a man who opened a restaurant, with a good kitchen, attractive tables and an excellent menu.

One of his friends came along soon afterwards, and said:

'Why have you not got a sign, like all the other eating-places? I suggest that you put on it "RESTAURANT: FINEST FOOD".'

When the sign was painted and put up, another enquirer asked:

'You have to be more specific – you might mean *any* old restaurant. Add the words "SERVED HERE" and your sign will be complete.'

The owner thought that this was a good idea, and he had the signboard duly altered.

Not long afterwards someone else came along and said:

'Why do you put "HERE"? Surely anyone can see *where* the place is?'

So the restaurateur had the sign changed.

Presently a further curious member of the public wanted to know:

'Do you not know that the word "SERVED" is redundant? All restaurants and shops serve. Why not take it out?'

So that word was taken out.

Now another visitor said:

'If you continue to use the phrase "FINEST FOOD", some people will be sure to wonder whether it really *is* the finest, and some will not agree. To guard against criticism and contention, please do remove the word "Finest".'

And so he did. Now, just the word "FOOD" was to be seen on the notice, and a sixth inquisitive individual put his head through the doorway. 'Why have you got the word "FOOD" on your restaurant: anyone can see that you serve food here.'

So the restaurateur took down the sign. As he did so, he could not help wondering when somebody who was hungry, rather than curious or intellectual, would come along . . .

In this tale, of course, the restaurateur is plagued by the literal-mindedness of the 'people of reason'; for whom, as for all of us, intellect plays a valuable part. The food which our man is trying to provide, however, is the 'food of the heart'; where the heart stands in Sufi parlance for the higher perceptive faculties of humankind.

Our contemporary Sufi poet, Professor Khalilullah Khalili, my most illustrious compatriot, puts it like this:

In every state, the Heart is my support:
In this kingdom of existence it is my sovereign.
When I tire of the treachery of Reason –
God knows I am grateful to my heart . . .*

Idries Shah
1978

*Persian *Quatrains of Ustad Khalilullah Khalili*, trilingual, Baghdad:
Al-Maarif Press, 1975, 22/23.

1

Real and Imagined Study

Sufis and their Imitators

Q: What can you do about imitators? It has been observed that, since you started to make Sufism known really widely in the West, numerous small groups have been enlarged, and entirely new ones have sprung up – and most people realise that these are just cults, and not Sufi groups at all.

THE SMALL BOY AND THE EXAMINATION

A: That reminds me of a joke. It is said that a small boy was faced with an examination question: 'What is rabies and what can you do about it?' He wrote as his answer: 'Rabies is Jewish priests, and there is *nothing* you can do about it!'

These Sufis are Sufists, not Sufis, and there is nothing that you can do about it. I am, however, interested in an inherent assumption: the one behind the question – that one should either have to do anything about it, or that one *could*, indeed, do anything about it ... If we do try to do anything about it, we risk attracting large numbers of disenchanted former Sufists, who would hope at first that we could give them THE REAL THING – but who would become doubly homeless, so to speak, when they found that one branch of the entertainment industry had closed down, and another failed to open up!

Sufi studies in the West and in the contemporary East, it should be remembered, are repeating a pattern.* Throughout the ages there have been Sufis and imitators. Perhaps, to clarify things in your own mind, you might like to ask yourself this question: 'Why do I imagine that there is any activity that does not have imitators, charlatans, confusion and "tourists" and passengers?' People do not find that they can do anything about tricksters or

*Not only do humorous tales contain valuable structures for understanding. Their use also helps to weed out people who lack a sense of humour. Sufis hold that people who have not developed or who have suppressed their capacity to enjoy humour are, in this deprived state, also without learning capacity in the Sufi sphere.

cranks who offer a trip to the Moon – except to increase public information on spaceflight.

I cannot help feeling that the questioner is defining his own mentality and showing us that he is thinking in a more confined way than his limitations require.

If we can do anything about the imitation, it is to spread the information of the real. But our doing this depends upon the audience being prepared. The preparation involves a wideness of horizon and the intelligent use of the clear thinking methods which are already current in all present-day societies, though only lately coming into use in our area of interest.

The negative attitude is to look at the imitators. The positive one, surely, is to remember the words of Jalaluddin Rumi, who said that false gold only exists because there is such a thing as the Real . . .

JAMI AND THE EXTERNALS

Both imitators and the followers of previous formulations whose externals alone persist can be reminded, especially if they read the Sufi classics, that externals are not the same as content. It is in this vein that the great teacher Jami speaks, in his *Baharistan,* 'The Abode of Spring':

The rose is gone from the garden, what can I do with the thorns and leaves?

The Shah is not in the city, what shall I do with his court?

The attractions are the cage: beauty and goodness the parrot.

When the parrot has flown, what can I do with the cage?

ANALOGY OF THE FUR JACKET

In *Fihi ma Fihi* we find the allegory of the jacket. 'In Winter,' says Rumi, 'you look for a fur garment, but when summer comes you have no time for it, it is an encumbrance. So it is with imitations of real teachings. They keep people warm until the time comes when they can be warmed by the Sun . . .'

So, like the fur garment, people will cleave to cults and

imitations because these things suit them, respond to something within them which calls for cults and imitations.

At the same time, of course, they imagine all sorts of things about themselves, such as that they are genuine, sincere, unconcerned about themselves and concerned about others or about truth.

SHIBLI AND THE STONES

In a famous instance, recorded for instance in the *Ilahi-Nama* of Hakim Sanai, the Sufi teacher Shibli of Khurasan made this self-deception a matter of illustration-teaching in a dramatic event which he initiated.

Because of his extravagant utterances, disliked by the authorities, Shibli was chained up as a madman. A number of people who respected him went to him on a visit, enquiring about his welfare. He asked them who they considered themselves to be, and they answered that they were his friends.

At this Shibli hurled stones at them, and they ran away.

Shibli shouted: 'You say that you are my friends, thinking of me! But I have shown you that you flee from my affliction, and hence you are concerned not for me, but for your own protection from stones!'

TO RECEIVE WHAT IS NOT IN YOUR DESTINY

Besides, we should bear in mind the teaching of the great sage Abu'l Hasan Khirqani, recorded in Attar's *Recitals of the Saints:*

'The people of the world have a fixed destiny. But the spiritually developed receive what is *not* in their destiny.'

Q: What is the harm in imitating? I am sure that most, if not all, of the human development systems which are publicly offered are only imitations. If, however, these give people pleasure and some taste of a deeper reality, they surely must have a value?

THE KNOTS STANDING IN THE WAY OF THE TEXTILES

A: If you take an analogy, you might see it differently. Supposing we were discussing the art of weaving which might be developed. Supposing people were at a stage where they could only tie knots in string, which gave them pleasure and might be regarded as a foretaste of weaving. If the people only imitated the knotting phase, and in addition regarded the knotting as the entire art – when would weaving itself come into being, no matter how much pleasure there was attached to it? Certainly, knotting would have a value as such: but it would also constitute a barrier to going further if the idea of anything further were 'abolished' by people thinking that knots were as far as anyone could go in textile work.

There are two points worth noting here.

The first is that 'pleasure' certainly is not to be opposed, but there are many sources of pleasure, and to seek pleasure as a part of something more specific leads to confusion and more.

The second is that if you get obsessed by the early stages of something, imagining it to be the whole, you will not go further.

THE WOMAN AND THE SPIRITUAL BEING

Look at the ancient tale of the woman and the spiritual being.

There was once a poor woman who helped a spiritual being disguised as a wanderer from far away, giving him hospitality when others had cast him out. As he left her house, he said: 'May your first task tomorrow last all day!'

She thought that this was a strange way of thanking someone, but soon forgot.

The following day a merchant brought her a short length of gold thread and asked her to embroider it onto a garment, for embroidery was her work, when she could get any.

She unwound the gold and embroidered the cloth. When she had finished, she saw that there was more gold thread on the floor than she had started out with.

The more she wound it up into a ball the more there was. She wound gold thread all day, and by nightfall she had an enormous quantity. By tradition, left over thread belonged to the embroidress.

She sold this thread and with the money she was able to rebuild her house and furnish it, as well as setting herself up with a fine shop.

Naturally the neighbours became curious, and she told them how her luck had changed, and what had caused it.

Some time later, a merchant in the same town saw and recognised the 'stranger with magical powers' from what the woman had said about him and invited him into his shop and home. He showed the spiritual being great hospitality, imitating the way in which open-handed people behave; even carrying his attentiveness to extremes.

He thought: 'There must be something in this for me – and of course for everyone in this town.' He added the second phrase to his thoughts because, although greedy, he imagined that just to think of others would get him something for himself. Because, however, he was imitating charity, and because he did not think of the good of others equally with his own good but only as an afterthought, things turned out differently for him than for the charitable woman.

When the stranger was about to leave, the merchant said:

'Give me a blessing.'

'I do not do that,' said the stranger, 'but I wish that your first concern today should endure for a week.'

He went on his way and the merchant set off for his counting-house, where he proposed to count money, multiplying it for a whole week.

On the way across his own courtyard, the merchant stopped for a drink of water at his well. No sooner had he pulled up one bucketful than he found himself compelled to draw another, and another, and this went on for an entire week.

The water flooded his house, then that of the neighbours, and finally the whole town, almost causing it to collapse . . .

Attaining Knowledge

Q: How can I attain knowledge of myself? I look at organisations and institutions, such as schools or universities, or business enterprises or professions, and I can see that they have established reputations. They also have enrolment and recruitment, and they have objectives. For instance, if I become a politician I am aiming for cabinet rank; if I want to study medicine it is in order to become a practising doctor or a research worker or a teacher. When I approach Sufi ideas, whether through books or individuals, I find that a similar kind of coherence is not there: or if it is, I cannot find it. I often become confused, and I have met many other people who are also confused, who are trying the same thing. Because of this I also feel that an answer to this question would be of great value to many other people who believe that there must be truth and value in Sufi thought and activity, because it has continually produced great people, but that the 'way in' and the curricula are baffling.

A: It is interesting, not as a lesson in what Sufis are like, or what the Sufi enterprise is about, to look at these words, for they display, very clearly, what people are like, and we will see in a moment, how easily one can answer them by using materials, analogies and ways of thought which they would have been able to use for themselves if they had really been as analytical and coherent as they imagine they are.

First it must be said that it is precisely because someone thinks like this that he is baffled. He has arbitrarily selected parallels and assumptions, and seeks to apply them to us. Interestingly, he had misapplied them, with the result that he arrives at what he could even have subconsciously sought, confusion.

One traditional way of answering this question would be to quote the proverb: 'However fast you run, or however skilfully, you can't run away from your own feet.'

We will go through the analogies, and show how they apply to us just as much as to anyone or anything else cited.

First of all, it is not for us to satisfy each and every would-be student about Sufi applicability to himself and Sufic probity or otherwise. It is for him to satisfy himself; and he will probably use the same methods he uses when he applies to learn anything else. But he should remember that if he goes, for instance, to a school of medicine and asks: 'How do I know that you can teach me?' he will be shown the door. He is not eligible. Such an approach is neither correct behaviour nor indicative of a stage of intelligence in which one can be taught. There are plenty of people who do not adopt the attitude of an idiot, and it is the duty of the medical school to give its limited time to such people. It is someone else's task to do the more preliminary work with you. One function of the books already published is to provide this briefing.

Secondly, the reputation of the Sufis is already well enough established, and continues in that role from a base of repute which they established even long before numerous contemporary institutions existed. Sufic continued flexibility, viability and effectiveness (if you must measure in this way) are themselves evidences of their value in terms of the levels on which such things are assessed in the familiar world.

The coexistence of genuine Sufic enterprises and imitation ones only parallels similar imitations of almost every other kind of institution in the world. It is no new thing, and it has virtually the same characteristics and origins.

Thirdly, the idea of 'enrolment and recruitment' naturally varies with the kind of institution. The enrolment and recruitment of, say, bank clerks differs from that of, say, soldiers. People may become bank clerks and find that they are not suited for banking life. They may become politicians and discover that they *are* suited to this life. They may enrol as deep-sea divers and discover that deep-sea diving is not what they thought it was, in spite of plenty of divers around, sufficient schools, and an abundance of literature on the subject. What are you seeking from Sufi studies or activity which differs from these things?

Fourthly, of course, there is the question which comes under the heading of objectives. Suppose you want to be a politician: nobody would say that you could become a Cabinet Minister before you were perhaps a leg-man for a minor parliamentary candidate, or an envelope-licker in Party HQ, or even a canvasser for an obscure Rural District Council Member. The objective, again, may be to be a Cabinet Minister or a Prime Minister. How many people who at the beginning of their political careers: (a) know what it is like to be a Prime Minister, even if they are aiming for it; (b) really will become a Prime Minister? In any case, the people who do attain such rank are the ones who obey the Chinese proverb 'The journey of a thousand miles starts with a single step'.

Fifthly, as to confusion: people frequently become confused either because they cannot understand the elementary steps they have to take, or because they invariably enjoy confusion, or for some other reason which they do not know. The origins of a state of confusion can often be discovered merely by transposing the problem into terms whose structure is more familiar, as I have just done.

Among the Sufis, as among those of other paths, it has always been required that the intending participant practise certain requirements to fit him or her for higher learning. In modern societies, equivalent and often exactly similar prerequisites are found. Because so many familiar institutions with clearly laid out requirements already exist in contemporary cultures, it should be easier, not more difficult, for people to understand, given real desire, the requirements. These include: humility, dedication, abstinence, restraint, obedience. Unless you exercise these 'virtues', you will get nowhere in banking, the Army, medicine, politics, human service or anywhere else in many forms of mundane endeavour. If, on the other hand, you want to escape these tiresome preliminaries and flee into Sufism, then we know what you are like, and we cannot talk to you at all. 'To say "yes" to the Sufi way is to say "no" to imagined escapes.'

It is no accident that Sufis find that they can connect most constructively with people who are well integrated into the world, as well as having higher aims, and that those who adopt a sensible attitude towards society and life as generally known can usually absorb Sufi teachings very well indeed.

You started your question with the matter of the visibility of study institutions. But the world itself, as well as special attitudes, properly understood, constitute the Sufi school. Remember the words of Maghribi, who said to a monkish individual: 'What you are seeking in your retreat/I see clearly in every road and alley-way'.

It is no use adding external things, say observances – to the life of someone who is carrying on too many unproductive observances. It is hopeless to add ideas to minds already too full of ideas. Study institutions may become visible when the head is more emptied of imaginings.

SAADI AND THE MAN WITH A FULL HEAD

Saadi has a tale about a man, whose head was full of imagined knowledge and arrogance as a result, who went to visit Koshyar, from a great distance. Koshyar taught him nothing, saying: 'You may think yourself wise, but nothing can be put into a full pot.'

If you are full of pretence, Saadi continues, you are in fact empty. Become empty of fruitless ideas, he teaches, so that you may come and fill with higher perceptions, and understand real meaning.

There is a widespread notion in non-traditional societies such as the current Western one, that their scientific base causes the people to think, for some reason, in a way different from that of 'ancient' or 'Eastern' peoples. Anthropologists, interestingly enough, have pointed out that human thinking habits are everywhere very similar, and that the models and assumptions used by, say, the Africans of old and the Europeans and Americans are not at all different. The fact that this expert information has not filtered down to general knowledge is in itself an indication of the conten-tion of, for example, R. Horton, who commented on the un-examined assumptions of Western and African people thus:

'The (Western) layman's ground for accepting the models pro-pounded by the scientist is often no different from the young African villager's ground for accepting the models propounded by one of his elders. In both cases the propounders are deferred to as the accredited agents of tradition. As for the rules which guide scientists themselves in the acceptance or rejection of models, these seldom become part of the intellectual equipment of members of the wider population. For all the apparent up-to-dateness of the content of his world-view, the modern Western layman is rarely more 'open' or scientific in his outlook than is the traditional African villager.'*

Knowledge of yourself may involve, if we are learning at the present time, a knowledge of the way of thinking of your society, and to realise that you are probably its product, and that this knowledge can be attained in fact by such anthropological and psychological observations made by the Sufis in the course of their teaching how to assume new and more promising extra perspectives.

This involves knowing more through knowing oneself; knowing oneself through knowing how one thinks about others; and 'seeing yourself with other eyes than your own' – all ways of applying the lessons which so far in the West are mainly only being pointed out, and are not linked with attempts to further one's perceptions of what lies beyond familiar consciousness.

The statement 'He who knows himself, knows his Lord' means, among other things, that self-deception prevents knowledge. The question asks about how to attain knowledge of oneself. The first self about which to attain knowledge, is the secondary, essentially false, self which stands in the way, however useful it may be for many daily transactions. It must be set aside, made something which can be used or not used: not something which uses you.

The way in which this is done is by self-observation: registering how and when this self is operating, and how it deceives. A man once remarked, in the hearing of the Sufi ancient Junaid of Baghdad that at that time it had become difficult to find brothers.

HOW TO FIND YOUR BROTHERS

Junaid instantly identified the onesidedness of this attitude. 'If you seek a brother to share your burden, brothers are in truth hard to find. But if you are in search of someone whose own burden you will yourself share, there is no scarcity of such brothers,' he said.

*R. Horton: *African traditional thought and Western science*, in: *Africa*, 37, 1967, International African Institute.

ANSARI ON LOOKING AT YOURSELF

You want to be able to evaluate institutions of the Sufis. You want to gain knowledge of yourself. You can do the former when you have done the latter. Sheikh Abdullah Ansari, of Herat, in common with all classical Sufi teachers, insists that you must see yourself other than with your own eye, that is to say, apart from your present way of looking at things, or your fixation with this secondary self will only increase in strength and blot out objective understanding.

ANALOGY OF THE GARDENER

Until you can see yourself clearly and constantly for what you are really like, you have to rely upon the assessment of a teacher: the 'gardener' of Rumi's comparison:

'A gardener going into an orchard looks at the trees. He knows that this one is a date, that one a fig, the other a pomegranate, a pear or an apple. To do this, he does not have to see the fruit, only the trees.'*

DIFFICULTIES

Q: What are the difficulties in the way of transmitting knowledge today in the West?

A: Very little different in essence, though different in appearance, from the difficulties at all times. To understand this you have to obtain some perspective.

If, in the Middle Ages in Western Europe, you had preached, say, hygiene, what would have happened to you? You would have been seen as heretical, for a start – because only infidels washed. You would have been castigated by reputable people for assuming that you were better than they were, because you washed and they didn't. If you taught about microbes, would you have got away with it? If you used *their* mass-media, you would have been accused of immodesty and worse; if you tried to set up your own, you would be accused of sinister intentions or worse...

*Fihi ma Fihi ('In it what is in It'), by Jalaluddin Rumi Balkhi.

And – equally important – who would listen to you? The freaks, the occultists, the failures who were out to find a short-cut to success ... Not the people who were to become the authorities on hygiene ... Much preliminary groundwork would have to be done, explaining assumptions, proving that bias was not reality, living down unwarranted mud-slinging.

RISE ABOVE YOUR OWN BARRIER

The great Sufi poet Hafiz says, and how rightly, that the difficulties are within people, for they imagine things which are really irrelevant to be important in this search: 'You yourself are your own barrier – rise from within it.'

THE PRIEST AND THE PUBLIC

People mistake information for knowledge, and one indication for another. This is mainly because they generally do not know what they want, and often think that they want something when they do not. This difficulty besets all kinds of activities in the West.

I have recently been talking to the priest in charge of a church in a new town development. He had carried out a careful poll of what his new parishioners wanted, what kinds of sermons, how they are to be delivered, what subjects they were interested in. This all took him several months. In the end he had a picture of what was required and he provided the themes, treatment and atmosphere which the people had asked for.

The people came to his church services for the first few weeks, and then came in smaller and smaller numbers. The only reason which they gave when questioned about their lack of interest is: 'It isn't what we thought it would be like.'

This shows (as you will find in innumerable Sufi stories) that neither the teacher nor the learner knows, without a real situation, how the teaching is to be carried on, if it is not done merely by indoctrination or emotional arousal, in specific instances.

The fact that teachers in many disciplines think that they know how to teach, and classes think that they know how to learn, obscures the fact that people in general accept this folkloric belief without testing. The only exception to both parties carrying on for centuries with diminishing returns is in areas, such as commerce, where nobody can afford to imagine things: tests have to be made.

THE DEMAND FOR LAUGHTER

There is an instructive example in British television where many people complained about the production habit of putting a laughter sound-track onto shows, following every joke, or having a studio audience. Viewing audiences did not like it. The Head of Light Entertainment at London Weekend Television in 1970 bowed to the bitter criticism and flood of letters by removing the laughing audience. The actors now complained that they could not act properly without laughter to help their timing. 'So', continued Mr. Barry Took, 'I brought the audiences back, and everything was fine again. Almost exactly the same people who had written in to complain wrote again to say how much they preferred the shows with audiences.'

HOW TO SELL BOOKS TO SCHOLARS

When circularising scholars with lists of new books, we found a similar result. Postal advertisements couched in impeccable scholastic language brought hardly any sales. But circulars which were written like advertisements for soap-powder had large numbers of these respectable gentlemen sending in their orders by return: even though the books were on serious subjects. When I mentioned this result in a newspaper interview, several academics wrote to me agreeing that they preferred an 'exciting' advertisement and that 'scholarly treatments' bored them ...

THE DEAD WHO WALK ...

Whether in the East or in the West, one of the difficulties in the way of transmitting Sufi knowledge has not changed in many centuries. As the Sufi ancient Abu'l Hasan Khirqani stated, 'Many people who are in reality dead are walking in the streets; many who are in their graves are in reality alive', he tells us, in Attar's lives of the masters.

The difficulties of transmitting knowledge about which you ask mean that only a small number of people can immediately learn what is being taught. The others have to go through exposure to experience and teaching until their inward perceptions are able to connect with the transmission.

Many people believe that their interest in a subject is preparation enough. Further, they cannot credit that others may have the perceptive capacity while they themselves must wait.

JUNAID AND THE JEALOUS STUDENTS

Junaid illustrated this on the overt level one day when some of his twenty students were jealous of his attachment to one of their number. The parable-in-action which he devised is worth thinking about.

He called all the disciples and ordered them to bring twenty fowls. Each pupil was instructed to take one bird to a place where he could not be seen, and to kill it.

When they all returned, the birds were dead: all except the one taken by the controversial student.

Junaid asked him, in the presence of the others, why he had not killed his bird.

'Because you told me to go to a place where I could not be seen, and there is no such place: God sees all', answered the man.

The difficulty of transmission of knowledge is bound up with the orientation of the student. Wanting knowledge is not enough. As we see in the case of Junaid's students, only one in twenty acted in accordance with his own beliefs.

TEACHERSHIP ACCORDING TO MUINUDDIN CHISHTI

The institution of teachership is there for this reason, that the learner must learn how to learn. Understanding this one realises why it is not an extreme statement to say, as did Muinuddin Chishti:

'It should be taken to heart that whatever the Spiritual Guide persuades his disciples to do and to practise, it is for the benefit of the spiritual disciple himself.'

Secrets and the Sufis

Q: Why do Sufis hint at secrets, and speak of remarkable places and strange books, and so on, if not to titillate?

THE CULTIVATED VOLUNTEERS

A: When they do so, it may only be to identify the superficialists who scramble for these things. This resembles the old Army technique when the sergeant says to recruits: 'Hands up those who are too cultivated for manual work' – and then, when some hands go up, says, 'These are the men who need the most training in manual labour!', and assigns them the roughest tasks.

Another reason may be that what to you is titillating, is to me my everyday life. Words like 'remarkable', 'strange' and so on, have no absolute meaning, and are utterly subjective. What is the meaning of 'secret, strange, remarkable'?

It is not unknown for Sufis to deal in things which cause people to react in this manner, in order to allow the audience to experience and to observe their own changes of mood and sensation, to realise that too many people have too many buttons to be pressed in them, as it were.

There is no single answer to the question. Yet it is one of the most widely misunderstood: because careless students have assumed that Sufi teachings aimed at single individuals or groups, or intended for short-term uses, are perennial injunctions, applicable under all circumstances. Much Sufi literature is no longer applicable, since the mentality of the audience has changed over the years.

Rumi speaks of the matter of so-called secrets, when he says: 'If you do not see the secrets of truth, laugh at us ...'

BREAD FOR THE HUNGRY

Secrets and strange places and remarkable books, too, are often the current coin of the language in which uninstructed people think about certain matters. In order to connect with these people you may have to use their language at the outset. This does not make it *your* language. You remember the saying: 'To a hungry man, "two and two" means "four loaves of bread"'? If you are speaking to a hungry man, your first words might well be about bread.

If you want a shorter answer to the inference that Sufis simply want to titillate, here is an old proverb:

'If you believe it, and think that you are sure of it, know that you are in fact in need of improvement. Being sure and believing are stages to be superseded on the Path to Certainty.'

Words like 'secret', too, are technical terms among the Sufis. A better rendition of 'secret' is often 'innermost consciousness'.

When to have Meetings

Q: People hear about something and immediately crave it, as you have pointed out. Why does just any meeting with a teacher or a source of knowledge not produce results for the student?

THE SPRING OF SWEET WATER

A: There is a Persian saying, from the classical *Gulistan* of Saadi, to this effect:

Wherever a spring of sweet water may be –
Men, birds and ants will circle around it.

Wherever there is a source of attraction, people will surround it, in accordance with their nature. I say, 'in accordance with their nature' because human beings resemble animals in being attracted to the aspect of things which immediately attracts them. As with animals, sometimes these things are suitable for them, sometimes not.

Let me be more specific. You hear about a teaching and what you hear attracts you. Or perhaps you want to find out more about it. This means, to you, that you should with the least delay make a contact with this teaching. The assumption here is that you can benefit from a contact made at your convenience or under circumstances dictated by you. This attitude is unpromising, because it does not correspond with what *could* happen.

The only value of a teaching to you, and to the teaching itself, is when you become attuned to it in the way, at the time and under the circumstances which are best suited to a fruitful relationship with that teaching. 'Even a fish can only drink so much of the sea.'

In this respect the teaching is more subtle than, say, learning a language. You can get a book, or recordings, or a tutor, and study a language anywhere, at any time, whenever you can conveniently do so. And yet, even with learning a language, conditions must be

L.H.L.—3

right. You must be in a certain mental and physical state: not too tired or too hungry, for instance. You must be in a comparatively comfortable place, not standing in the open in a downpour of rain, for example. You must have certain essentials: an electronic machine, electricity, or to be able to read, preferably not be deaf and so on. The ordinary man can grasp these needs in a learning situation which he organises for himself. He does not so readily bother to think about them in respect to higher knowledge. Why not?

Learning how to learn involves examining assumptions. Mulla Nasrudin tales very often fulfil this function.

SHABISTARI ON ATTUNEMENT

Shabistari, in his *Secret Garden*, alludes to the problem of attunement between teacher and learner, and between people and their experiences, emphasising that the harmony must be right: 'Illumination is sometimes of grandeur and sometimes of beauty [its] perfection is between the two.'

People crave things, you say, and you are right. But if the thing which they crave, in this case Sufi knowledge, is qualitative and not quantitative, an adjustment to quality must take place before learning can take place.

Consider the fact that Sufi teachers give subjects and other materials to students to study so that a result may be seen when it can take place, and not just by an arbitrary 2.30 pm the following afternoon. People who are victims of the belief that learning takes place mechanically or by instant illumination cannot profit from this, because they reject a whole range of the interaction between the teacher and themselves.

Any meeting with a teacher can produce results, but it is the student who will inhibit these results, because of the shallowness of his expectations. We have published numerous tales which illustrate this point on learning how to learn.

Q: Is this why you seem to discourage people from coming long distances to see you, while they continue to arrive from the ends of the earth from Japan, Argentina, India, Canada, Samoa . . . ?

A: I do not discourage all such people. But there is a pattern, and I am glad to be able to share it with you, since it is one which lies at the very root of our studies. When I was a young disciple, I had exactly the same question, and was in just the same sort of position as you. My teacher used to get letters and visits from people from all over the world. I asked him why he discouraged people who made (or were prepared to make) long and sometimes difficult journeys. What he told me I have found to be true, and even, if that is possible, doubly true. It was this:

ATTITUDES OF DISCIPLES

People tend to think first and mostly of themselves. This can mean that when they hear of our work, they passionately desire to take part in it, to learn more, to benefit themselves personally. When they do this it always means that they are feeding their own selfishness, and have become fixated on personal advantage.

On the other hand, when people come into contact with our ideas and spread them to others in the right kind of way (that is, not cultishly or by setting themselves up as teachers) they are sharing as well as taking something in.

Such people never clamour first of all to be received, seen, taught, and so on. They cultivate a group of people, spread this knowledge as best they can, and then they ask whether they should come or whether someone might visit them. They are, in fact, in a condition to learn and to serve as well as to be served. This establishes the continuum of serving and being served.

Others, on the other hand, spend large amounts of money to travel, collecting it sometimes from others, and think only of themselves, even if they do not realise it. If they do not see this behaviour in themselves it is for us to point it out to them, so that they can profit from so doing, and learn to readjust their greed by establishing the serve and be served continuum. This is what my teacher taught me. He used to say: 'Many people think I am only testing them when I send them messages to this effect or if I do not answer them, giving them an opportunity to change their approach from "Give me" to "What can I do?" but you will see, in this very place, how the people who come here under such

conditions turn out to be unteachable, mere metaphysical tourists.'
He was completely right. So, by refusing to teach, he gave them
an opportunity of learning this behaviour of their own through self-
observation. Some of them, although only a minority, actually
learned this. Of course, we have been able to cut down very much
on this difficulty by publishing anecdotes where it has been shown
by classical and other teachers how anxiety to learn is sometimes
a mask for self-interest. This has enabled quite large numbers of
people to adopt a correct posture towards the Teaching.

Learning how to learn is well illustrated by this kind of approach, and this does show how one and the same person can be
unable to profit from the Teaching while he or she insists on extending this greed side of the personality towards it, and how the
same person may be able to learn when applying the better and
more promising side towards it.

But do not forget that there are just as many who do not
know how to teach as there are who cannot, in their present state,
learn. There is even the circumstance that people who think that
they can teach, are unconcerned about the learning side.

HOW A LANGUAGE WAS TAUGHT

Only the other day I found a delightful example of this mentality
when talking to a language teacher. He said: 'I have a marvellous
system, all my own. I taught it to a man who enrolled as a private
pupil. I taught him absolutely perfectly.'

I said, in the usual rhetorical way people use in general conversations: 'So he knows the language very well now, does he?'

'Not a word,' said the teacher. '*I* taught him perfectly, but *he*
just *would not learn.*'

The Ceiling

Q: Can you give me an example, in parallel or parable terms, of the area in which Sufi teaching operates, and how it is done?

A: Our teaching speaks of, and exists partly in, 'another world', a 'higher realm', a 'different dimension'.

Here is a parallel of what this means, in one significant way, and what the object of the Teaching is.

THE UNKNOWN CEILING

Suppose we have a house with walls, ceilings, floors, and we are inside that house. Let us say that through long-established custom, people can touch and deal with only the floors and walls. If someone were to walk in and say: 'Look at the ceiling,' the people would be incapable of doing so – rather like a child which often cannot see something, certainly cannot observe it, unless it has been demonstrated to it.

Suppose, further, that the custom of generations was to hang things on walls and not to have anything on the ceilings. Objects on the ceilings might then be 'invisible' to the people at large.

So it is with our teaching. We frequently and abundantly assert that people do not think things through, that they make assumptions (such as 'there is no ceiling') which they do not attempt to verify. But, like the intelligent man who would be trying to point out the existence of the ceilings, we do more than constantly draw attention back to the theoretical postulate ('there may be ceilings').

We provide, in instructional courses, meetings, contact with teachers, observation materials, exercises, call them what you like, the practical means to establish and maintain for the community which is being addressed the experience of the existence of 'ceilings'.

Careful preparation is necessary before people can perceive something which is there all the time. Saadi of Shiraz rightly referred to this in poetic terms when he said: 'The Adept sees that same thing in a camel/as in the beautiful ones of China or Chagil.'

Again, by the application of a certain concentration capacity, some people induce others to externalise their inner thoughts, as a teaching method. These thoughts betray the character and operation of the secondary self, the false personality which, although enabling people to handle many of the circumstances of life, has as its objective the maintenance of itself: and not the progress of the individual beyond quite narrow and shallow limits.

WORKING ON THE 'COMMANDING SELF'

This Commanding Self (in Sufi classical literature styled the *Nafs-i-Ammara*), is manifested by reactions, hopes and fears and various opinions and preoccupations.

By bringing its operation into view, its limitations, distortions and peculiarities can be observed, both by the individual himself and by observers. This 'self' is actually largely what most people imagine to be their own personalities, their own and only selves; and it is interposed between objective reality and the real self, the essence, of the individual, whose realisation is the purpose of Sufi study.

Sometimes the manifestation of this self is characterised by ideas or behaviour attributed to other people, as can happen in a dream. One modern technician with knowledge of such things has remarked: 'It is as if the mental computer has been induced electronically to repeat a part of its programming . . .'

The reverse effect is also possible, when the Teacher [Murshid] imparts to the mind of the disciple [Murid] concepts which can reach the essence and which therefore cannot be conveyed by the ordinary methods employed in communicating with the conventional self.

People have tried to cultivate this capacity for purposes of personal ambition and, since this is indeed partially possible, its methodology is carefully protected.

Such works as Ibn Arabi's *Durrat al-Fakhira*, 'Precious Pearl' give numerous instances both of this mechanism and of how it tends to be independent of what people customarily regard as systematic operation. It can, for example, arise unbidden. It works in people whom one would not immediately suspect of possessing it – because of our usual assumptions about any such capacity. It may not operate at all. Sometimes it is willed, sometimes not. On occasions it functions whether the faculty is being used for 'good' (socially acceptable) purposes or not. Traditionally, it can also work for what seem to be trivial purposes, as has been noted with similar extrasensory activity in more recent Western studies. These facts can make it all the more interesting, since such characteristics are not in accord with the usual folkloric beliefs about such matters and tend to lack inherent relationships with occultism, more directly resembling more modern communications phenomena, though in a very refined form. ·

UNDERSTANDING WITH THE HEART

'The Sufis,' runs the saying, 'understand with their hearts what the most learned scholars cannot understand with their minds.'

The results of the encounter with the Sufi may or may not be at the time or place desired by the learner. They may or may not follow immediately. Other things may have to happen before the full benefit of the meeting can be perceived.

One of the more obvious factors at work in such relationships is pointed out in the tale in my book *The Dermis Probe*, entitled 'Pomegranates'.

WORK AND WORK

Q: Why do Sufis expect people to do physical and mental work; why do they so often have establishments which have to be kept going by labour?

A: I first came across this question in myself, when I was living in a Sufi settlement where everyone had to work. There were so many important and influential – and moneyed – people who visited the place that I used to wonder why our Teacher did not 'professionalise' things, and employ gardeners and so on, rather than having so many people doing things that some of them were manifestly not accustomed to doing.

I asked him one evening when he called for questions: 'There are people constantly offering large sums of money to us. Would it not give more opportunities for study if we used this money to run the establishment?'

DEVELOPING ONE'S OWN UNDERSTANDING

As is the custom among Sufis, he told me to go away and find the answers myself, and then to come back when I had them, to see whether I was only asking frivolous questions. So I spent three or four weeks on the subject.

First I wrote down all the possible reasons I could think of, then I wandered about looking at the way in which things were being done, studying life through life, until I came up with the answers. They were these, and by giving them to you I am doing you no favour, since if you had worked them out yourself you would have gained more. As it is, I will have to give you the opportunity of learning something equivalent by some other procedure:

Some people offer money as a substitute for action, and those need to learn that they can serve by greater humility. Hence money is not taken from them, in their own interests. Others may give or offer money and it may be accepted, but it is the Teacher who decides how it shall be used, and students are not able to suggest a study or organisational programme when they are there to learn.

Again, having a working framework means that people can learn all kinds of things which cannot be learnt in the ordinary world, and which are vital to their ability to understand concepts and experiences of an extradimensional nature. For instance, if you want to get something done in ordinary terrestrial terms, you may have to have a hierarchical system. This, in turn, may allow people to exercise a latent desire for power which may not be indicated in them. How are you to improve such people if you are in fact encouraging that tendency? You have to work with whom you have, and therefore the kind of organisation must afford opportunities for exercising good characteristics and starving negative ones.

This cannot be done in an atmosphere where matters are run on the fuels (greed, hope, fear) which are essential to compel people to act and keep acting in the outside world. If, again, you take money from certain people, they (not you) may imagine inwardly that they have 'bought' something. This can encourage their desire for preferment. It can also, on the contrary, cause the person to feel that he or she is not pulling his weight and that he has just purchased his passage, as it were. This is not good for anyone either.

Further, there are always the people who offer money and when you take it assume that you have used it for yourself. People should not be placed in a position where their worst characteristics, in this case suspicion, are exercised. It is one thing to create a situation where people can observe their own undesirable characteristics working, but it is quite another to produce one in which they have this subconscious canker, perhaps not ever exteriorising it.

That would make such a person worse, not better. That is just as bad as the implied moral blackmail where you appear like a saint, in order to make them feel respect or that they are unworthy. Incidentally, it is for the last-named reason that Sufis refuse to exercise pressure on people by moral persuasion, which accords with modern discoveries in psychology, though historically we find that it was very little understood in most cultures. It still remains the main source of hypocrisy.

Conflicting Texts

Q: Some Sufi texts seem to show that a person should be disciplined and dedicated, others that he should be critical and objective. How can these be reconciled?

ARE ALL LINES STRAIGHT?

A: In exactly the same way as, say, mathematics can be reconciled if it is asked 'One book says all right angles are ninety degrees, but Einstein says that there is no such thing as a straight line, all lines are curved, hence there *are* no right angles'. You are mixing up two treatments of the same subject, treatments which depend upon the area in which you are working or the degree of advancement of the student, or both.

If the student is unable to adopt both disciplined and also critical postures, both linear and holistic thinking, he will not be able to perceive that which is to be perceived. Shabistari makes this point when he teaches that people have to be flexible and to find the path between extremes and opposites: '[The Seeker is] always balanced between rejection and faith.'

USE AND ABUSE OF HABIT OF MIND

Habit of mind is at one and the same time one of the most useful and most useless instruments in approaching problems. If you choose the right approach, you may solve the problem. But if you cannot choose it, and only obey it, you may not be using the best habit for the purpose.

The habit which possesses present-day thinking is generally to assume that a disciplined approach will solve all problems. This is run a close second by its opposite: the beguiling but equally partial belief that if discipline is lost, insights are gained. In the story of the moth and the spider, entitled 'Scientific Advance' in my *The Magic Monastery*, you can see why neither approach when adopted as certain to provide a solution, will succeed in areas where the mechanical mind or the incoherent one, dominate thinking.

The would-be Sufi needs guidance precisely because books, texts, while telling you what is needed, do not tell you when. Think of the proverb: 'Words have to die if humans are to live.'

Self-Deception

Q: Can you mention something hurtful?

A: Surely most people can do that.

To me, it is hurtful to have to deal with people whom you would like to teach when – pretending to themselves that they seek knowledge – they only want a social community, friendship, 'togetherness', attention and the like.

All these things are delightful: and all the more delightful when consciously indulged in, rather than found by means of deception. Deception in this case is pretending to oneself that one is studying when one is seeking stimuli.

Such people may have the capacity to learn. But they overlay it with shallow aims. They may have been trained to seek smaller satisfactions and to give them grand names. They may, on the other hand, simply be carrying on the demands of babyhood. Rumi said: 'When will you cease coveting nuts and raisins?'

The condition can be so well established that people are to all intents and purposes unconscious of its presence.

UNDERMINING LOWER ASPIRATIONS

Sufis jolt people from this 'sleep'. Such shocks are often experienced as hurtful – until they take effect, when we are always grateful that we have been allowed to encounter them. What is in fact hurtful to humanity does not necessarily *feel* hurtful at the time. Self-deception is the chief of these.

When something real is being studied, lower aims will tend to vanish, and so will the hurtfulness of the effect of the lower preoccupation's being assailed. As Sheikh Gazur-i-Ilahi says, in his *Irshadat*, if the development by means of the Sufi Way is profound enough, defects of thinking vanish, having nothing to sustain them.

It is not a question of where you go, or whether you join a

group. It is a question of whether you have been correctly prepared to learn how to learn.

THE HOUSE AND THE LORD OF THE HOUSE

Bayazid Bistami emphasised the different ranges in perception of Truth when he said that the first time he visited the Kaaba at Mecca, he saw the Kaaba. The second time he saw the Lord of the Kaaba. The third time he saw neither of these, not the Kaaba nor the Lord of the Kaaba.

Journeys to the East

Q: Do you want us to go to the East, or to join Sufi groups?

A: I have said and written so much about Sufism and the Sufis that some people imagine that I am trying to influence them to join a cult or a religious grouping.

It is, in fact, not possible for me to mount such a campaign, as I will now explain to you.

Hearing and reading what I have had to say about the Sufis has caused hordes of the religious-minded to flow towards the often grotesque versions of Sufism in the East. It has also, with equal force, caused masses of the curious and greedy to flock around the guru-ist cults of the West.

This leaves those who are uninformed, those who want to learn more of what Sufism is, and those who are unconcerned.

This operation has been highly successful, but this part of it has had no higher function for the majority than any other instrument which sorts things – or people – out.

THE AIM AND THE DESTINATION

A mere journey to the East generally has the effect of the jingle: 'Two men looked out from prison bars/One saw mud, the other stars.' What is the wayfarer like, quite apart from the road or the destination? Sheikh Saadi reminds us: 'I fear that you will not reach Mecca, O Traveller, for you are on the road to Turkestan!'

Take heart from the fact that this tendency to wander about looking for knowledge, and to set off for distant destinations (supposedly for knowledge but in reality just to get moving) is a very human tendency. There are plenty of examples of it and of its consequences, in my *Tales of the Dervishes*, and how this characteristic cropped up again and again in the lives of the classical Sufis and their disciples.

So we have to assess who it is that is proposing to go to 'The

East', when this person wants to go, with whom – if anyone – and to where.

More people go to the East and find nothing than ever realise any heart's desire, because they do not know how to structure their enterprise.

CAN YOU WAIT 150 YEARS?

Have you heard how Mulla Nasrudin heard that some parrots live to 150 years – and bought a young one to check whether this would turn out to be true?

'Joining Sufi groups' is unlikely to be useful to people who find groups that they have the option to 'join', without being admitted after assessment as to whether they could usefully join.

One would have to know about the 'Sufi group' before giving an answer which implied that people are likely to encounter real Sufi groups among the derivative 'orders' or 'schools' or 'teachers' which have set themselves up publicly . . .

VARIETY OF STATEMENTS

Whether studying in groups or travelling to the East, or whether otherwise engaged, I note that not many people seem to heed a wide enough variety of Sufi statements.

One such which would repay deeper study before searching is the advice of the illuminate Mumshad Dinwari:*

You learn, he says, by association with a realised teacher. But you can gain nothing from such a person if you bring a sense of personal pride.

The widespread compulsion to do things for which one is not fitted, and also to assume that one's choice of action is appropriate, is seen everywhere, in all epochs.

THE LEGLESS BURGLAR

In the contemporary world there is an excellent opportunity to see this working in the human behaviour reported in the daily and

*Recorded in his *Tadhkirat al-Awliyya* by Faridudin Attar.

weekly Press. Take this almost random example. It shows behaviour which underlies such things as unthinking group-joining or journeys to the East. Are they the product of spiritual aspirations or of sheer non-thinking elevated into a virtue?

A cat-burglar, who climbed girders and houses to steal, and who carried out at least forty-one thefts, was caught and brought to court. Of course he was caught, in spite of his great skill: because he happened to have no legs, having had them amputated years before.*

*Daily Telegraph (London) 9 September 1977, p. 19, col. 3.

What a Sufi Teacher Looks Like

〜〜〜〜〜〜〜〜〜〜〜〜〜〜〜〜〜〜〜〜〜〜〜〜〜〜〜

Q: How should a teacher appear to the students, according to the Sufis?

THE BRICK AND THE HOUSE

A: This question, like so many others which assume that they can be usefully answered in a few words, reminds me of a story about Mulla Nasrudin. Someone asked him what his house was like, basically. In reply he brought this man a brick, saying: 'It is just a collection of these.' What the fool may do without realising it is foolish, the wise man may have to do or say in order to show how unthinking the question is.

How can you say what a teacher should look like? The most one can do is to make a few remarks about it.

What is so perplexing to conditioned attitudes about the Sufis is that, unlike teachers of other kinds, they refuse to stick to one kind of appearance. As an example, if you go to see a Sufi divine, he may not look, talk or act like a mystical master at all. This is because he says either: 'You can teach only by the method indicated for each pupil, and you may have to teach by what seems to him unlikely'; or else because he says: 'There is a time and a place and certain company. According to these, we will teach. When it is a time to be serious, we will be serious. When it is a time to work through what looks like ordinary things, we have to do so.'

So important is this lesson that it can be said to go before all others: in the sense that failure to know this can prevent you from learning more – and can leave you attached to the externals of hypocrites. This includes, of course, unconscious hypocrites.

If the Sufis are right in their claim that time affects behaviour, and that personal appearance should change (and even temperament) then obviously all the people who cultivate a reverend appearance, and all those who acquire it, mistaking this for spirituality, are wrong.

53

It is this unspoken contradiction which makes it almost impossible for people who want continuity and easily identifiable teaching figures, to accept the change in circumstances and attitudes which the Sufi Way demands.

These people, of course, will not have thought it out like this. All they know is that 'A holy man must seem holy to me'; or 'If he always behaves in the same manner, or always exhorts me to the same things, I believe that he may be right'.

The other problem is that the observer is confusing, as he is bound to confuse without having understood, continuity and consistency with reliability or truth. Because butter always tastes the same when it looks the same, he expects a similar 'reliability' in his spiritual teacher. He is, of course, self-deceived in this assumption.

The genesis of the attitude adopted by the people of externals is that their inward drive is for finding tidiness, order. This is not a spiritual activity, it is perhaps, rather, a therapeutic one. Order is essential for disordered people. Looking for it as a major factor in 'esoteric' directions is the mistake.

In trying to make what – for them – is order out of what they imagine to be the disorder of Sufi tradition, they have to oversimplify. They ignore parts of the teaching and succeed only in creating an imitation of Sufism.

Because so many people desire order so strongly, you will find more imitations than reality. One cannot blame anyone for this. But pointing out facts can help.

WHAT A TEACHER SHOULD BE

Ibn Arabi's dictum on this matter has not been bettered:

'People think that a teacher should display miracles and manifest illumination. But the requirement in a teacher is that he should possess all that the disciple needs.'

BEYOND APPEARANCES

In order to possess what a disciple needs, the Teacher must be one who has gone beyond appearances and has realised his innermost self, after transcending the barriers imposed by attachment to secondary factors. He really exists and is aware of this existence. As Ibn Arabi says: 'Absolute existence is the source of all existence'.

Hallaj put it in this way, indicating the peculiarity of the realised individual:

'I am the Real, for I have not ceased to be real – through the Real.'

Sufi teachers who have reached stages where strange things happen in their vicinity, generally called miracles and wonders, due to actions other than any attempt to impress, have to try to compensate for this. Otherwise people are attracted to them or to the Sufis in general because of a craving for wonders.

THE ONION SHOP

One example of this is when the great woman Sufi Rabia had no vegetables in the house, and mentioned it. Suddenly a string of onions fell from the sky, it seemed, and people cried out that this was a proof of divine blessing.

Conversions through miracles, Rabia realised, are only emotional happenings and have no essential spiritual reality. So she said, in a famous phrase:

'A miracle, you say? What, does my Lord therefore keep an onion shop?'

Books and Beyond Books

Q: What is the compatibility, if any, of the Sufi book and the Sufi teaching beyond books?

A: Many people say that they cannot learn from books.

INSTRUMENTAL FUNCTION

Of course they cannot: because they have first to learn that, correctly guided, they can learn from books, or from grasshoppers, or from anything.

A book, for the Sufis, is an instrument as much as it is something to give information.

Information and action are both necessary.

The key is the teacher.

If he says: 'Read this book' then you should read it.

If your answer is: 'I cannot learn from books', then you are in fact refusing his teaching.

If you refuse teaching, do not be surprised if you do not learn anything.

You may be one of those whose problem is that you do not want to learn, and your saying 'I want to learn' is a protection against ever learning: an incantation, in fact.

No real teacher will mistake a man or woman who merely says: 'I want to learn' for one who undoubtedly wants to learn.

That is why so many people have to go through stages which will show them that their condition (while they claimed that they wanted to learn and could not find the materials) was an unsuitable basis for learning.

REALITY AND POTENTIALITY

Man has to come to understand how to see himself as he really is, so that he can achieve something in the area which he calls 'what he might be'.

Again, it is the teacher who knows what is indicated: whether his student has to develop through linear or other modes. As Khaja Khan says, traditionally, direct teaching beyond books, the mystery of unification, was taught to the spiritual elite, while the linear Holy Law (the Islamic *Shariyya*) was given to the ordinary people. In this way the limited could rise via discipline, the *Shariyya*, and the elite were able to descend to the Law by means of the Truth of immediate perception.

According to the Sufis, there is only one Essence, Reality (*Haqq* = Truth). Derived from this is appearance, Form, referred to by Ibn al-Arabi, in his *Fusus al-Hikam*, and others, as *Khalq*, that which is created, secondary. To mistake the secondary for the primary is usual and humanity has to learn how to avoid this. But living in a secondary realm, 'the world', humanity must learn the value and limitations of the secondary, of phenomena. The limitations include the fact that such derivatives cannot help one beyond a certain stage with anything. The value is the occasions and circumstances in which such things can be of help, and the kind of use they can be.

VALUE OF THE RELATIVE

'The Relative is the Channel to the Absolute' (Al-majazu qantarat al-Haqiqa) encapsulates this statement. The Sufi's experience informs him in relation to knowing how to deal with the secondary factors, and hence enables him to teach.

The Sufi teaching through books, or through the use of scholastic methods applied to indicate their absurdity or limitations, was demonstrated one day by Shaqiq of Balkh when Haroun al-Rashid visited him seeking wisdom.

THE VALUE OF A KINGDOM

The Caliph, in all his magnificence, was in need of a lesson in the relative nature of power and possessions. 'Ask a favour of me', he said.

Shaqiq asked him whether he would give one-half of his realm to someone who would give him a drink of water, if he were dying of thirst in a desert.

Haroun said that he would.

And, continued the Sufi, would he give the other half to someone who enabled him to pass that water, if he had become unable to do so?

Haroun said that he would.

Now Shaqiq asked the Caliph to reflect why he valued his kingdom so highly, when it was something which could be given away in return for a drink of water, which itself does not stay with one.

People assume, like the Caliph, that they have something of value and that by giving some of it away they can gain something of even greater value. They tend, too, to offer not what they have to get rid of, but something which they can give because they want to.

Therein lies the genesis of trade, and a desirable thing it is, too – if confined to trade. Therein, too, lies the desire to prescribe one's own studies, one's own path: 'Ask a favour of me', as the Caliph put it.

But, as the Sufis never tire of saying, the Path has its own requirements, and the things which people want to do are likely to be those which will help them to continue in the way in which they are already set, rather than in a direction which will break through their limitations.

Because Sufi affairs do not seem to resemble the kind of organisation of studies familiar to most people, they imagine that they have to be carried out in a completely incoherent manner. It is worth listening to what Aftab-ud-Din Ahmad has to say about this, in his Introduction to a version of Gilani's *Futuh al-Ghaib*:

SUFISM AS A SCIENCE

'The word "mysticism" [employed in English for Sufism] has an elusive atmosphere about it, whereas *tasawwuf* [Sufism] is a regular science with its set laws and a full scheme in detail. It is based on palpable experiences which can be reproduced, like in any other science, under set circumstances. Every pilgrim has to pass through the same stages in his spiritual journey and these stages are readily recognisable by their detailed descriptions given unanimously by all masters. The landmarks and pitfalls are described in equally exhaustive particulars. Just as in any other course of study, there are methods in it to test the progress of the disciple and his merit. As in any other branch of knowledge, there are geniuses in this branch of study who create a stir in the world . . .'*

GARBLED MESSAGE

Books and other methods of mass-communication are used selectively by Sufi teachers. And there are cases where the message is garbled, so that they do not use certain versions of them at all. Some translations, for instance, contain ludicrous errors, even when made by experts. This sort of garbling can happen with anything, and only a human guide can put things to rights.

THE NEWS-STORY

The British Broadcasting Corporation, within hours of the death of King Faisal of Saudi Arabia, put out a recording of a highly emotional account of the assassination taken from the Saudi network. This, you would imagine, must be something on which one could rely. But there was only one problem about the BBC's version: it was in fact the final minute of the Czech language commentary on the Ali-Wepner fight in Cleveland, Ohio. Reading some 'Sufi' materials, they sound the same . . .

*Aftab-ud-Din Ahmad: *Futuh al-Ghaib*, Lahore: Ashraf 1949, p. ix.

Saintliness

Q: Can you say something about saintliness and Sufi teachers?

A: The people who are most anxious about finding, following, refuting or dealing in some way with Sufi teachers tend to be those least able to identify or locate them.

This is because the searchers are usually looking for obsessionals: people who cannot help behaving in a way which announces, twenty-four hours a day, 'I am a spiritual man'.

Those who lead ordinary lives, or who lack the trappings, are invisible to the anxious.

But the reverse of this opinion is more likely to be the case. Those who signal by manner, impedimenta and otherwise that they are to be regarded as authorities are in fact usually the superficialists.

The 'saintly' appearance is one of three things, in all branches of esoteric activity, Sufism included:

1. Imitation by superficialists.
2. Adopted by indoctrination or obsession.
3. Affected as a temporary or superficial measure to signal to those who can perceive only this aspect.

The task of the teacher and the student is to get beyond the appearance as soon and as completely as possible.

SERVICE

It is on this subject that Saadi of Shiraz wrote the poem, in his *Bostan*, 'The Orchard':

The Path is not other than
   the service of the people:
It is not in the rosary, the prayer-rug
   and the dervish robe.

WHAT A SAINT IS AND DOES

Saintliness, which superficialists identify with what are too often superficial actions and appearance, lies, as Saadi reminds us, in the service of the people. People who seek saintliness are only to be taken seriously if they are also concerned with human service.

Saintship, being a saint, as Dr. A. E. Affifi rightly remarks, according to Sufi lore, 'does not mean holiness or piety, although such characteristics may *accidentally* be found in a saint ... Any man is a saint ... if he possesses such a degree of 'gnosis' (supreme knowledge) as would enable him to understand his exact relationship to God (Reality) of whom he is but a manifestation, and to realise his essential oneness with the One Reality. In other words, a man is a saint if he is what Ibnul Arabi calls a "Perfect Man" ...'

KNOWLEDGE AND BEHAVIOUR

Saintship is not in miracles, not in looking devout. The test is in knowledge. People ask: 'How can knowledge be as good as behaviour and belief?' The Sufi answer is that without knowledge there is no certainty that behaviour is right, and no guarantee that belief is real. Real religion and real correct behaviour come through knowing what religion is and knowing what should or should not be done: not in accepting the local cultural norms without experience.

Sufis have constantly maintained that knowledge accords with holiness and generally accepted behaviour: but not with the counterfeit of these which are all that mainly exist in the self-deceived 'good' people.

Saintliness, if by this we mean appearances, including supposed wonders or the effect which someone has on other people who conclude on this basis that he is a saint, is entirely subjective and cannot be called saintliness at all in the Sufi sense.

A DOG HAS PRECEDENCE

Bayazid Bistami, walking through the streets with some of his followers, made an occasion to demonstrate the shortcomings of such superficial assessments, as reported in Attar's *Musibat-Nama,* 'The Book of Calamity'.

A dog was walking towards them, and Bayazid made way for it. One of the disciples thought to himself that this must be wrong: Bayazid was a great saint, accompanied by students, allotted a high status, and a dog was after all only a dog.

Bayazid perceived this man's feelings and explained.

The dog had seen them coming and had projected the thought to Bayazid that he must be sinful to have been created a dog, while this great man must be saintly because he was able to appear in such a resplendent and honoured form.

'It was because of this idea of that dog's,' said Bayazid, 'that I gave him precedence.'

Secrecy

Q: There seems to be no traditional psychology or similar study without a conception of secrets and secrecy. Why is this, and what is the nature of this secrecy?

A: Among the Sufis, the technical term 'secret' is applied to 'the innermost consciousness of man', and may be found authoritatively rendered as such. It is common knowledge among people of traditional spiritual systems that there are differences in the significance and emphasis of the idea of the 'secret', according to the condition of the person involved.

Here are some examples:

STIMULATION

(1) People who are seen to be strongly influenced by the idea of secrecy, and stimulated by it, thus automatically reveal themselves as curiosity-mongers, and the Sufi, for instance, will know how to deal with such a person. It may well be that he has ruled himself out while he remains a mere anticipator of secrets.

ENERGISING

(2) The idea of a 'secret', for those who can adopt a correct attitude towards it, can sometimes have an energising effect, because for them it constitutes the discovery or attainment of something which is prized and valuable. This point has been specifically emphasised by Ibn el-Arabi among the Sufis.

PRIVACY

(3) Secrecy has often been confused with privacy; privacy is needed to eliminate sources of interruption when people are concentrating upon something.

(4) Secrecy can be the word applied to the fact that something is not ready to be revealed, or that it is 'hidden' from someone at a particular time for a good reason: and this reason may not be any more than effectiveness of operation, to ensure progress.

Many things which are called 'secrets' are only things withheld from people until they can understand or effectively experience them.

To clamour for 'secrets' or to do the equivalent (to want them unknowingly) is a characteristic of man, strongly marked in almost all undertakings and stages of maturity, by no means confined to esoteric areas. If you narrow your conception of secrecy to a crude definition of something which is being kept from you, for instance, you do no more than show that you are unlikely to be flexible and sensitive enough to understand the 'secret' aspects of refined and subtle things. Many 'secrets' are best kept by the denial of any secret, or by people appearing, as Sufis often do, to be people of simplicity and ordinariness. The advantage of this to the Sufi is that it relieves him of the need to avoid or combat secret-seekers: they regard him as superficial or 'ordinary'.

PENETRATION OF MEANING

One 'secret' of the Sufis is their method of making people aware of truths contained in experiences and also in literature, which are denied these people by the barriers which habit or subjective emotions raise up.

Saadi says, in his *Bostan*: 'The door of illumination is open to those for whom other doors are closed.' These doors are often those of intellectuality, of believing that one's own ideas will open doors, and doors to purely scholastic or merely systematic approaches, without the insight which enables one to clear the mind of rubbish.

THE SECRET OF THE SECRET

The Sufi paradox: 'The secret of Sufism is that it has no secret at all' means that what is secret and hidden to those who are not realised Sufis becomes understood and experienced to the Sufi, and therefore ceases to be termed a secret at all.

The word *Sirr*, generally translated as 'secret', stands in accepted Sufi terminology for 'the innermost consciousness'. So that, if the innermost consciousness is not known to its possessor, it remains for him 'secret'. And, on the verbal level, where by definition consciousness cannot be experienced, only referred to, it remains for that reason 'secret', 'hidden'.

One of the abilities of Sufis is that they can see through the outward show and self-deception of others, and are thus able to teach these prisoners of the secondary self to attain to the real 'secret', innermost consciousness, within.

THE TURKISH MAIDEN

Yusuf al-Razi illustrated this capacity to read minds, and also how others lack this and judge by appearances, in his famous story, found in Attar's *Recital of the Friends*.

It is related that Hiri was once asked to look after a Turkish maiden by a Persian merchant who was going on a journey. Hiri became infatuated with this girl and decided that he must seek out his teacher, Abu-Hafs the Blacksmith. Abu-Hafs told him to travel to Raiyy, there to obtain the advice of the great Sufi Yusuf al-Razi.

When he arrived in Raiyy and asked people there where the sage's dwelling was, they told him to avoid such a heretic and free-thinker, and so he went back to Nishapur. Reporting to Abu-Hafs, he was told to ignore the people's opinions of al-Razi, and seek him out again.

In spite of the almost unanimous urgings of the people of Raiyy, he made his way to where al-Razi sat. There he found the ancient, accompanied by a beautiful youth who was giving him a wine-cup.

Scandalised, Hiri demanded an explanation of how such a reverend contemplative could behave in such a manner.

But al-Razi explained that the youth was his son and the wine-cup contained only water, and had been abandoned by someone else. This was the reality of his state, which everyone imagined to be a life of dissolution.

But Hiri now wanted to know why the Sufi behaved in such a manner that people interpreted it as heretical.

Al-Razi said: 'I do these things so that people may not burden me with Turkish maidens.'

'You Can't Teach by Correspondence'

I HAVE before me a packet of dehydrated onions.

Let these dried onions stand for something which has been written down. They are neither the original experience (the onion) nor are they nothing at all. They possess a virtuality.

Add hot water, and this is absorbed by your dried material. After a few minutes, we have something which we know to have been dried onions, but which is not now the same. What we now have is 'reconstituted onion'.

We do not have whole onions, it is true. Neither do we have fresh onions. But we have something which will enable us to recognise fresh onions when we see and taste them. This is an advance upon dried onions.

The original experience was fresh onions. The water was the addition made by the right circumstances of study. The result is edible, and this is a suitable substitute for fresh onions. It contains some nutrition, too.

Those who say: 'You cannot make anything out of dried onions' – the equivalent of 'You cannot get anything from a book' – are wrong. Those who say: 'I will wait (or search) until I find fresh onions' are wrong. *They are wrong because they do not realise that they would not recognise 'fresh onions' if they saw them.* This has to be said, though reluctantly, because such statements are usually taken as challenging, when they are more often intended only to be descriptive.

Let us therefore postulate the statement: 'You *can* get something from a book. That something may be so important as to lead you to the recognition of the real thing. It is therefore in many cases all-important.'

INGREDIENTS

But *why* should people imagine that there is nothing in a book of the same order as 'fresh' experience? Simply because they do not know that specific circumstances (such as water added to the onion shreds) are needed before they can get anything. It is the Sufic purpose to help towards the provision of the water as well as the dried onion, so that in due time fresh onions may be presented.

HUMILITY

One of the real reasons for the attempted inculcation of a really 'humble' attitude towards life and learning in traditional teaching techniques is to try to enable people to adopt a point of view which will allow them to 'approach onions through whatever condition of onion is available'.

Of course, such teachings in inept hands rapidly turn into moralistic ones. Instead of saying the above, people cast around for a logical prop to teach patience and humility. They soon find it: 'Humility is good for society. It makes people good, pure, etc.' This, however, is the social level, not the metaphysical one. If you are 'humble', it may help you in ordinary life. If you are not, you will get nowhere in higher things.

If people cannot adopt a 'humble' attitude towards something which they are being invited to study, they are not able to study it at all. Therefore there is no such issue as is frequently supposed, where people ask: 'Why should I obey something which I do not know?' The question is invalid because whoever is at that stage *cannot* obey or disobey: he can only remain a fairly querulous enquirer. He is not master of the option, so there is neither any validity in the question nor any need for an answer, other than a description of his state. The hope lies in the possibility that he may recognise his condition through a description of it, and adjust his attitude accordingly.

People, however, more often than not adopt secondary indications as primary, and Sufi teachers have to take into account this tendency. Sometimes they provide deliberately contrived shocks to display the limited nature of the would-be student's thinking, to help him (or her) to gain a deeper understanding of themselves and hence to liberate a wider perspective enabling them to learn.

Such a shock is contained in the tale told by Bayazid Bistami.

A man, he recounted, met him on the road and asked where he was going. Bayazid told him that as he had two hundred dinars, he was going on the Pilgrimage to Mecca.

The man said: 'Circumambulate *me* seven times, and let that be your Pilgrimage, for I have dependents.'

So, continued Bayazid, he did what the man asked, and returned to his own house.

More often than not, such an adjustment, because it involves admitting that previous thinking-patterns are inadequate, is not sufficiently welcome to him. He seeks something which will bolster the desire to feel that he is significant.

He very easily finds such a creed, individual or institution: because almost all of the current ones specialise – whether they know it or not – in judicious flattery. Even if flattery is alternated with disapproval, it remains flattery.

This is one reason why it is so important to understand one's personal motivation.

An important aspect of this theme of the value of intermediary materials as catalytic elements is to note that there is a form of learning by direct and provoked perception. This is distinct from learning through rote methods or by selective study where that study is planned by the student or by someone else who does not have a full perception of the student's needs.

APPEARANCE AND FUNCTION

We speak here of function, not appearance. There is an interesting parallel in an event which I remember from a time when some literalists were questioning Sidi Abu-Yusuf on Sufi teachers. His answer both shows their mentality and how it fails to accord with reality:

The questions covered the claims made by or on behalf of Sufi exponents to be Supreme Chief of the Sufis.

Abu-Yusuf said: 'This is a metaphor only and does not imply any rivalry. It does not encompass, either, any idea of hierarchy in formal organisation. Furthermore, it does not mean that each claims (or has claimed for him) to be Chief of All the Sufis. It only means that, for those who are following their instructions, Sufi teachers must be regarded as the chief and only source of wisdom. This role is no greater than that of any teacher whose pupils must maintain their concentration and learning ability by not dividing their attention to other subjects, such as – in this case – a hierarchy of teachers. The real chiefs of the Sufis exist and operate in a generally non-perceived realm and are never known in their higher functions; though these personages may present themselves as mere Sufi masters from time to time – as they may assume any other guise – to carry on their functions.'

Background to 'Humility'

BEFORE the period generally regarded as historical time, there has been an operation of a form of cognition linked with human development which is outside the current methods of acquiring and utilising information. The result of this effort has often been called 'wisdom': although the word *wisdom* has also often been applied to other fields.

RELICS ARE NOT THE THING ITSELF

Many religious, mystical and other formulations are, up to a point, shrines for the relics of a completely or partially successful attempt to present and make available to various individuals and communities means for acquiring this knowledge. Like almost everything on earth, they are subject to deterioration or fossilisation. They become both museums and exhibits, at one and the same time.

Because of the tendency to stress discipline and group-attention without contemporaneous adjustments of other factors, many such formulations (some of them called schools or cults) crystallised in the short or long term, and not infrequently they have claimed a monopoly of truth or effective ritual. This process, mirroring limited thinking-patterns, frequently goes so far as to lead to a virtual destruction of the dynamic of the formulation of the School. In practice, exclusivism and dogmatism, beyond a certain point, militate against certain necessities of flexibility. There is a continuing need for regeneration.

What appears to some people as the sum total of the human heritage of philosophy, metaphysics or even magical thinking can also be viewed, for the foregoing reasons, as heavily burdened with the wreckage or misinterpretation (through selective choice) of formulations previously operated by coherent Schools. The factor causing this state of affairs is endemic in the human community, and has often been unsuspected by large sections of whole civilisations; though made the subject of close attention and rectification by specialists outside of mechanical and confined thought. Such specialists are those who can grasp internal principles and dynamics: not those who merely rearrange.

THE TRADITION MAINTAINED BY COMPETENCE

In contradistinction to the public and overt formulations familiar to all as stabilisations of many forms of religious, psychological and community action philosophies and other systems, there has always been a continuous, altruistic stream of guardianship of this comprehensive and adaptational knowledge, throughout history. This is based on capacity and knowledge, not on arbitrarily deciding to become a specialist.

There are excellently sufficient reasons why the foregoing facts have never been more publicly known or accepted in any real depth. Among those more easily understandable by customary thinkers is the fact that 'to make an announcement such as this, to those who are basically selfish will serve mainly to increase their selfishness at the expense of their real, inner desire for truth' – thus further masking the potentialities of the Teaching from such people.

Another, easily-understood, reason is that the existence of narrow systems of thought (over-simplified to contain the aspirations without regard to potential, and to permit a wide-scale disciplining of populations) has produced a type of 'expert' or concentrator of this kind of bias who will automatically feel insecure if any attempt is made to widen his horizons. The result will be opposition, distrust and confusion.

From time to time, certain cosmological and human factors being in alignment, there is both a need for and a possibility to re-establish, by means of a special and skilled effort, formulations and activities which maximise the prospects of more rapid and thorough penetration of the teaching which leads to the development referred to as 'knowing oneself' or 'having wisdom'. Several such periods, cyclic in character, have occurred in recent times: none of them has been generally recognised for what it is. This, again, is not to say that because one believes this one is automatically able to find it. The correct approach is everything.

ROLE OF AN INTERVENTION

The first stage of this knowledge concerns answers to the questions generally phrased as involving the origin, nature, being and future of mankind itself, collectively as well as in the individual. The manner and order of procedure of approaching these questions themselves involves a capacity whose absence or ineffectiveness in the ordinary individual spells his incapacity to participate in his own development. He is in need of an organising intervention to break the vicious circle which results.

KNOWLEDGE OF THE END CREATES THE MEANS

The desire for an 'awakening', often used as a technical term, may or may not be accompanied by the information and experience essential to precede this stage. The Teaching, for its part, is carried out – and is able to cross ideological boundaries – because of a knowledge of the objective: an objective which is at worst postulated as an assumption that it exists; at best glimpsed: and thenceforward is the subject of repeated attempts to devise a means to recover this glimpse.

The working hypothesis or traditional framework provides the structure by which the would-be illuminate attempts to approach this goal. In the case of the School, knowledge alone provides the basis upon which the structure can be devised.

'Once you know the end, you can devise the means.' The end does not justify the means – it provides it. The means, employed in this sense, is the structure referred to in some literature as 'The Work'.

THE SCHOOL

One of the structures within which this knowledge is studied, collected, conserved and transmitted has often been termed a School. There are others, continuously at work, whose existence

73

and mode of operation is not of applied value, though frequently a matter of curiosity and inquisitiveness, occupying much time and giving rise to much effort, due to the faultily-based assumption that a lively interest in something once heard about may lead to familiarity with it, and hence usefulness to be gained from it. Since, however, its *modus operandi* is far from having an exactly operable analogy in current thought, it is in fact, if not in theory, 'completely concealed'.

It is extremely common for encounters to take place between people who are interested in this area, and those working in it, without the former being in any way able to enter into it – or, most frequently, for them to have any conception or recognition of the role or method of operation of the other individuals.

The 'School Work' is a lower-level activity which nonetheless has to be passed through before a recognition of the higher level is possible. Acceptance of this principle is among the first requirements leading to the necessary effective time-scale and order of events in which the Teaching may take effect. One of the chief barriers to accepting this fact – even as a working hypothesis – is the over-valuation of the role, potentiality and knowledge of the learner.

It is for this reason that such stress is placed, in so many traditional systems of which viable fragments subsist, upon the need for what is approximately rendered in familiar parlance as humility. Its distortion is self-abasement.

WHAT HUMILITY IS NOT FOR

As one of the great Sufis said: 'My humility is not there to impress you – it is there for its own reason.'

The person that you feel yourself to be, according to the Sufis, is a false person, which has no true reality. When humility is exercised, people begin to realise that they do not, as it were, exist at all. This perception of oneself as *'Adam* (not-being) is stressed in Hujwiri's *Revelation*, in the second chapter dealing with the real meaning of poverty. When people take pride in their humility, they have merely adopted another concocted 'self' as part of their not-being: and this is what produces hypocrites.

The purpose of seeing through one's own nothingness is to see beyond into what is really there to which one's real self can relate. Humility is therefore directly concerned with the quest for Absolute Truth.

NO VALUE IN MAKING A VIRTUE OF A FUNCTION

The coincidence of some similarity between the words '*Adam* (not-being) and *Aadam* (man) has caused poets and others in Eastern languages to equate the two neatly in verse and prose. It is interesting to note, by the way, that even orientalists and reviewers, discussing this point, sometimes observe so little of this play on words that they even charge Sufi writers with being ignorant or adopting strange usages when they say such things as 'Man is '*adam*'. I often feel that this uncharacteristic failure to register the contention is in such cases due to the fact that the subjectivity of the commentator is censoring his understanding: he is, after all, generally a man – as a man he does not want to think of himself as 'not-being'. This is all the more marked in people (who do of course include scholars) who actually identify themselves by means of the learnt patterns and information-stock which is, to the Sufi, part of the non-being, the personality and not the essence, of humankind.

In other words, as we all know, pride prevents humility. Pride is attached to a sense of oneself which may be wholly or partially created by secondary things like believing that one is learned.

It has truly been said that 'Humility is not so much a virtue as a necessity, in order to learn.'

RABIA AND THE DOOR

The posture which is required in the Sufi was well illustrated by Rabia al-Adawiyya. She heard that Salih of Qazwin was teaching by the phrase: 'Knock at the Door and it will be opened to you.'

Rabia said: 'How long will you persist in saying this, O Salih – when that Door has never been shut?'

The lack of humility is also something of a conspiracy: where people not only ignore it when it is found in others, but cannot credit its reality. This is in addition to those who cannot even conceive how or when to exercise it.

TALE OF THE PROFESSOR

Not long ago (pursuing the first remark) I was showing a visitor around the grounds of this house. As we passed a quiet and diligent man sitting on the ground mending a piece of wood, the visitor asked: 'Who is that?'

I said: 'That is Professor So-and-So.'

His brow creased into a frown, and he looked at him again. Then he looked at me. Now he said: 'Are you *sure*?'

And, pursuing the second remark, there is the incident involving Maaruf of Karkh.

COLLECTING DATE STONES

Sari al-Saqati saw Maaruf picking up the stones of dates from the ground and asked him what he was doing.

'A child was crying,' he said, 'because, being a penniless orphan, he had no nuts like other children. So I am going to collect date-stones and sell them [to be ground into flour] so that he can have some nuts, and be happy.'

How Serious is the Student?

Q: I have heard you say that many of the people who imagine that they are serious about the study of Sufism are in fact not serious at all; and because of that cannot benefit from it. Can I have an example?

A: One of the best examples is a matter of our daily experience. People read books or hear things about Sufism, and immediately proceed to 'beat a path to our door'. Now, at this juncture I have published sixteen books on Sufi ideas and action. One would infer, surely, that if I am publishing this material – and in such quantities and with such energy – that we regard its publication, and hence its study, as important.

But out of the average of 10,000 or so letters received each year, a significant proportion of all people are found to be 'serious' (as they claim) without bothering to read the material. If they were serious, they would give it serious attention. If, as they so often state, they don't want written materials, why do they apply to ME, since I am dealing partly in written materials? People come to see me, not having a sound grasp of what we are saying – because they have not studied our literature – and so I cannot help them.

They come from all over the world, spending money and wasting time, but they won't spend money on books, won't give time to their study. Do you imagine that one can regard such people as 'serious'? Admittedly, they constitute only a minority of all our contacts, but the large total number of people contacting me means that this minority still adds up to a sizeable total number of individuals. If you want to assess someone, look at what he does, and ignore his protestations of 'being serious' – at least for the moment. If he is *acting* seriously, you will be more inclined to accept his claim to *be* serious. If he is only *saying* it, no matter how strongly he may believe it, we can only conclude that he has little or no idea of what he is really doing, and hence I would be the last person to be able to be of use to him, especially since he is first in need of elementary instruction in straight thinking.

KNOWLEDGE AS PERCEPTION

In these days, as in the past, what is generally called knowledge is a great 'veil' to understanding. Gazur-i-Ilahi reminds his hearers that there is scholastic and observational learning. Inner knowledge – perception – is the real form of knowledge. The one is like knowing about honey by studying it, the other to know it by taste.

One is knowing. The other is only knowing about knowing.

What seems to be a lack of 'seriousness' is really better referred to by your second definition: that people cannot benefit. The reason why is that they lack a desire to pay attention to what is said and done.

CHEESE AND THE MOON

When we talk about the 'seriousness' of the student, we have to remember that many people have very little idea what serious study might mean. It often means, for them, compulsive study, whether there is any product or not. You may have noted that the British Association for the Advancement of Science (of which I admit to being a Life Member, by the way) held a meeting at which the discoveries announced included:

That moon rock shares properties with Cheddar and Emmentaler cheese; that in general fat people do not go to universities; that rats prefer listening to Mozart rather than Schoenberg. This wasn't in the Middle Ages, with angels dancing on pins, but in 1970 of the Christian Era . . .

Social and Psychological Elements in Sufi Study

Q: Are you reducing metaphysical and spiritual studies to the level of sociology and psychology?

A: No, I am, on the contrary, trying to show the contaminants and confusions from socializing and popular psychology in these studies. If people think that they are worshipping God when they are in reality seeking emotional excitement, this can hardly be to everyone's advantage. If the sensations aroused by transfer of emotions from one person, or one system, to another are thought to be 'special', when they are extensively described and illustrated as normal social actions and developments, what harm is there in affirming the truth?

Q: It is often said that it is better to leave people with their beliefs, rather than to disturb them.

A: If the belief is equivalent to believing that an appendix pain is the work of the devil, it is wrong to leave the patient with it, for he is likely to die.

THE MAN WHO FELL OFF A MOUNTAIN

It may not be our role to do anything for him, but on the lower level, we can't be prevented from alluding to his state. People like this sometimes resemble the man who fell off a mountain. When he had reached half-way down, he said to himself: 'five thousand feet and nothing has happened yet – in fact it is quite pleasurable'.

We may have to leave such a man alone, but we can't help noting his real situation. Such people are often those who turn up and say: 'I am following the X Path, and I find it rewarding, but I would like to add a little of your wisdom . . .'

The belief that something which is really, for instance, a selfish self-absorption in religious activity is anti-religion in effect. Sheikh Ibrahim Gazur-Ilahi truly says: 'That which takes you to God is religion/whatever stands between you and God is "the world"' How many pious people realise that?

The levels of sociology and psychology, which your question regards as a 'reduction' are, in fact, essential to examine at the learning how to learn stage, because unless the psychology is correctly oriented, there is no spirituality, though there can be obsession and emotionality, often mistaken for it. Those who trade in such things, mistaking them for spirituality, have of course – knowingly or otherwise – a vested interest in discouraging interest in the psychological and sociological levels. Those interested in truth, however, cannot afford such luxuries. As for the social level, this and the psychological are dealt with by this quotation from one of the greatest of all Sufis, who is not dealing in spirituality, if you define this term narrowly:

Sheikh Abdullah Ansari says:

What is worship?
To realise reality.
What is the sacred law?
To do no evil.
What is reality?
Selflessness.

This is the Sufi approach – not the other way about. There can be no spirituality, according to the Sufi masters, without psychology, psychological insight and sociological balance.

So, if you are looking for spirituality which requires such insights, you have to look at the 'reduction' by the great classical Sufi masters, not by me, for I am no innovator in this respect. If, too, you imagine that the Sufis are not to be regarded as 'spiritual' because of their insistence on psychology and sociology, you are out of luck again: not only Islamic authorities but scholars from all faiths continue to regard the

Sufis as among the greatest exponents of the spiritual among humankind.

There is no wisdom where there is no common sense: it cannot under those conditions find any expression.

They say: 'Seek wisdom while you have the strength, or you may lose the strength without gaining wisdom.'

THE INVISIBLE CAT

But you must start where it counts: you cannot start halfway along and expect results. Mark Twain advertised, as a hoax, that he had lost a cat so black that it could not be seen by ordinary light, and wanted it back. Nearly a thousand people contacted him claiming to have seen it. Would you begin to teach such people, or at least people in such a state of mind, anything?

THE ROBBER-PRIEST

In England, no time ago, there was a priest who was a burglar, who even burgled another vicarage, an abbey and a school. He was caught trying to rob a bank, which he travelled to by taxi, having enlisted his housekeeper, convincing her that they were doing something good. Should the social and psychological levels of such a person not be looked at before proceeding with the spiritual, the higher, levels? Another priest got divorced and married a witch ...

2

On Attention

Characteristics of Attention and Observation

~~~~~~

Q: Can you define characteristics of attention and observation as of importance in Sufic studies?

A: Study the attracting, extending and reception, as well as the interchange, of attention.

One of the keys to human behaviour is the attention-factor.

Anyone can verify that many instances, generally supposed to be important or useful human transactions on any subject (social, commercial, etc.,) are in fact disguised attention-situations.

It is contended that if a person does not know what he is doing (in this case that he is basically demanding, extending or exchanging attention) and as a consequence thinks that he is doing something else (contributing to human knowledge, learning, buying, selling, informing, etc.,) he will (a) be more inefficient at both the overt and the covert activity; (b) have less capacity of planning his behaviour and will make mistakes of emotion and intellect because he considers attention to be other than it is.

If this is true, it is most important that individuals realise:

1. That this attention-factor is operating in virtually all transactions;

2. That the apparent motivation of transactions may be other than it really is. And that it is often generated by the need or desire for attention-activity (giving, receiving, exchanging).

3. That attention-activity, like any other demand for food, warmth, etc., when placed under volitional control, must result in increased scope for the human being who would then not be at the mercy of random sources of attention, or even more confused than usual if things do not pan out as they expect.

CERTAIN PRINCIPLES MAY BE ENUNCIATED. THEY INCLUDE:–

1. Too much attention can be bad, (inefficient).

2. Too little attention can be bad.

3. Attention may be 'hostile' or 'friendly' and still fulfil the appetite for attention. This is confused by the moral aspect.

4. When people need a great deal of attention they are vulnerable to the message which too often accompanies the exercise of attention towards them. E.g., someone wanting attention might be able to get it only from some person or organisation which might thereafter exercise (as 'its price') an undue influence upon the attention-starved individual's mind.

5. Present beliefs have often been inculcated at a time and under circumstances connected with attention-demand, and not arrived at by the method attributed to them.

6. Many paradoxical reversals of opinion, or of associates and commitments may be seen as due to the change in a source of attention.

7. People are almost always stimulated by an offer of attention, since most people are frequently attention-deprived. This is one reason why new friends, or circumstances, for instance, may be preferred to old ones.

8. If people could learn to assuage attention-hunger, they would be in a better position than most present cultures allow them, to attend to other things. They could extend the effectiveness of their learning capacity.

9. Among the things which unstarved people (in the sense of attention) could investigate, is the comparative attraction of ideas, individuals, etc., apart from their purely attention-supplying function.

10. The desire for attention starts at an early stage of infancy. It is, of course, at that point linked with feeding and protection. This is not to say that this desire has no further nor future development value. But it can be adapted beyond its ordinary adult usage of mere satisfaction.

11. Even a cursory survey of human communities shows that, while the random eating tendency, possessiveness and other undifferentiated characteristics are very early trained or diverted –

weaned – the attention-factor does not get the same treatment. The consequence is that the adult human being, deprived of any method of handling his desire for attention, continues to be confused by it: as it usually remains primitive throughout life.

12. Very numerous individual observations of human transactions have been made. They show that an interchange between two people always has an attention-factor.

13. Observation shows that people's desires for attention ebb and flow. When in an ebb or flow of attention-desire, the human being not realising that this is his condition, attributes his actions and feelings to other factors, e.g., the hostility or pleasantness of others. He may even say that it is a 'lucky day', when his attention-needs have been quickly and adequately met. Re-examination of such situations has shown that such experiences are best accounted for by the attention-theory.

14. Objections based upon the supposed pleasure of attention being strongest when it is randomly achieved do not stand up when carefully examined. 'I prefer to be surprised by attention' can be paraphrased by saying, 'I prefer not to know where my next meal is coming from'. It simply underlines a primitive stage of feeling and thinking on this subject.

15. Situations which seem different when viewed from an over-simplified perspective (which is the usual one) are seen to be the same by the application of attention-theory. E.g.: People following an authority-figure may be exercising the desire for attention or the desire to give it. The interchange between people and their authority-figure may be explained by mutual-attention behaviour. Some gain only attention from this interchange. Some can gain more.

16. Another confusion is caused by the fact that the object of attention may be a person, a cult, an object, an idea, interest, etc. Because the foci of attention can be so diverse, people in general have not yet identified the common factor – the desire for attention.

17. One of the advantages of this theory is that it allows the human mind to link in a coherent and easily-understood way many things which it has always (wrongly) been taught are very

different, not susceptible to comparison, etc. This incorrect training has, of course, impaired the possible efficiency in functioning of the brain, though only culturally, not permanently.

18. The inability to feel when attention is extended, and also to encourage or to prevent its being called forth, makes man almost uniquely vulnerable to being influenced, especially in having ideas implanted in his brain, and being indoctrinated.

19. Raising the emotional pitch is the most primitive method of increasing attention towards the instrument which increased the emotion. It is the prelude to, or accompaniment of, almost every form of indoctrination.

20. Traditional philosophical and other teachings have been used to prescribe exercises in the control and focussing of attention. Their value, however, has been to a great measure lost because the individual exercises, prescribed for people in need of exercise, have been written down and repeated as unique truths and practised in a manner, with people and at a rate and under circumstances which, by their very randomness, have not been able to effect any change in the attention-training. This treatment has, however, produced obsession. It continues to do so.

21. Here and there proverbs and other pieces of literary material indicate that there has been at one time a widespread knowledge of attention on the lines now being described. Deprived, however, of context, these indications survive as fossil indicators rather than being a useful guide to attention-exercise for contemporary man.

Attention upon oneself, or upon a teacher, without the exercise of securing what is being offered from beyond the immediate surroundings, is a sort of short-circuit. As Rumi said: 'Do not look at me, but take what is in my hand'.

3
Sufi Study Themes

Sufi Study Themes

Q: If you were to give a number of study themes to the people present, which ones would you stress?

A:

1. All approaches to a study or an individual may start with a desire for attention. However they start, they must never end up in this manner.

2. Study the assumptions behind your actions. Then study the assumptions behind your assumptions.

3. 'Why did I do such-and-such a thing?' is all very well. But what about 'How otherwise could I have done it?'

4. You have come a long way, and you do not know it. You have a long way to go, and you do know what that means.

5. In respect to some, you may have advanced. In relation to others, you have not progressed at all. Neither observation is more important than the other.

6. If your desire for 'good' is based on greed, it is not good, but greed.

7. Exercise power by means of kindness, and you may be causing more damage than you could by cruelty. Neither approach is correct.

8. The man who knows must discharge a function. The one who does not, cannot arrogate one to himself; he can only try to do so.

9. Do not try to be humble: learn humility.

10. Assume that you are part-hypocrite and part heedless, and you will not be far wrong.

11. To copy a virtue in another is more copying than it is virtue. Try to learn what that virtue is based upon.

12. No practice exists in isolation.

13. If you seek a teacher, try to become a real student. If you want to be a student, try to find a real teacher.

14. The more often you do a thing, the more likely you are to

do it again. There is no certainty that you will gain anything else from repetition than a likelihood of further repetition.

15. At first, you are not worthy of the robes and implements of the Sufi. Later you do not need them. Finally, you may need them for the sake of others.

16. If you cannot laugh frequently and genuinely, you have no soul.

17. When a belief becomes more than an instrument, you are lost. You remain lost until you learn what 'belief' is really for.

18. When a dervish shows interest in your material welfare, you may be pleased. But it is frequently because you are not yet ready for anything else.

19. When someone asks for you to help in doing something, do you imagine that it is because he cannot do it unaided? Perhaps he is a Sufi who wants to help you by connecting you with his task.

20. If you are lazy, count yourself lucky if someone points this out, giving you a chance to improve. Laziness is always your fault. It is the sign that a man has persevered in uselessness for too long.

These points are in fact exercises in outwitting the false self, which thrives on smaller satisfactions. The Sufi aims at *Fana* (passing away – of the False Self) and *Baqa* (remaining – of the Real). Behind the supposed 'I', which is impermanent, lies the real one, which is characterised by the awareness of truth, of reality.

And listen to the words of Junaid of Baghdad, when he said: 'A good-natured sensualist is better than a bad-tempered so-called Sufi.'

4
Things of the World

An Eastern Sage and the Newspapers

%%%

LETTER TO A SAGE

A WESTERN student of the spiritual wrote a fierce and reproving letter to a certain Eastern sage, when he saw his name in a newspaper. 'You should be completely unconcerned with the things of this world!' he said – and much else.

When I visited the sage, I asked him what he had thought of the letter, as I wanted to report his reaction to the writer of it.

'I do get letters, it is true,' he murmured, 'but I am afraid I do not read them, because, you see, they are things of this world, and I am not concerned with them.'

'Things of this world' include, according to the Sufis, anything other than Truth.

CONDUCT OF THE SUFIS

The conduct of Sufis does not necessarily show their degree of detachment. It more often shows what the observer imagines it to show. Shaikh Yahia Munir, in common with many authorities, states that the behaviour of the realised Sufis (the Auliyya) are not all the same in appearance. Some eat well and sleep; others fast and stay awake at night; some are clothed in rags, others in excellent clothes. Some accept gifts, others do not. Those who judge others by such appearances are called, by the Sufis, 'people of externals'.

Such judgments are made by people whose emotional life has expanded at the expense of their humanity, their logical capacities and certainly their spiritual perceptions.

TAKING THE NAME OF GOD...

The dilemma of people who only use words, and not full understanding, for their religious conceptions, is well illustrated in this story – the one of the fruit – from Rumi's *Fihi ma Fihi:*

Someone took some fruit from a tree and ate it. The lord of the property said to him: 'Why do you do such an unlawful thing? Do you not fear God?'

The fruit-eater replied: 'Why should I? the tree is God's, and I am God's servant, eating from God's tree.'

The owner said: 'Wait, and I will give you your answer.'

He had the other man tied to the tree and beaten.

The man cried out: 'Do you not fear God [that you do this to me]?'

The landlord said: 'Why should I fear? You are the servant of God, and this, this stick which is God's is being used to strike God's servant!'

Just as intellectual and systematised religious argument fails when brought into a broader context, so do even wider religious concepts fail when compared with the extradimensional perception of Truth which the Sufis bring to human experience. That is the message of all the Sufi sages.

Basis for People's Interest

SOMEONE wants to know how it is that it is difficult to get to see me. He also wants to publicise my 'spiritual attainments'.

I'll tell you, about both.

It is not either easy or difficult, it is more likely to be a matter of figures. Just as it would be with anyone.

Taking an eight-hour day and seven-day week, we find that in a year if one sees one person each hour; in daily session and doing nothing else, giving one-hour interviews, I could see just under three thousand people a year, and each one only once.

But something between three and ten times that number of people express a desire to 'see me'. And, if every year you saw each person only twice, you would only be able to see around one and a half thousand people.

Although the subject is always supposed to be important, I note that the urgency drops off, mysteriously, on holidays and during Summer vacations...

Mind you, if I were doing nothing else but seeing all comers for an hour a day, the procedure would carry the makings of its own solution. This is because I would become so boring, so worn out, so useless, that people would want to see me less and less, and so I would eventually retrieve my freedom.

So, rather than have to go through this, why should I not carry on and remain at the position where I am anyway?

Especially since there are adequate supplies of other people who are delighted to be surrounded by troops and groups of people imbibing their wisdom from morning to night.

I have been criticised for saying this. It is said that such people always create dissatisfaction among the majority of their followers, who soon switch to the next guru. Exactly what I mean: if I were to behave in this way, I would also create dissatisfaction, when people had had enough of my ritual of sitting about being the great guru.

I have neither the inclination nor the training to enrol myself in the guru circuit.

The foregoing, of course, looks upon the 'seeing people' activity as a socio-psychological activity, already adequately observed by sociologists but entirely ignored by the occult-minded: except when they confuse it with a 'spiritual activity', which it most certainly is not.

In my own experience, amply confirming that of the traditional Sufi authors, this clustering around will have to be justified by the clusterers as a 'spiritual activity'. The onus is on them to do so; or else to seek out their natural affinities: the seekers of adulation whose main other characteristic so often seems to be that they cannot bear to be alone for very long.

In my youth a teacher said to me: 'If collecting together were the way to greater enlightenment, grains of sand would all have become saints, flocks of birds would break up and each one would become a spiritual teacher, sheep would exercise the functions of the enlightened. Similarly, the characteristic which we see in the least enlightened to crowd around things and people deemed to be strange, valuable or exciting would not be gatherings of gapers but, rather, assemblies of the elect . . .'

SHEIKH ABU-ISHAQ'S FRIENDS

As to 'spiritual attainments', I am reminded of the words which Sheikh Abu-Ishaq of the Green Island, near Algeciras in Spain, spoke to Ibn Arabi and reported in his twelfth-century *Durrat al-Fakhira*:

'I regard people as of two types. First there is the friend who has a good opinion of me and speaks well of me. He is a friend. Then there is the person who speaks badly of me, who tells of my "spiritual condition".'

Thinking in Terms of
Supply-and-Demand

Q: If people interested in spiritual things are asking what are in fact 'commercial' questions, is that the fault of the people or of the systems? How does your range of questioners compare with those received by others working in the spiritual field?

A: This is several questions in one. First, people have been trained to think in crude supply-and-demand terms about almost everything. This is due to the culture and social outlook, so it is hard to call it the fault of the people or of the systems which they are approaching with questions.

Second, if you read published literature by people working in the spiritual field from the supply-and-demand analysis point of view, you might be amazed to find that in general neither the questioner nor the spiritual man seems to be aware that they are engaged upon 'commercial type' transactions.

Third, discussions with professional people, such as doctors and lawyers, shows that they get the same kind of questions, structurally supply-and-demand questions, from their clients; and, indeed, the whole range of annoyances and subjectivities of which I have been speaking. This is so well understood by real teachers in the East that it is summed up in the joke: 'So-and-so went to a certain teacher for conversation, but all he got was illumination!'

Q: Are your books designed, then, to 'fill in' gaps in possible behaviour-patterns in people approaching Sufism?

A: On the general level, they all carry this design, and the result of asking interested people to read them carefully has been to establish and maintain, successfully, a basis of holding a viewpoint which would otherwise need monastic circumstances to reveal and develop.

Q: What other activities do you employ, in addition to your books?

A: An enormous range. But these activities, many of which, though traditional among Sufis, would be unrecognisable as spiritual by narrowly conditioned people, are experienced following the grouping of the books, and in specific measure: 'prescribed', as it were, for the needs of the people. Thus they are not susceptible to descriptions like listing them, or writing about them.

KNOWLEDGE AS ACTION

People who deal with spiritual matters as if they were commercial questions, people who seek behaviour-patterns as in the second question, the query about activities, are all, I think, due to enquiries based on the desire for action. To the degree to which this is true, we should note what Sheikh Ibrahim Gazur-i-Ilahi says about the matter of knowledge and action: how action cannot take place without knowledge.

He stresses that 'People argue about whether knowledge or action should come first. But they are the same. [Worthwhile] action is in fact knowledge in operation. Right action stems from right knowledge. Right knowledge is acquired through the teacher.'

AN INFURIATING BOOK

One of the few instances where we can quote the operation of a non-book as an instrument, yet bridge the area of literature, is in the case of *The Book of the Book*. This tale, which I published in the form of a book, tells how people become disappointed by books, and how they can learn from them what is and is not in them. Critics were furious because the story was so short, as they assumed that a book must be of a certain length. This fury overtook them before they had read the contents, which described their behaviour and showed how inadequate it was. This gave us – and many other people as well – published evidence of the mentality of literary people and literal thinkers which they would never have admitted to if directly challenged. We let them do it for us. This shows how a book can be used to create a situation.

The Effect of Tales and Narratives

Q: You have published several hundred tales and narratives, mostly from the Middle East, illustrative of situations which often show strengths and weaknesses in people. Why do you export this material from other cultures, instead of producing it in current terms, and what effect is it having on the Western world, if it is not simply promoting 'Eastern Wisdom'?

A: This material is well developed as an instructional medium in the East; so it would not be good sense to attempt to improve on or substitute for something which is tested and effective. Take it the other way around: people in the East do not usually try to invent radio for themselves just because it was invented in, and imported from, the West.

The effect which our material is having in the Western world is already extensively written about by people in the West, who say that they find it useful, and I must refer you on this point to these people.

Another reason why we have not been using material from the West is that until recently we have not had a home-grown product, sufficient material of this kind, to recycle.

Even if we had been able to collect it, its reception, due to established patterns of disdain for narrative instruction, would not have given it a fair chance. Only after indicating its usage, vitality and durability in certain cultures which have found it useful could we induce people elsewhere to look for the local product and – above all – make use of it.

We have had to re-open the question of the possible value of tales, stories, jokes and narrative, and hold this door open in the face of a long-standing Western convention that such material is only of entertainment value. What has happened is that the equivalent of a technological infra-structure, or a basic literacy in this field, is being established in the West.

But you should not assume, merely because you are living and studying in the West, that (a) this material is intended only for the West: because it has also had a phenomenal success in the East; or that (b) people in the East have not had to go through a similar retrieval and refamiliarisation process to enable them to reclaim the non-entertainment content in these artefacts of their own cultures.

Indeed, in the East as in the West there are still many people who are unable to adjust to the restoration of extra and educational dimensions in the material. It is fair to say that whereas in general the West has only recently acquired the time, energy, flexibility and variety of curiosity to examine the materials in the manner intended by its original producers, so – again in general – the East has tended to have forgotten the attributions, depth, content and structures in which it was traditionally presented.

Sections of both communities have been coming to a fresh understanding of the materials; sections of each remain, largely for reasons of personal insecurity and attachment to over-simplified ideologies, uninterested or hostile.

It is further worth noting that much of Western religion and tradition is thoroughly saturated with Eastern tales and stories, many of them, according to Sufis, originally tales of inner meaning, now taken as literal truth or only analogy. And tales and stories are almost the only cultural phenomenon which are found as the property of all peoples of the world, not belonging, strictly speaking, to anyone.

OPPOSITION TO ARABI

Ibn Arabi taught through what was apparently love-poetry, and people became bitterly hostile towards him. This behaviour of theirs was due to their inability to understand the projection which he was using, not to the reality of their imaginings. But their suppositions about him and his work were firmly believed by them to represent the truth, to be factual in nature. In his case, he was able to teach them further by providing a commentary which satisfied them and caused them to hail him as a great mystic. But in so doing, since they had not arrived at this understanding through inward and personal perception, they were cut off from the benefits of the material's actual use within themselves. They were only intellectually and emotionally satisfied. Their perception of him was limited to a reassurance that his ideas did not conflict with their own ingrained beliefs.

It is this mentality of what is in fact superficial assessment which causes the poverty of potential understanding in people who seek only explanation and not perceptions.

Stories of the Miraculous

Q: Are the 'miraculous' stories of the doings of Sufis literally true, or are they designed to illustrate structures equivalent to what may happen, or are they intended to make people credulous or to 'think in a new way'?

A: The answer is the same as the answer to such a question as 'Is a carrot yellow, is it intended to give nourishment, or to propagate itself, or to make up stories about?' The truth is that, under the right circumstances all of the factors may be true, according to what use is made of them.

You can use dervish tales to impress people, if they want to be impressed or if you gain anything from such deception, and many people do actually do so.

Again, the hearers can misuse them if they insist upon being impressed, or upon being cynical about them. They almost always, too, contain structures and immediate values which may be analogical; and they may be again and again repeated in actual events, which makes them literally true when they recur in their cyclical fashion.

Q: Can I have an example of one which you can remember as actually having happened, as well as being traditional and as representing a pattern?

THE KING AND THE WOODCUTTER

A: Here is one, very well known among the Afghans, and attributed nowadays to Ahmad Shah the first king of modern Afghanistan:

Ahmad Shah was crowned King with a wreath by a certain dervish, respected by all. From that time on, he often wore the dervish mantle, and roamed among his subjects, seeking to improve the quality of his rule.

One day he visited, in this disguise, a woodcutter, living in a forest shack. 'What would you do if you could not sell your wood?' he asked. 'Respected Dervish,' said the woodcutter, 'I would trust in God and find something.'

The next day the king had it proclaimed that no woodcutters were to be allowed into the city, and a day or two later visited the man again, in his disguise.

'How are you living, now that the King has taken such a strange attitude towards woodcutters?' he asked.

'Well, now I make leather belts and sell them to the shops. Trusting in God, I have enough to eat.'

The king left him and some time later issued an edict that no item of leather was to be sold in the shops.

When Ahmad Shah visited his poor woodcutter-leather-belt-maker again, he said: 'How are you getting on, now that Fate seems to be pursuing you and has stopped your new career?'

'Sir,' said the other man, 'I trust in God and work as a market porter. All is well, and I have enough to eat.'

Ahmad Shah now caused all market porters to be conscripted into the Palace Guard, without any pay, and not even to be given anywhere to sleep.

That night the king went in his dervish cloak to see his friend, and found him in his hut, eating some food and whittling wood.

'What are you doing?' asked the king. 'I have been taken into the Royal Guard, but without food or anywhere to sleep,' said the man; 'so I have pawned the sword they issued me, bought the necessary food, and I am making a dummy sword until my future shall further be known.'

The king went back to his palace.

The following morning the Commander of the Guard called the woodcutter and ordered him to behead a prisoner. They walked together to the place of execution, where the king, as was the custom, was waiting. The woodcutter did not recognise the king in his crown and royal robes, but saying 'Trusting in God', he drew his wooden sword and awaited the order to strike. The prisoner said: 'In the Name of God, may this sword refuse to cut – for I am innocent!' The wood-cutter dropped his sword on the ground. After an investigation the condemned man was found to be innocent after all. Ahmad Shah was so impressed that he made this man his Grand Vizier. From that time the Afghan kings always used before their names 'Al Mutawakkil ala Allah' – he who trusts in God.

EMOTIONAL CRAVING

People who are interested in the miraculous will either 'consume' wonder-tales from emotional craving, or may allow them to operate as alternative ways of thinking about things, to exercise the part of the mind which says: 'stereotyped reactions are constricting'.

The automatic and emotional reactions alike are part of the secondary self and do not represent perception of truth.

Sirri al-Saqati, who died in 867 of the Christian Era, said:

'True wisdom is: non-attachment to self and devotion to Truth.'

Continuous versus Effective Activity

CONTINUOUS activity, labels, a conditioned sense of importance or progress, the attainment of lesser goals on a shallow plane, these tend to be the body and bone of many a human system whose members expect much more of it than it can deliver.

Since it supplies social needs, keeps people occupied and relieves strains, it is believed to be – not just that, but something of a higher order.

On the other hand the teaching method and the study which is discontinuous, which does not use the reward-and-punishment motif, which works with whom it can and when and where it can – the Sufi way – is regarded by the children of automatism as less fulfilling, less interesting, less attractive.

It would be less important, and should be less interesting, if there were an alternative. That is to say, if it were possible to achieve insight, fulfillment, illumination, know yourself, higher consciousness, and so on, through the mechanical organisation. In such a case there would be no need for the Sufi system: it would be irrelevant and ineffective.

But these are not the alternatives. It is only when this is understood that people can approach the Sufi study and can profit from it. Until then they are always hankering after either:

*A system which will be revealed to them if only they will endure the confusions of the Sufis;

*Themselves being able to force order out of what they unconsciously imagine to be the chaotic state of the Sufi projection;

*or something to which they can transfer which may resemble the Sufi one to them, but which offers the kind of stimuli which they crave.

This is no new problem. But it must be stated constantly. If it is learned, real learning outside of the strait-jacket and blinkers of shallower activity can begin.

But how is this done, where do we start?

It is done by lodging the idea firmly in the mind with at least as much durability as the fantasies which oppose it and which masquerade as fact; we start by making sure that we have absorbed the statement, and that we don't just gobble it up and ask for the next piece of attractive news.

HUMANS AS DEMONS

Remember what Rumi said, and you will see how people chain themselves with their desires, which are not the same as their potentialities:

Humans are demons and lust is their chain
It drags them to the shop and field
This chain is composed of fear and anxiousness
Do not see this creation as chainless:
It pulls them to effort and chase
It pulls them to the mines and to the sea.

Capacity comes before Opinion

Q: Some people say they can learn through studying books, others that there isn't anything worthwhile in books, and others that they haven't found the right books yet. What are your reactions to this sort of thing?

A: I can't do better than repeat an old story told by a Sufi. He described how at one time he looked for books and did not find them; then he found them and thought that everything was in them; then he decided that there was nothing in them. Finally, but only after going through all these phases – and phases they are – he realised which *were* the books useful to him, and what their use really was.

What had been wrong was his attitude of accepting or rejecting books before he himself attained the capacity to study the matter properly. He was forming opinions without first developing ordinary capacities further; and asking for things without being able to profit from them.

He should have started with more common sense.

Rumi speaks of people who rely upon the written word as sometimes being no more than donkeys laden with books. Why do people always wonder whether books are any good, without wondering whether they are themselves in a state to profit from them?

When I was first taught this, I was given this saying, so that by calling it to mind I could again experience the shallowness of the discussions about books, as carried out in so many circles:

'Premature independence is the daughter of conceit.'

If you write the question down and look at it, you will, I think (and hope) at once see that it is not a question about Sufi learning, but about books. This person is concentrating on the idea of books, not the ideas in the books.

Sanctified Greed

SUFI study is in some ways more difficult, in others easier, than other forms of study involving man's development of himself.

It is more difficult, for instance, because many of the approaches and behaviour-patterns needed by Sufic study are not naturalised in ordinary culture: they have not been needed by societies in order to form and sustain themselves up to a certain point.

It is easier, again, to approach many Sufi patterns because we already have the analogy of thought-patterns and behaviour-instruction being passed down by the culture for establishing and maintaining itself: the principle is there.

But sometimes the two are in conflict – or seem to be. For example, the undifferentiated desire for attention and frequent stimuli intakes in common-denominator rhythm is known to everyone. In most human cultures, especially in the cruder forms, this stimulus-intake has been harnessed to the culture's own service. It has not been analysed and divided up as, for instance, you would divide (in the case of food) appetite from nutritional requirement and again from taste, flavour, habit and greed.

So, taking our example, people have sanctified greed – so long as it is the kind of greed prized by the society. All other kinds of greed are labelled 'bad', but acceptable greed is labelled 'good motivation', only too often. This diversion of greed into national, tribal and similar objectives only perpetuates addictive behaviour. People develop a taste for, say, attention; the society says: 'Yes, you may have it – all you have to do is to seek our approval by works of charity, heroism' – whatever the society in question thinks it wants or needs. Such approved works not infrequently cause injustice to others.

Because the victim seeks and gets stimuli, he is generally fully occupied with this, and fails to see that he is being manipulated, or that he has a compulsion. His spectrum of perception of the (in this case) acquisitive is never developed. It is as if he had a sense of touch but could not tell fine from rough, or hot from cold. He is correspondingly at a disadvantage in respect to people who have a finer sense and also in respect to his and his society's possible variety, including the solution of problems.

As he has never been told that there is sensitive touch, (to continue the analogy) he cannot perceive it. As he gets approval from using coarse touch, he is at the mercy of those people and institutions which lay down the rules. As he does not conceive the possibility of anything more sophisticated, he has no chance of finding it. Because it does not exist, of course, within the terms of his conventions, in his tribe. Or he may imagine the possibility, but be wrong in his choice of method of developing it.

This is, of course, the pre-rational, pre-scientific, pre-organised state. It is referred to by Sufis as the 'All Soup has Lumps in It' situation: after the tale of the yokel who wouldn't accept lumpless soup because he hadn't encountered it before, and refused to eat it.

So he is not only coarse, he is an addict. How can he be cured?

He can be cured by experience. But first he must conceive the possibility. Next he must be exposed to it, but only after he has attained 'spare capacity', time and alignment which will allow him to focus on the problem. He can never do so while the only alternatives which he is offered are simply other forms of addiction.

He must get used to the idea that he is automatised even while he is gulping the panacea called 'I am not going to be automatised!'

He may have to try again and again. Saadi, in his *Bostan*, 'The Orchard' says: 'Not every oyster holds a pearl/Not every time does the archer hit the target.'

Psychic Idiots

Q: Is there any quick, rule-of-thumb way of telling whether a person is serious and capable of learning in the Sufi Way?

A: If there is any, it is this: serious people are prepared to start at the beginning and go a step at a time, to 'start the journey of a thousand miles with one single step'; people who are not serious are looking for miracles and stimuli and 'advanced work'.

Q: What produces, and what sustains, this unsuitability?

A: Vanity, which is why most systems require humility.

Q: If most systems require this, why does it not work?

A: Because most systems end up by making imagined humility into a form of vanity, so they end up with vanity just the same.

You can perceive a person's aspiration if it is genuine, because this creates a change in the emanations from such a person.

USELESS PRAYER

Omar Khayyam said:
They went, and none returned again
To tell you the telling of that beyond
You won't gain anything through automatic prayer
Prayer is worthless without sincerity and true aspiration.

This second question, about unsuitability, interests me rather more than the first, about 'Quick, rule-of-thumb methods.' Has the enquirer ever asked himself what he could do with such a method?

Q: But surely prayer, properly carried out, can prepare for proper learning?

A: 'Properly learned' is the operative phrase. People who pray and who do not attend to the necessary change in themselves as its basis, are not the same as those who really do pray. People who pray have to be altered by prayer, and this alteration is partly manifested in their behaviour and temperament.

Many Sufi teachers have insisted that disciples observe psychological and social development before even allowing them to pray, or, at least, before acknowledging that they are capable of effective prayer. Khwaja Muinuddin Gharib Nawaz Chishti actually equates prayer with right thought and right action on the ordinary human level:

'Prayer consists,' he said, 'in hearing the complaints of the aggrieved and to assist them; to help the needy and the oppressed; to feed the people and to set free the captives from captivity. All these things, Gharib-Nawaz emphasised, are of great importance.'*

*Dr. Z. H. Sharib, *Khwaja Gharib Nawaz*, Lahore: Ashraf 1961, p. 114.

When Criticism can Stop

ↈↄↄↄ

Q: When do people stop criticising what others are doing?

A: When Jalaludin Rumi started to recite his couplets of wisdom, it is reported, people had not had enough time to form any opinion of him.

Some were interested, some were not. Others, following an inevitable human pattern, resented him. They said: 'We hope that you do not think that you are a second Aesop or something.'

WESTERN SAGE

According to one sage of the West, criticism has to go through these stages:—

1. It is impossible
2. It is possible, but it is useless
3. It is useful, but I knew about it all the time.

Criticism can then stop.

THE SICK MAN WHO CURSED

Enduring the criticism of others may be part of doing good to them. You can read in *The Bostan* of Saadi the story of the sick man whom the great Sufi Maaruf of Karkh was helping. He cursed Maaruf, whose wife asked him why he continued to serve one who was so ungrateful.

Maaruf answered that this patience was part of the help for the sick: the patient, he had observed, could not find rest until after he had been allowed to vent his wrath.

I am not myself much interested in the stopping of criticism. How about interesting oneself in improving the quality of criticism; so that it can be more useful? Much of it is so bad that even undesirable things criticised are not effectively criticised, especially when the critic shows his spleen or bias instead of being constructive.

Sheikh Abdullah Ansari, of Herat, the great Sufi teacher, has rightly said:

The evil of another person can be averted:
There is no escape from one's own . . .

Information and Experience

Q: Why do you stress the importance of information as well as of experience?

A: There is a saying that, according to what a person's mentality is, even an angel may seem to him to have a devil's face.

It is also useful to note that whereas an angel may seem to have a devil's face, and a devil an angel's face, there are other forms of this complaint.

INFORMATION BEFORE OPINION

People tend to form opinions about people, things and ideas, only on the basis of the information and prejudice which they already have. If you show, say, a camera to a child or a primitive man, he might think that it was a monster.

What people need is information, more often than they realise. This is the reason why generations of Sufis have laboured to broaden the basis of information and experience available to man. With information and experience, man may make more reliable judgments about people, ideas and things. The less information he has, the less likely he is to be able to understand. To try to teach anyone who is in a condition of insufficient information is futile, never attempted by real teachers, and wasteful of time and energy to both parties.

INSTITUTION WITHOUT INSIGHT

'Halls and colleges and learned discourses and porch and arch,' says Hafiz, 'what advantage are they when the wise heart and seeing eye are absent?' And to make real sense of experience, information must be there as well.

The Teaching is a Matter of Conduct

ꗗꗗꗗꗗꗗꗗꗗꗗꗗꗗꗗꗗꗗꗗꗗꗗꗗꗗꗗꗗꗗꗗꗗꗗ

Q: Can people pursue a form of study in Sufism without being trained and constantly stimulated, as they are in all systems which I have examined?

A: This famous saying from our tradition repays the closest possible attention: 'The Teaching is a matter of Conduct'.

By acting in a certain manner, a person may be able to give the impression that he is enlightened, studious, worthwhile, valuable or many other impressive things. All teachings, in their lower ranges, seek to teach people to adopt acceptable conduct and behaviour.

CONDUCT, HERE, DOES NOT MEAN CONFORMISM

Because of this emphasis upon conduct, misunderstandings arise very easily. People come to imagine that if they *seem* to be conforming, they are acceptable, or that they are progressing.

The fact is, of course, that conformism is a part of the civilising of people. If they conform to the rules of the culture which surrounds them, larger numbers of people can associate together more easily. Strife is generally reduced. Communication between people becomes possible when, for instance, they are not all talking at once.

It may be necessary to conform to certain kinds of expected behaviour in order to learn something. But when this conformism becomes the only, or major, characteristic of the people, the teaching has stopped taking effect. Instead of learning, we have practice: practice of conformism.

Conformism has two possible evils: (1) that people will mistake it for 'higher' behaviour; (2) that people will believe that all they have to do is to appear to conform, and that as a consequence they will get 'a place in Heaven'.

We are all familiar with human systems in which either or both of these deteriorations are evident. They are so persistent, indeed, that conformism may be taken as the outward mark of organisation. But not only need this not be so: it may be positively dangerous to the potential function of the group.

Then why do we say 'The Teaching is a Matter of Conduct'?

KNOWLEDGE AND ACTION ARE RELATED

First, because when a form of conduct is laid down in the Teaching, whether it be doing a task or carrying out a study or exercise, the relationship between mental 'set' and bodily action is specific. It helps the exercise or undertaking to operate correctly.

Secondly, because when a person is given something to do as an assigned or expected activity, how he does it, whether he does it at all, the degree of competence or activity without constant exhortation: all these are diagnostic. One can tell, and the individual himself should be able to tell by self-examination, whether he is progressing or whether he is behaving in an automatic manner. If he finds that he needs constant stimulus of threat or promise, he is not attuning himself in the right manner. If he will conduct himself in a certain manner only providing that he receives a certain amount of attention, he is placing the demand for attention before the study.

The many different outward forms which the Teaching has assumed through the generations has had two main reasons behind it.

First, that according to the time and culture involved, the Teaching must be projected afresh.

Second, and more to our point at this moment, the 'new' forms are adopted partly in order to prevent automatic conformism.

In a real teaching situation the individual is tested and can test himself against the degree of activity, leading to personal volition, which he is able to maintain without indoctrination, repetition, constant appeals.

In order to show that they are not 'trained and constantly stimulated', as you call it, and to show that conduct is of inner as well as outer significance, Sufis have adopted the *Malamati*

(Blameworthy) method of behaviour. A Sufi may deliberately court opprobrium, not for masochistic or attention-arousing purposes, but in order to show others how readily they will respond to outward signals which may have no meaning at all.

Similarly, some people working in the dervish path have been called *Beshara* (Without Law) because they have chosen down the centuries to practise their training privately, and to avoid public stimuli, to indicate that appearances can mean only superficiality.

TALE OF THE FLY

Saadi reports one quite characteristic example of conduct-teaching, from the life of Hatim al-Asamm: 'The Deaf'. Some didacticians, he says, hold that Hatim of Balkh was deaf: do not believe it. One day he saw a fly caught in a web and spoke to it, for the edification of those present, saying that it had been deceived by something attractive and desirable, but had only managed to get itself caught.

But this analogy of the human condition was further given point by the audience when they realised that Hatim's attention had been attracted to the buzzing of the fly, which other people could hardly hear: and yet it was he who was supposed to be deaf.

Hatim explained that he was not deaf at all. He pretended that he could not hear because then he would not be expected to listen to praise or opposition intended to influence him. If people thought him deaf, those who surrounded him would say what they really thought about him.

An interesting difference between Sufis and others is that, like sociologists and other scientists carrying out tests, Sufis are able to pretend – to deceive, as some will always have it – while the convention is that people should never pretend to be what they are not: in this case, of course, to be deaf. But the Sufi always points out that while he may pretend to a purpose, to point out a fact, the ordinary person will pretend because he wants people to accept and respect him. His pretence, therefore, is far worse and far less productive, except of deception and self-deception.

The study-course laid down by the teacher for his student, in Sufism, may have degenerated into conformism and automatism in various imitative communities and supposed 'schools', but they are easy to identify. The guidance which the teacher gives, no matter what form it takes and how it may conflict with other people's assumptions of what it is or should be, is the method of learning from a Sufi.

The teacher's role is to render himself superfluous to the learner, by helping him to escape from the toils of lesser ideas and of the shallow mind. Until that moment comes, like a guide to a path which is invisible to the learner, the teacher is followed with absolute trust.

The great Sufi Abdul-Qadir of Gilan stresses, in the seventeenth address of his *Futuh al-Ghaib*, that this is like the role of the wet-nurse, who has to cease suckling the infant when it is able to eat solid food. When secondary and low-level attachments have vanished, the Seeker goes into a relationship with objective Reality. At this point, continues the Sheikh, there is no further need of the disciple relationship.

Knowing one's own Sincerity

Q: How can a person know whether he is sincere or not?

A: To be a hypocrite is perhaps the worst thing there is. But I can think of something more destructive than that: it is to imagine that one is not false in 'good resolutions'. Neither imagine that you are false, nor lash yourself, for both may be forms of self-indulgence.

Have the courage to recognise that, no matter how many people are impressed by the seeming humility and self-reproach of pious people, the real effort is in knowing about oneself, so that one can do something about it. Once you yield to the comparatively easy way of assuming personal guilt, you may become guilty of amusing yourself, revelling in your worthlessness.

If you do that, people may admire you, they may point you out as a good example, traditional texts may support your thoughts and actions, society may believe that it benefits from your existence – but you could yourself be nowhere.

The real people of knowledge can be said to exist for the purpose of indicating to really earnest seekers that a man is really self-deceived when he feels that he is being righteous. They do not exist to paper over the cracks by agreeing that a certain train of thought or series of actions or both are invariable indications of genuine belief and practice.

One of the great Sufis said: 'A saint is a saint unless he knows that he is one.'

The Sufis have throughout the centuries, commanded the respect and understanding of the majority of religious people by insisting that sincerity can never be simply assumed, in oneself or in anyone else. People know the sincerity of themselves and others by observations of acts and study of thoughts, and testing of words against performance.

The superficially religious apply 'tests' for sincerity which enable ignorance and misunderstanding to continue.

Rumi brings us a fine analogy of this, showing how people in judging things from ignorance of the facts, come to false conclusions.

In this tale, a bedouin was listening to another man saying prayers. He began by repeating a passage from the Koran, where it is said, in Chapter IX ('Repentance') verses 97 onwards:

'The Arabs of the desert are the worst in unbelief and hypocrisy...'

Infuriated, the Arab gave him a blow on the head.

The man at prayer continued the quotation, coming to the passage:

'...But some of the desert Arabs believe in God and in the Last Day...'

'That's better!' said the bedouin, 'now I have taught you how to behave...'

Here the bedouin stands for the superficial and assumption-prone part of the mind of the literalist religious person, whose 'faith' seems demonstrably based on conduct, and whose assessment of the faith of others is based on his own imagination of what the other person's beliefs mean.

Rumi's bedouin – and our questioner about sincerity – could have made this test, had they known of it, to think of the aphorism:

'If you think that you are not self-deluded, just check whether you think well of yourself or not.'

The Would-Be and Should-be people

THERE can be all the difference in the world between the would-be followers of the Tradition and the should-be followers.

Each of them may have the necessary capacity.

The should-be ones could very well never have heard of metaphysics. They could even hate the idea of esotericism. Nowadays there are still very many people who have no ideas about – nor interest in – religion, mysticism, 'things of the mind': though they are fewer every day.

The would-be ones are those who have been attracted at some time or other to a scrap of genuine inner activity. They may have met some person, engaged in some such activity, read some literature. They are would-bes because they believe that because they have heard about something, might even have tried to practise it, for that reason they have a right to it.

In general, close contact with the would-be shows that his interest is comparatively shallow. He is guilty, as the psychologist would claim, of desiring a system which fits in with preconceptions, seeking no more than to achieve any kind of personal equilibrium.

He may have the capacity. Most frequently he does not have the necessary attitude. He will tend, of course, to believe that he has got the right attitude. He will accuse others of not having it.

Both types need education in Sufi evolutionary philosophy, initially by means of familiarisation with its viewpoints and some of its materials. This is difficult, because few general-purpose expositions of this material exist, contrary to the popularised belief that 'it must be in books': or, 'I won't bother with books, but I will get it from someone in the flesh.' But this is why there are, and always have been, Sufi schools. This is one reason why the schools take, to the crude observer, mystifyingly diverse outward forms.

123

As the Akhlaq-i-Muhsini says:

The bird which knows not of sweet water
Has his beak in salt water all the year.

IS YOUR BEAK IN SALT WATER?

This salt water, in the mind of the Sufi, is what is otherwise
called 'The World'. The ordinary person imagines that that which
he more instantly perceives, like material objects and obvious (to
him) thoughts, must logically be what is more real. But the Sufi
says that so-called concrete things are not experienced but inferred.

You infer fire from smoke, and smoke may appear to be real,
but its underlying reality is the fire. When this habit of assuming
that instantly perceptible things are more important than more
subtle ones goes, the latter become perceptible. Sufi study is de-
voted to this task.

It is for this reason that the great Sheikh Abdul-Karim Jili
says:

Truth, reality [al-Haqq] is felt, perceived:
The world is inferred [ma'qulun].

As long as one regards what are in fact secondary things
(including one's secondary, conditioned self) as primary, the
subtler but more real primary element – Reality and the Essence
of the individual – will not be perceived.

A MEETING WITH THREE DERVISHES

I met three dervishes in the Middle East, and asked them whether
they had ever encountered any Seekers from the West. 'Frequently'
they told me. I asked them if they ever taught these people
anything. 'This is what happens' one them said. 'They come to us
and say "Teach us", and we start to try, sitting before them or
leaving them there and retreating to communicate by direct perception.' I wondered what happened next. 'Always the same thing.
After two or three days they set off again, complaining that we
are not doing what we said we would do.'

Satisfactions and Purpose of Ritual

Q: We see people all over the world deriving satisfactions from ritual. How can we get beyond ritual?

A: Initiation and celebratory rituals carried out by religions, societies and other groupings can have various – very different – origins, purposes and functions.

We might liken all these purposes, origins and functions to, say the various processes which are known to and carried out in any given science. In chemistry, distillation is not the same as fermentation; the use of alkalis is not the same as the use of acids. There is both industrial and research chemistry.

In the case of the science of man, there are similar distinctions.

WHEN RITUALISM STARTS

When the knowledge of these distinctions disappears, ritualism takes over, or else the limited use of such processes. When the use and possibility is limited, the effect is slight: it may even be harmful. As Saadi says: 'Though the fire-worshipper may tend his flame for a hundred years, if he falls into it, he will be killed.'

Take prayer. When prayers are carried out among people with a certain preparation, and when due regard is taken for such things as correct attunement, there will be one effect of prayer. If people are encouraged to pray without these or other elements, their prayer may become a psychotherapeutic tool: immensely valuable, but nonetheless at a lower level than its optimum function.

EMOTION MISTAKEN FOR HIGHER FEELINGS

In such a case, emotional feelings are mistaken for spiritual ones. The only objection to such an activity is that a person or community triggered to associating prayer with emotion will be almost incapable of developing further, because the conditioning invariably elicited by the sight, sound or participation in prayer will be an emotional one.

Communities and individuals reared in the emotional and conditioned use of rituals and other procedures have to undergo a reorientation before they can perceive a higher content in such observances.

This is difficult, because such people generally seek a deepening of their familiar experience, not an improvement upon it.

Saadi says, in his *Bostan*: 'Do not expect, my child, a reward from Omar, when you are working in the house of Zaid.'

DEFINITION OF A SUFI

To learn, people must give up a great deal, and this includes ritual as something from which they imagine they might learn. It is to emphasise this that Abu-Yaqub al-Susi, quoted in Kalabadhi's *Taaruf*, states that the Sufi is 'One who does not care when something is taken from him, but who does not cease to seek for what he has not.'

Real and Ostensible Self-Improvement

Q: Does the Sufi school do anything about the automatism of man?

A: Ostensibly, and as far as they understand, people may be trying to improve themselves.

In fact (as can be determined by studying what they are actually doing and what they really mean by what they say) they are often automatising or diverting themselves.

This is only because they are working with a shallow use of the mind, an area which becomes conditioned comparatively easily.

Ironically, many who have heard of this process, and see it in others, think that they are immune from it by the very act of repeating that 'man becomes moribund, conditioned'. Yet this very repetition will automatise, condition him. Liberation, for such theoreticians, is farther than it is from the 'non-initiate', who has never heard of the argument.

It is possible to turn away from automatism by using techniques devised to outmanoeuvre it. But first we must register sufficiently deeply, not just frequently or excitedly, that such a process is needed. Second, we must discover whether the individual involved has the capacity to be deautomatised. Third, we must prescribe the treatment for that particular individual. Fourth, we must assess whether he will abide by the treatment.

These are among the reasons for the techniques and specialised studies of the real Sufi school.

Some people are inwardly determined to retain their automatism, while trying to profit from a Sufi school's work. I think that that is the real problem. 'You are in the bonds of attending to the beard and turban,' says the Diwan of Shams-i-Tabriz, 'how will you gain the quaffer of the great goblet?'

The automatism of man is overcome, in the words of Dhun'Nun, by aiming for 'being as you were, where you were, before you were'.

Roles of Teacher and Student

Q: How does the Sufi teacher overcome the fixed but unperceived biases of the student?

A: Let us look at the relative positions of the teacher and the student. The student regards the teacher as someone who has a quantity of something, and will give him a part of it. Or he may look upon him as someone who knows a method of achieving something.

The teacher sees the student as someone who is eligible for gaining a portion of something. In another sense he looks upon him as someone who can achieve something.

Each in its own way, the attitudes of the two have a connection. The problem of the teacher is greater than the problem of the student. One reason for this is that the student is anxious to learn but seldom realises that he can learn ONLY UNDER THE CONDITIONS WHICH MAKE THIS LEARNING POSSIBLE.

He cannot make real progress until he has undergone a preparation for learning. When this preparation is complete, the student may progress slowly, rapidly or instantly through a number of phases in which he understands what he has called the meaning of life, or to know himself.

The most important thing, therefore, is to get the student into an alignment in which his progress can be effective and continuous.

This can only be directed by someone who knows the whole picture, and who knows what is possible and what is not, with an individual and a given group of people.

Because the student is likely to be imprisoned by attitudes which have trained him, he will tend to approach the teacher, and the teaching, in all kinds of ineffective and minor ways. He will ask for 'peace of mind', progress in his worldly life, money, knowledge, illumination, assurances – all things which may be important in one way or another, but which are not necessarily relevant to his situation. In other words, he asks to be taught, or to be given, knowledge and things which HE HAPPENS TO BE WANTING FOR THE SOLE REASON THAT HE HAS DECIDED THAT THESE ARE NECESSARY OR URGENT.

This, from some viewpoints, is a ridiculous situation. It is as if a schoolboy were to say: 'Yes, teach me French, but teach me only at 4 p.m.', or 'I want to learn mathematics, but I will not do so in this particular class', or, again, 'I would like to learn the principles of biology, but first I must have some information about tadpoles, because to my mind they are the most important thing'.

The fact is that you can learn only what you can be taught. If you impose or interpose conditions gained from speculation, emotion, imagination, intellect and so on, you will still have to learn how to learn. This means finding out how to collect knowledge, stage by correct stage, without the foregoing limitations.

The human being, not knowing what he really is, not knowing where he came from or where he can go to, is hardly in a position merely to assume that he should get his instruction in this or that form; or that before he does anything else his warts should be charmed or his house set in order in a way which he happens capriciously, or even dedicatedly, to demand.

The first duty of the teacher is to make this plain and not to compromise with the superficial sentiments which many people believe are fundamentals.

Rumi says: 'You are a lover of your own experience not of me/You turn to me to feel your own emotion.'

If you look at the way in which you approach things, including your desire to learn and its expression in action, and if you note what mistakes you have made and also what the Sufis say about the roles of teacher and student, you will realise that the fixed but unperceived biases of the student to which you refer need someone outside of the student to supply the stimuli which will enable him (or her) to escape from the trap of customary thinking-patterns.

STUDENTS WHO DO NOT LEARN

Sheikh Abdullah Ansari of Herat, recognised as one of the clearest exponents of the School, as well as one of its greatest sages, lists the things which people do and think which block their progress.

These cause bafflement, sorrow and confusion. People who do not follow their teacher's prescriptions either remain in one of those conditions or else adopt some – often unperceived – psychological stratagem which causes hypocrisy, fanaticism or imagined understanding.

These are the things which the student cannot measure in himself, and which the teacher attends to:

'To want before it is due
To desire more than is due
To want for oneself what belongs to others.'

Some people, of course, are so wilful that even if you tell them that you are not going to compromise with fixed biases, they will continue to battle. In such cases the teacher will disappoint their expectations by making himself out to be unsuitable to the student, borrowing from the *Malamati* techniques. Even then, the delinquent student may not be able to understand what is going on, and will put all kinds of fanciful interpretations on the matter. Saadi, in the *Gulistan*, has a tale about this.

TALE OF THE MUEZZIN

There was once a Muezzin who called the faithful to prayer with such an awful voice that the mosque trustee, a kindly man, offered him ten dinars to go to another town. Subsequently he came across the trustee and said, 'You offered me only ten dinars to go to another town, but where I am now they are offering twenty, but I still refuse to leave.'

The trustee laughed and said: 'Hold out, and you will find that they will even go as high as fifty.'

5

Action and Meaning

Real and Relative Generosity

UNGENEROUS MEN

ONE man heard of the plight of another while he was sitting among friends. He immediately felt moved, and handed out a sum of money to be given to the distressed one.

Another, who had not heard of any special case, went out when he had some money and looked for someone who was in need. He asked him about his needs, and fulfilled them.

Which of these was the really generous man?

The answer is – neither

Both were generous within conventional limits. They were doing what they had been taught to do.

These forms of generosity are sufficient only at the very beginnings of generosity.

Beyond this is the stage for which these other forms are supposed to be the preparation.

Because people rarely rise above the preliminary stages, these shallow forms of generosity are assumed to be the height of generosity.

The real generosity is when a man does something generous when nobody knows about it; or when, other people knowing something about it, he refuses to gain any credit for his generosity, from the recipient or anyone else.

Real generosity is anonymous to the extent that a man should be prepared even to be considered ungenerous rather than explain it to others.

This kind of generosity, in goods, in work and in thought, is deliberately cultivated in the ranks of the Elect, and is practised by those who wish to enter their ranks, with no exceptions at all, and there is no relaxation of this exercise.

Generosity is also marked by doing what one says one will do. Saadi teaches: 'when the generous promise, they perform'.

Not to be greedy is, paradoxically, the highest form of looking after one's true interests.

Greed harms you: generosity helps you.

This is why it has been said: 'Greed is the mother of incapacity'.

Why do Sufis Excel

Q: What stops people making progress, especially in great writings or producing teaching materials?

A: An eminent orientalist has recorded in print his difficulty in understanding how the Sufi classical author Saadi of Shiraz could have written two great Persian classics in three or four years.

This may be a problem to the scholastic: but it describes *his* mind, not Saadi's.

To the Sufi such perplexity marks a situation not dissimilar to that of the ingenuous person who says: 'I can't understand how that man with the thunderstick can bring down such a big metal bird from the sky.'

This 'concealed savage' in man is not present, of course, only in the limited type of scholar. He is the savage which prevents everyone from making progress in any field.

Correct teaching brings out human excellence.

The teaching must, of course, work with the best part of the individual, must be directed to his or her real capacity.

In the first chapter of his *Gulistan*, the 'Rose Garden', Saadi declares:

How can anyone make a good sword from bad iron?
From teaching, the useless one will not become useful.
The rain, whose nature does not change.
Grows flowers in the garden, thorns in the marsh.

People who have fallacious objectives are like the barren soil. The flowers grow from soil which is composed of the right objectives.

The people whom you mention as not making progress are working from an unsuitable basis. 'If you insist on buying poor food, you must be prepared to dislike it at the serving.'

Confusion as a Personal Problem

Q: What can I do about my confusion and worthlessness?

A: People who ask that their confusion be removed should take note of these three points first: —

1. They should satisfy themselves that I (or others) have offered to remove confusion, etc. Sufis have not. They therefore have to trace the source of the offer, if any, to remove confusions and apply to whoever has made the offer. If the 'offer' has in fact arisen within the mind of the applicant, he should recognise this.

2. They should note that confusion, etc., may often be a protection. You may not like a fog, but if it is shielding you from a man-eating tiger, it is better to have it. In too many cases people should be giving thanks for their confusions, which are shields, rather than trying to remove them before they are able to face what lies behind.

3. Plenty of people, and this is of course well recognised today, create and maintain their own confusion, even while imagining that they are trying to escape it.

The answer, therefore, to 'what can I do about my confusion?' is, 'Find out what its cause is, and why it is there. Then decide if you want to do anything about it.'

Confusion comes of not paying attention to what should be attended to first. The problem of the confused, therefore, is that they should become aware of this, first using their wits to observe themselves, and think less about confusion. Remember the proverb: 'A sign is enough for the alert, but a thousand counsels are not enough for the negligent.'

As to feeling worthlessness, there are limits to this as there are to the reverse. Saadi has designed this poem, which I translate from Persian for you, to see that the problem is one of perspective:

A drop which fell from a rain-cloud
Was disturbed by the extent of the sea:

'Who am I in the ocean's vastness?
If IT *is*, then indeed I am *not*!'
While it saw itself with the eye of contempt
A shell nurtured it in its bosom.
The heavens so fostered things
That it became a celebrated, a royal Pearl:
Becoming high from being low
It knocked on the door of nothingness:
Until Being came about.

The Persian poetic convention is that a pearl is a transformed raindrop.

Your confusion is because you are not getting what you want; and your sense of worthlessness is something which you feel you have and do not want. One of the Sufis has remarked, on this same double problem:

'You must strive to be patient both with what you want and what you do not want: for each of them will try you. Exercise both kinds of patience and deserve the human name.'

FEELING YOUR OWN NOTHINGNESS

The Sufi saint Attar records the great ancient Bayazid* as saying: 'You must feel your own nothingness'.

To perceive one's own nothingness is valuable. To indulge oneself emotionally by frightening oneself with it is shallow self-amusement – all the more attractive to many people because they can pretend to themselves that it is sincerity or piety. One has to get beyond this childish state.

---

*In Attar's *Tadhkirat al-Awliyya*. Bayazid died in 875 of the Christian era.

Being a 'Guru'

Q: I find that people tend to depend upon me, and that when I give them attention, or under other circumstances, they 'transfer' onto me; they regard me as a Guru when I try to teach them. I do not want to have people dependent upon me, so I do not want to teach them.

A: When people start to depend upon you in this unwelcome manner, it is up to you to dismiss them, retaining only those who actually can learn, and who do not use you as a source of dependency. I have no idea who told you that there are only two alternatives – to teach and have people dependent, or to 'shut up shop'. I tell you that this is an over-simplification. Shun the people who show these signs, and you will be able to teach usefully.

If, of course, you have nothing to teach, it is your job to convince such people of that.

THE DERVISH'S DISCIPLES

A dervish once went to a Sufi and said: 'People adopt me as their teacher, and I want to dissuade them'. The Sufi said: 'All you have to do is to behave as if you were mad, and they will soon desert you.'

'But my reputation would be gone!' cried the distraught dervish.

'Ah, I see,' said the Sufi, 'the question was about teaching, but what lay behind it was self-esteem!'

Well, do you want people dependent upon you or not?

I wonder whether you realise that Sufis do not call themselves Sufis, because that is arrogance? I was present when a Sufi was asked: 'Why do you not say that you are a Sufi?' He answered: 'That would be self-assertion, and would invite attack.' 'Then,' the questioner said, 'why do you not deny it?' He said: 'That could be untrue, and, moreover could deprive worthwhile people of a means of learning.'

The questioner is perceiving things through his secondary self. The two anecdotes I give draw attention to the working of this self, which cannot teach or learn.

Systems

꧁꧂꧁꧂꧁꧂꧁꧂꧁꧂꧁꧂꧁꧂꧁꧂꧁꧂꧁꧂꧁꧂꧁꧂꧁꧂꧁꧂

Q: I am convinced that the Sufi materials which I have read and heard about are based upon a knowledge of real truth, far more than anything else which I have come across. Why, however, should the Sufis expect you to follow their methods? Is there no other way? What about other systems? I want to exercise humility.

A: The Sufi advocates a certain way, or one or other of a large number of methods, because these are the methods which gave rise to the results which you so unreservedly applaud. So, in effect, they say: 'You like this result? Very well, this is the method by which it was arrived at. You want some other result? Very well, you must apply to those who are responsible for the other result, and seek their methods.'

IN AND OF THE SUFI WAY

I remember hearing this question asked of a certain Sufi. His answer was this:—

'If you want to *learn Sufism*, you must follow the Sufi path. If you want *information* about why you should follow the Sufi path, you must apply to someone who is not teaching, but who is giving out scholarly opinions about the relative merits of various paths.'

As to humility, we can link it with learning by noting the statement of Kalabadhi in his *Taaruf*:

'Humility is the acceptance of the truth about the truth, from the truth.'

The question can both be asked and answered by the same person if he will first attend to the matter of the difference between learning *of* the Sufi Way and learning *in* the Sufi Way.

You see this tendency very often, where things which might be admissible under one set of circumstances are turned into 'perennial truths'.

Someone was asking me just now, for instance, about the question of 'selling knowledge'. He felt that people should not make a charge for wisdom, and expected me to condemn those who did so.

You see how it works? First the fact that knowledge and wisdom are the product of processes is ignored, and they are unconsciously redefined almost as commodities. Then only is it possible to talk about 'selling them'. Now, I can sell you information, or sacks of coal, but neither I nor anyone else can sell knowledge.

JESUS AND THE APPLES

I have recently been reading, too, a remark attributed to Jesus in one of those gospels which are, for one reason or another, condemned by the various churches. Listen to what is said there about selling:

'Jesus said: "There went forth two men to sell apples. The one chose to sell the peel of the apple for its weight in gold, caring nought for the substance of the apples. The other desired to give the apples away, receiving only a little bread for his journey. But men bought the peel of the apples for its weight in gold, caring nought for him who was fain to give to them, nay even despising him." '

Think about this story and see something of the vehicle and the objective, the nature of human thought and behaviour, and the question of human studies and the materials within the structure.

The Vehicle and the Objective

Q: What is your attitude on the structure of human studies and the materials within the structure?

A: A characteristic disease of human thought is to mistake the vehicle and the objective, or the instrument and the aim.

This tendency is seen in all human communities, whether they are what we call 'advanced' or otherwise. It is as strongly present in civilised as in barbaric societies, only its manifestations are different.

The rule is that:

Something which was functional becomes prized for itself: whether it is an exercise becoming a ritual, or an individual worker becoming idolised, or a tool becoming a totem.

Whoever encourages this tendency will always find supporters, because this warp is already in the human environment, and its derivatives will seem 'right'.

On the other hand, the concept of vehicle and instrument, of not seeing the wood for the trees, and other manifestations of this possible confusion, are so well established that there will always be people who will understand the importance of thinking straight on the container and that which is contained, and on other manifestations, including the grub-chrysalis-butterfly one.

The means and the end are not the same. Studies, courses and processes exist for determining, perceiving and profiting from the knowledge of 'means' and 'end'.

Do you remember Omar Khayyam saying:

'Temples and the Kaaba of Mecca are the houses of devotion/ striking the bell is the sound of worship/the girdle and church and rosary and cross/every one is the sign of devotion.'

The tool becoming a totem is especially marked as a tendency when people want to generalise theories, laws and rules out of situations which require a greater flexibility than just one or two alternatives.

Concern and Campaign

Q: If one feels something very strongly, is it not right to pass this on to others, to get them 'concerned', and to form bodies of people who have similar interests?

A: Any of these things might be right, or might be wrong, entirely depending upon what the subject in question is, and who the people involved are. I would have thought this inherent in the question. You only have to look about you to see the confusion and unhappiness caused by people indulging themselves by rushing about worrying other people and making them worriers – and hence inefficient – when concern and propaganda are no substitutes for knowledge and action. However, one of the great advantages of the fact that this 'wet-hen' behaviour is so widespread is that it provides almost daily illustrations of its ugliness and often destructive role, enabling us to avoid it when it is functioning in that way.

Interestingly enough, it has not always been felt that agitation and recruitment are the answers to problems, or even that one does not benefit from sustaining problems, rather than always sharing them.

We can also meditate on the words of the *Anwar-i-Suhaili* – 'The Lights of Canopus' – where it is said:

The nightingale which cannot bear the thorn
It is best that it should never speak of the rose.

Above all, I think that there is a need to know whether one is right, as well as a compulsion to believe that one is right and to convince others of this. The former attitude is just as important, but the latter perhaps is the one more familiar to most people.

'Concerned' people may be right, but they may only be satisfying personal desires. To train other people to share these desires may be admissible: but only, I think, when they are recognised as desires, and not represented as necessities. In the latter case, if they are in fact not truths, both deception and self-deception are taking place. Can this be good?

THE MAN OF STRAW

Saadi tells in *The Bostan* of 'A wise youth from a decent land, who joined a community of people in Darband.' He was a person of 'excellence, intelligence and discernment' and the people received him well.

One day the chief of the pious said to him: 'Go, scatter the rubbish from the mosque!'

The youth went outside and disappeared. When he was seen the next day, he was accused of lack of respect for service, and selfishness, for not doing the sweeping:

'Do you not know, O selfish infant, that men succeed through service?'

Now these people had assumed that he saw what they saw — the dust in the mosque. But he was not a superficialist like them:

'He began to weep, burning with sincerity: "I saw no dust or soil within that building .. I set off, so that the mosque should be clear of straw".'

This man regarded himself as the pollutant of the mosque, while the others only thought of the campaign of cleaning and the concern for the superficial: even when there was no dust in the mosque, they still wanted it swept.

Saadi continues:

This only is the Way of the Dervish:
To humble his person.
For eminence, choose humility!
For to that roof, there is no ladder but this.

The last line contains a play on words, and can also read, in the Persian: 'To that heaven there is no advance than this' ...

Alas, people have not changed much since Saadi. Here is a sentence from a letter written to me by a famous man who is renowned for his spiritual virtues: 'I used to be proud and vain. Since I started to study Eastern teachings I am so humble you would hardly believe it.'

Use, Misuse and Disuse
of forms of Study

Q: How can you explain the many forms in which people have attempted to teach? Since people believe in these forms, believe that they are true renditions of fact, they are enabled to reach truth through them. But is it that some are true and some are not, as the exponents of the organisations claim? If certain forms through which studies are carried out are true, are all the others false?

A: I must have answered this question – or, rather, the questions in this cluster – several hundred times, both in speech and in writing, including what I have written and quoted in books.

The fact that such questions continue to be asked constitutes a quite remarkable demonstration of what questioners are like: some at least will ask questions even though they have been answered in accessible form dozens of times.

But this may mean that the questions need to be answered again and again, until the answers penetrate.

The answers, once again, are: –

1. Truth has no form;

2. The means through which people may perceive Truth have forms;

3. All forms are limited. Some of the limitations are time, place, culture, language;

4. Different forms are not necessarily antagonistic, for the above reasons;

5. Forms have changed through the centuries in obedience to the external world to which all forms belong;

6. When people believe that the form is more important than the Truth, they will not find truth, but will stay with form;

7. Forms are vehicles and instruments, and vehicles and instruments cannot be called good or bad without context;

8. Forms outlive their usefulness, increase or diminish in usefulness;

9. These statements are abundantly to be found in the writings of Sufi teachers. They were written down in order to be read and remembered. They are seldom so energetically stated or so strongly maintained elsewhere, which may account for the fact that they have not been sufficiently heeded by people who have not given Sufi materials the study they deserve.

The outward forms of things of the world, about which Sufis so often speak, include the forms of teaching, which must be understood in their inward meaning, as well as exercising an instrumental function.

Nasir-i-Khusru has truly said:

Your diver [for treasure] has only given you salty clay
Because he has seen from you only envy.
Seek the meaning from the Outward like a man:
Don't be like an ass, content with noise.

THE CAT WITH A UNIVERSITY DEGREE

In February 1975, a fine ginger tom-cat named Orlando was nominated in the Surrey University elections for President of the Students' Union. That the cat was a bona fide student seems evident by the fact that it has a BSc. No doubt it will go on to a higher degree. This news story could very well, in traditional times, have been originated by a Sufi, as a comment on study and the times...

Potentiality and Function

ᴔᴑᴂᴑᴂᴑᴂᴑᴂᴑᴂᴑᴂᴑᴂᴑᴂᴑᴂᴑᴂᴑᴂᴑᴂᴑᴂᴑᴂᴑᴂᴑᴂᴑᴂᴑᴂᴑ

Q: What is the value of spiritual exercises?

A: Here is a story for you:

THE CHESS GAME

A certain countryman was being taught the game of chess. He was rather confused because the piece known as a castle was sometimes referred to as an elephant, sometimes as a castle, sometimes as a rook, and so on.

Finally he got the hang of the names, and the game started.

Within a very few moves his teacher took one of his castles. Picking it up in fury, the countryman ground it under his foot, saying: 'Yes, you have enough names and wide-ranging moves, but in action we can see you are good for nothing!'

What is the value of anything?

The value of spiritual exercises is to be of value to whom they can. The human interest should be to provide the right basis for the exercise, not to seek the exercise itself. The exercise is there and the need is there. What of the state of the individual?

Saadi, in the *Rose Garden*, says:

The Sanctuary is in front and the thief is behind:
If you go, you win, if you sleep, you die.

If you perform spiritual exercises while still not able to distinguish them from emotional activities, you will only be adding to your emotional life. This is why they are always prescribed in authentic schools, unlike the circus system of making everyone do them in imitative cults.

Perhaps one of the best ways of remembering this is to liken it to the story of the fat man who was eating an enormous meal. Someone said to him: 'Aren't you on a diet?' He said: 'Yes, but

I have had my diet for today. This is my dinner.'

Conditioning can be so all-enveloping that it takes over systems which were originally flexible and specific, generalising them out of all recognition, though unfortunately not out of popularity.

This has given rise to a rather wan joke, which nevertheless has a certain minatory quality:

DO YOU KNOW WHAT I AM?

A wandering dervish sat down beside a tousled figure at the roadside, who began to say:

'I can't pray, I can't understand Sufi classics, I don't like esoteric exercises . . .'

'Then give it all up' advised the dervish.

'But how can I? I am a famous "Sufi teacher" in these parts . . .'

Conditioning and Education

Q: You seem to say that people are trained by many ordinary institutions in a manner which people call brainwashing or conditioning. But if psychologists have discovered that this is the way man is trained, what can be done about it, and what is wrong with it?

A: There is no doubt that people are conditioned, and that what they call their opinions and beliefs are frequently not their own but implanted by other people and institutions. Among others, the Sufi Al-Ghazzali pointed this out almost a thousand years ago.

But the assumption that all human education, training and development must be done by these methods is as unnecessary as to imagine, say, that because a tomato can be force-ripened that there is no other way for a tomato to ripen.

Conditioning is necessary, but it will function only for certain purposes.

Other purposes need other approaches.

The *Anwar-i-Suhaili* says:

The world is a hill and our actions are a shout;
The echo of the shout comes back to us.
Even though the wall throws a long shadow,
The shadow itself still runs back to the wall.

Sufi learning comes through nutrition, as it were, in the sense that Tustari answered the question 'What is food?' He said: ' "Food" is the contemplation of the Living One.'

The community of those who have self-realisation is regarded, by Ibn Arabi and others, as 'organic', except that this organisation is far more subtle and effective than that which gave us the analogy in the first place.

The secondary self stands in the way of learning, and it will be conditioned unless it is 'polished' – another technical term, liken-

149

ing it to a mirror on which dust has settled, again emphasised by
Ibn Arabi (in his *Fusus*) as well as by the classical and contemporary exponents of Sufism.

The Search for an Honest Man

THERE always comes a time when instruction-materials which were originally employed to direct the attention of certain people towards a certain aim are adopted as 'gospel', or else simplified out of all usefulness and shallowly interpreted.

A possible example of the latter is the current idea of the meaning of Diogenes' looking with a lamp, in broad daylight, for an honest man.

People think that he did this to indicate how rare were honest men. In fact, this procedure can be seen as a perfectly obvious example of someone directing attention to the whole question: not only to the rarity of honest men, but to the problem as to whether, how and where they might be found. The ambiguity of interpretation appears only when the student does not give both interpretative explanations equal value.

Diogenes, who died in 323 B.C., is known as the founder of the school called the Cynics. Their purpose was to teach that attachment to 'things of the world' was slavery. Today's cynics are, ironically, attached to, slaves of, cynicism.

Again, honesty as an aim must have an archetype beyond the actual dishonesty of humankind. Saadi gives this prayer:

Do to me what is worthy of Thee

Not that which is worthy of me.

The action of teachings differs greatly from their description. Teachings must therefore always remain fresh and flexible, unless we are to deal in terms of the 'secret herb' which I mentioned at Geneva.*

Honesty is, of course, not easy: because real honesty is exercised without difficulty when it is the manifestation of an inner reality, not when it is a duty or difficulty. But certain principles can be used to illustrate the activity of an honest man or woman.

*Idries Shah, *The Elephant in the Dark* (Geneva University Lectures) London: Octagon 1974, p. 69, contains this story.

TALE OF HATIM

When Hatim al-Asamm, of Balkh (now in Afghanistan) went to Baghdad, people surrounded him, saying:

'You are a non-Arab of halting speech, yet you silence everyone.'

He answered: 'Three things enable me to overcome my opponent. I am happy when he is right, and I am sad when he is wrong, and I try not to behave foolishly towards him.'

Ibn Hanbal asked Hatim what things would save humanity from the world. He said:

'There are four things. Accept the ignorance of others and spare them yours; spare for them from your substance, and do not expect any of theirs.'

The posture of honesty is not the same as its reality, as everyone knows. But how many people can tell whether they are honest or behaving as if they were honest?

A certain tale has been coined to give this important subject expression. In order to illustrate, it has been put into the mouth of two lunatics; which should not really make any of us feel that its equivalence could not occur among us marvellously normal people:

First lunatic religionist: 'God spoke to me!'

Second ditto: 'I did no such thing!'

How can one method be as good as another?

Q: What you have said about the same person, or the same group of people, being able to employ entirely different techniques to achieve the same object interests me. But how can one method be as good as another?

A: If a house is on fire, two ladders may be propped against one window. Both lead to the ground. The different colours of the paint on them may obscure the fact that they are ladders.

Q: But how do we know that *either* is a ladder?

A: You know by learning to recognise a ladder when you see one.

Q: How is that done?

A: By familiarising yourself with ladders.

Q: And climbing ladders?

A: While you are learning recognition, climb them as a part of it.

Q: But some people insist that there is only one ladder, their own.

A: They are right, if they are only saying that to focus attention on a specific escape-ladder as an instrument. If it works, it is equivalent to being the only true one. For practical purposes, it is.

Q: Are they right under any other circumstances?

A: Seldom, because if they really were right they would teach not 'There is only this ladder', but 'Look at all these ladders; they can – or could – work. Ours, however, is applicable to you and to me.' Failure to do this reveals ignorance.

Remark: But they are short of time.
Comment: So is everybody.

Q: Are some ladders too short?

A: Ladders are in all conditions: new, old, rotten, short, long, blue, green, weak, strong, available, in use elsewhere, and all the rest of the possibilities.

Q: What should one do about all this?

A: Try to conceive that the house is on fire. If you can do so without becoming obsessed or irrational about it, particularly without becoming suggestible through dwelling on this idea, you may get out. But while you are full of hope or fear, of sentiment or desire for social activity or personal prominence or even recognition, you will not be able to use a ladder, you may not be able to recognise one, certainly you should be spending your energies in circles which abound for the purpose of welcoming such tendencies.

People learn by methods which correspond with the kind and extent of their aspiration: this is the constant Sufi dictum.

In the *Anwar-i-Suhaili* it is said:

Nobody found the way to ascend
Until he found the step of aspiration.
Seek the stage, to mount to the Moon:
None drinks rain from a well.

Equally, of course, there are many people who cannot learn something at a given time, because they have some other expectation, some preoccupation, probably an emotional one. Reflect on this news item:

'More than 3,000 worshippers fled in near-panic from the famous Church of the Blessed Mary of the Rosary at Pompeii on Saturday night, when a bottle of Coca Cola exploded.'*

Daily Telegraph, (London) Monday, 9 May 1977, p. 6, col. 8.

6

Twenty-three Study Points

Twenty-Three Study Points

Q: May I have any brief aphorisms or statements which I can register and study, which will help to progress on the Sufi path?

A: If you are not a viable unit in the ordinary world, you will not become one elsewhere. If you have a poor capacity for making human contacts, we cannot offer you the substitute of a community where 'we understand one another'. That belongs to play-life, what some, of course, generally call real life.

* * *

If you are accustomed to being supported and kept going by social, psychological and other pressures in the everyday world, there is a sense in which you do not really exist at all. The people who collapse in the often unpressured-dervish atmosphere and who slack, become tiresome to others, or seek to attract or obtain attention: they will fall to pieces and one cannot help them.

* * *

Try to remember; and, if you cannot remember, try to become familiar with this idea:

Lots of people who imagine that they are with us because they are physically present, or because by the ordinary tests (feelings of loyalty, indoctrination) are ostensibly present, lots of those people are not effectively here at all. If you are one of those people, there is nothing we can do for you. If you are like an ordinary person: that is, if you have the tendency to 'be here' only for limited and primitive amusement, but have it only as a tendency and not a way of life: then we can perhaps make some progress.

* * *

Remember that the human being is so intensely standardised

that an outside observer, noting his reactions to various stimuli, need not infer an individual controlling brain in each person. He would be more likely to infer the existence of a separate, outside brain, and the people as mere manifesters of its will.

* * *

Register the fact that:
Virtually all organisations known to you work largely by means of your greed. They attract you because what they say or do appeals to your greed. This is concealed only by their appearance. If you stop listening to their words and look at the effect, you will soon see it.

* * *

Remember that greed includes greed for being not greedy. So, if someone says: 'Do not be greedy, be generous', you may inwardly interpret this in such a manner that you will develop a greed for generosity. This, however, remains greed.

* * *

There are some things which you have to do for yourself. These include familiarising yourself with study-materials given to you. You can only really do this – and thus acquire real qualities – if you suspend the indulgence of desire for immediate satisfactions.

* * *

All members of contemporary societies, with few exceptions, are in need of graduating from primitive morality to a higher one. The primitive one is the one which tells you, like a child, that honesty will make you happy, make you successful, get you to higher things. Honesty, you may now be informed, is essential as an instrument, not to be worshipped as a seldom-attained emotion-loaded ideal.

* * *

Sufis have their own methods of deterring unsuitable people. You may only know one or two ways. Pay attention to the techniques which, for instance, deter by compelling people to conclude that they are worthless.

*   *   *

What you may take to be attractive, or even spread out by us to be attractive to you, may well not be intended in this manner at all. That which attracts you, or others, about us may be that which is laid down by us as a tool which enables us to regard you (or others) as unsuitable.

*   *   *

One can give or withhold in a manner far more effective, sophisticated, useful, which is quite invisible to people who think that giving or withholding is done by external assessment. If you seek some mark of favour or 'promotion', know that you are not ready for it. Progress comes through capacity to learn, and is irresistible. Nobody can stand between you and knowledge if you are fit for it.

*   *   *

Anybody or anything may stand between you and knowledge if you are unfit for it.

*   *   *

You can learn more in half an hour's direct contact with a source of knowledge (no matter the apparent reason for the contact or the subject of the transaction) than you can in years of formal effort.

*   *   *

You can learn and equip yourself with latent knowledge, whose development comes at a later stage. Only those who insist upon instant attention want anything else.

*   *   *

The role of the teacher is to provoke capacity in the student, to provide what there is when it will be useful, to guide him towards progress. It is not to impress, to give an impression of virtue, power, importance, general information, knowledge or anything else.

*   *   *

Systematic study or behaviour is valuable when it is of use. When it is not, it can be poisonous.

*   *   *

Those who seek consistency as a major factor, in people or in study materials, are seeking system at a stage where it is not indicated. Children and savages do this, when they ask for information which will explain or make possible 'everything'. Consistency is, however, on offer from those people whose business it is to offer comfort and reassurance as objectives.

*   *   *

If you seek illumination or understanding when what you really need is information or rest from pressures, you will get none of these things. If you know what you want, you should go and get it.

*   *   *

If you carry the habit of judging things into an area where it does not apply, you will judge in a manner which will not correspond with your needs.

*   *   *

You cannot work on a higher level entirely with the concepts, language and experiences of a lower level. Higher level work is in a combination of manners and relationships.

*   *   *

The ultimate absurdity, incapacitating from real learning beyond the stage you have reached, is to imagine that one thing is another. If you think that a book is a sandwich, you may try to eat it, and will not be able to learn what a book can teach. If, too, you imagine that you are being 'open' or 'working' or eager to learn when you are only playing a social game, you will learn nothing. The people who refuse to play that game with you will also, of course, sooner or later annoy you.

*　　*　　*

Human organisations can take two forms: entities which are set up to express or attain the aspirations of their members; and those which exist in order to acquire or provide something which is needed. Wants and needs are not the same. The difference is in information. If people know what they need, they do not have to confuse wants with needs.

*　　*　　*

If you do not know already the difference between opinion and fact, you can study it in the daily and weekly newspapers.

7
Overall Study

Learning and Non-Learning

Q: Why is it that so many people read so much and yet are not changed by it? Can people not absorb Sufi information through the written word?

A: To learn something, you may have often to be exposed to it many times, perhaps from different perspectives; and you also have to give it the kind of attention which will enable you to learn.

In our experience, people fail to learn from Sufi materials for the same reason that they do not learn other things – they read selectively.

The things that touch them emotionally, or which they like or are thrilled by, they will remember or seek in greater quantity and depth.

Since these are often the last materials which they will probably need, and since such an unbalanced attitude towards anything makes the person in need of balance in his approach, we have the situation to which you refer.

We may at once admit that cultures which seek to highlight crudities, things which immediately appeal, and to project them in attractive forms and endorse and sustain them are unlikely to produce, on the whole, people with appetites for other than more of the same thing. But this behaviour will merely perpetuate the same kind of personality and attitude which created it in the first place.

If you have a chocolate cake decorated with sixteen cherries, and you gobble up the cherries because you like them, and then want to know why you have not eaten the cake – what does that make you? And if I tell you, would you like me?

This is the barrier to surmount. It is crossed by observing it in action, deciding to surmount it, and taking action to study comprehensively and not to pretend to be a student and then wonder why one has not learned.

Reading does not change people unless they are ready to change. Rumi said: 'You have seen the mountain, you have not seen the mine inside the mountain.'

Just because a book is available, even one of the very greatest books, does not mean that one can, or perhaps should, try to learn correctly from it at any given moment. The Sufi Sadruddin said, in his *Testament*, 'Hereafter let not every man seek to learn from the writings of the Sheikh Ibn Arabi or from mine, for that gate is barred to the majority of mankind.'*

This is because teachers may not need what is in books, but can use them for students, while students may not know, but might well not profit from studying them as arbitrarily as they ordinarily do.

Even the self-styled 'specialists', some of them scholars, do not translate the various levels and implications of Sufi materials correctly. In fact, there are indications that many of these people do not see the extra dimensions and alternative readings in the classical literature at all. Some even admit that they have not been able to do this.** Somewhat characteristically they do not seem to stop translating or to enrich their perceptions of the material.

The Sufi usage of Hafiz's works is not at all the same as the ordinary translator's or reader's.*** I have noted elsewhere**** that, although it has been translated many times and quoted many thousands of times, there is hardly a correct rendition of the very first couplet of Rumi's major classical Sufi work, *The Masnavi*.

We could give hundreds of examples. In fact, let us just open the *Gulistan* (Rose Garden) of Saadi and look at a passage and see what we find. Here is a passage; it runs in Persian:

Kasani ki yazdan-parasti kunand/Bi-awazi dulab masti kunand.

One English translation gives the meaning, literally enough, as:

---

*Katib Chelebi: *The Balance of Truth*, tr. G. L. Lewis, London: Allen & Unwin, 1957.
**Cf. L. F. Rushbrook Williams, *Sufi Studies East & West*, London: Octagon, and New York: E. P. Dutton Inc., 1973 and 1974.
***See 'Dye your Prayer-Rug with Wine' in this book.
****In my *The Sufis*, London and New York: Doubleday & Co. Inc., and Octagon.

Those who are God-worshippers
Become drunken (even) at the sound of a water-wheel.

Now, the word *dulab* (water-wheel), also means, figuratively, 'deceit' in Persian.

Saadi is saying, therefore:

1. That people who worship the divine (*yazdan*) go into a state of intoxication even at the sound of a water-wheel. This can mean, in this context, either that they can be so conditioned [in the case, of course, of superficialists] that anything will throw them into what they regard as a religious state, or else that anything might remind [rightly-attuned mystics] of Divinity;

2. Either type of person just referred to can be diverted into his or her state (imagined or real) by deceit.

So, instead of having the unexceptionable but fragmentary translation 'Anything will throw the religious into an ecstasy', we find a whole range of meanings open up as we look at the words and their alternative significations, including: –

1. Fixation upon the Divine can lead to becoming intoxicated by it, by the sound made by an inanimate object not intended to elicit such a reaction;

2. People who have fixated upon the Divine may revert to the intoxication [which may or may not be a veridical mystical experience] by a rhythmic sound;

3. Genuine mystical experiences can be invoked in the devout by rhythmic methods;

4. Experiences thought to be mystical can be elicited in people who have [genuinely or otherwise] engaged in divine worship by deceit(s).

This kind of multiple meaning abounds in Persian poetry. The Sufi has to be able to keep all the alternative possibilities of meaning in mind, so as to be able to look at the whole range of possible significances of human experience which ordinary people compress into a far smaller range of understanding.

Some Characteristics of
Sufi Literature

ᖇᑫᑕᑫᖇᑫᑕᑫᖇᑫᑕᑫᖇᑫᑕᑫᖇᑫᑕᑫᖇᑫᑕᑫᖇᑫᑕᑫᖇᑫᑕᑫᖇᑫᑕᑫᖇᑫᑕᑫᖇᑫᑕᑫᖇᑫᑕᑫᖇᑫᑕᑫᖇᑫᑕᑫᖇᑫ

Q: We find, in your book *The Sufis*, some illuminating material on Sufi literature. Could you say something more on this subject, to help in its study?

A: Nothing betrays the superficial or the uninformed student, when it comes to study and presentation of formerly current texts, like the use made by such people of literature.

To be entirely specific, we must point out that those who are primarily littérateurs and academic workers have a manner of study and an appreciation of literature which corresponds only with the outer husk of Sufi literature.

People are reluctant to admit this possibility, partly because so much of the Sufi literature is a part of the classical literary heritage: they think that it must be susceptible only to study for its derivations, variety, elegance, vocabulary and so on.

To say that all this superb material contains something which its' self-styled greatest supporters do not perceive is asking for their outraged condemnation. But, as this happens to be true, we are obliged to say it. Whether they like it or not, Sufi literature was not written for certain pedants, for orientalists, or even, often, for the generation of today. There is the husk for all to see. The kernel may be garnered by those who, first, know which is the husk; and also how to reach the kernel.

Viewed from this 'instrumental' usage of literature, the activities of memorising passages, selecting parts which appeal to one, comparing editions and manuscripts, seeking emotional or intellectual stimulus – all this is a different field from the inner functional one represented in this literature.

Let it not be denied that such masters as Rumi have baldly stated this fact. Nobody takes any notice – they go on studying Rumi. The result is that they imbibe the teaching material together with the antidote, corrective or protective material in which it is enshrouded. The only effect is cultural, in the anthropologist's sense of the word.

From the Sufic point of view, such people are of course completely entitled to their level of appreciation. The seriousness of the situation becomes evident when they teach others, people who are capable of greater understanding, to treat the materials in the same relatively shallow manner as they do themselves.

It is at this point that we have something to say and much to do.

Such trained individuals, we find, have their scope of 'being' attenuated, their perceptions (in the Sufic sense) dwarfed. They sometimes become conditioned to certain stimuli, they develop what can be alarming tendencies of a doctrinaire or academic nature.

Here are a few characteristics of Sufi literature:–

1. Some books, some passages, are intended to be read in a certain order.

2. Some books and passages have to be read under specific environmental conditions.

3. Some have to be read aloud, some silently, some alone, some in company.

4. Some are only vehicles for illustrations or other content generally regarded as extraneous or secondary to the text.

5. Some are of limited use or ephemeral function, being addressed to communities in certain places, at certain stages of development, or for a limited time.

6. Some forms have concealed meanings which yield coherent but misleading meanings, safety-devices to ward off tamperers.

7. Some are interlarded with material deliberately designed to confuse or sidetrack those who are not properly instructed, for their own protection.

8. Some books contain a completely different potential, and they are communicators through another means than the writing contained in them. They are not designed primarily to be read at all.

9. Sufi literature is a part of a carefully worked out plan. Its abuse leads to nothing of permanent value.

L.H.L.—10

Sufi teachings, and sometimes keys to it, are sometimes embedded in quite other material, not recognisable as Sufi at all to the uninitiated. Many of these teachings are really meditation-themes. They have a deep function almost unknown to pedestrian conventionalists, enthusiasts, imitators or the occultist.

Many people familiarise themselves with the classics, or any Sufi literature which they can obtain, thinking that they will benefit by doing this. Many again think that they have really benefitted. But since the frequency or pattern upon which the studies are planned cannot be penetrated by such people, they do not gain the nutritional and developmental content of the materials.

Even the sheer familiarisation with Sufi materials, for the purpose of future development, must at some point take place in accordance with the school pattern, itself based upon the 'great design' which unlocks the treasures of this extraordinary store-house.

No form of selectivity, no A to Z treatment of study, no mere immersing of oneself in 'Sufi thought', no participation in Sufi exercises or rituals, can, if carried out arbitrarily (and by this we mean without the direction of those who know the pattern) none of this can yield the deep Sufic content.

People may think that they have gained something. But this is characteristic of the adherents of each and every school, system, religion and so on. What they have gained is much more superficial than they imagine.

These are among the reasons for a special and specialised school to preside over exposure to the Sufi materials.

Sufi materials, of necessity, are designed to be perceptible in real meaning to those who are at a stage or in a condition to profit from them. If people are not, they accept shallow, emotional or misguided 'meanings' from Sufic materials.

This tendency is paralleled in the behaviour of animals and people at different stages of understanding and states of mind. You can find such examples, showing the failure to use one's mind correctly, every day in equivalent situations in ordinary life. Many Sufi jokes reproduce such situations, but the newspapers are also full of them. Consider the following:

THE PROTECTED MONUMENT

'Councillors at Ryde, Isle of Wight, burst into laughter last night on hearing from [a Government Department in] Whitehall that Seaview Pier was officially listed as a building of historic or architectural interest. The pier was demolished in 1952.'*

Lack of accurate information and the underlying failure to seek it, coupled with the assumption that things were in the condition imagined by whoever drafted that scheduling order provided the protection of the non-existent pier. The same kind of thinking is involved when many people deal with ideas, literature and personalities rather than buildings. The same kind of mental equipment approaches a different proposition in the same kind of way.

You do not even have to be a human being to assume things about something resulting in harm and uselessness to yourself. Look at this:

THE MONKEY AND THE HEAD

'A man had to be given hospital treatment for a sprained neck in Kuala Lampur, Malaysia, when a monkey trained to pluck coconuts from high trees jumped on to his shoulders and began twisting his head.'**

That monkey, no doubt, if trained, would have scheduled a non-existing building as 'of interest'.

Communication has to take into account the person to whom something is to be communicated. Consider this and compare it with someone buying a book and reading it according to his own conceptions of what it is trying to convey:

DOG AND DINNER

A Swiss couple told the newspaper *Blick* that they had taken their pet poodle into a Hong Kong restaurant and signalled to the waiter that they wanted it fed, making eating signs. The poodle was taken away. When the waiter came back with a dish under a

*Daily Express (London) 6 October 1971, p. 1.
**Ibid., 29 November 1969, p. 1., cols 5–6.

silver lid, they found their dog roasted inside, garnished with pepper sauce and bamboo shoots.***

The couple were reported to be traumatised and to be suffering from emotional shock. Many Sufi teachers, such as Rumi, reflecting in his *Fihi Ma Fihi* and the *Masnavi* on how people behave with spiritual materials, have almost an equal air of traumatisation.

***<i>The Times</i> (London) 21 August 1971, p. 1., col. 8 (via Reuter).

Impartiality as a Point of View

Q: How do we reach impartiality?

A: Most people's impartiality is not such at all, but a cover for a partial point of view.

If you have a bias towards impartiality, your goal must be the control of bias, not the struggle towards impartiality – because you will never reach impartiality through bias.

People who believe that they are impartial, however, seldom are.

To find impartial people is usually easy only for those who do not need them.

As the Anwar-i-Suhaili says:

'If practice were verification, we would be able to discern liars by their faces.'

As an example of impartiality, remember the action of Bishr al-Hafi, quoted by Ghazzali, in his *Book of Knowledge*, who buried a large number of books, saying:

'I feel the urge to recount Traditions. But I will not do this until the desire abates.'

Lack of experience and information causes lack of impartiality; but this does not stop people from believing that they are in fact objective. They believe this because they have a strong desire to be or to appear to be impartial. Hence Bishr's pointing to the disabling role of the emotion of desire.

We can illustrate what people do when they have too little information and too much desire in a safely 'objective' case of an anthropological observation from New Guinea:

BUYING THE PRESIDENT

In April 1966 some islanders refused to pay taxes because they were saving up to buy the President of the United States. They had already refused to vote as the President's name was not on the ballot paper . . .*

*The Times, (London) 14 April 1966, quoting Reuter, April 13.

To reach an impartial viewpoint, you have to be able to look at situations beyond their immediate 'message', so that you can eventually see things 'in the round'.

If I were asked to illustrate this by a Western parallel, I would choose this tale:

TWO MEN IN A MADHOUSE

A guide in a certain madhouse was describing two cases to some visiting psychiatrists. 'In this padded cell,' he said, 'we have a man who went mad when another man married the girl whom he was in love with.'

'And in the next cell?' asked a visitor.

'In that one we have the man who actually did marry the girl.'

Characteristics and Purposes
of a Sufi Group

త్రివ్రావ్రివ్రావ్రివ్రావ్రివ్రావ్రివ్రావ్రివ్రావ్రివ్రావ్రివ్రావ్రివ్రావ్రివ్రావ్రివ్రావ్రివ్రావ్రి

Q: May we have some characteristics and purposes of a living Sufi group?

A:
Appearance: May take any form consistent with the culture in which it is operating, the commanding principle being that certain people have to be related in some kind of a viable entity.

Objective: To form and maintain, under appropriate guidance, the special conditions in which the Teaching can operate.

Intention: To enable as many people as possible, in due order, to achieve the understanding which will facilitate the higher (as well as the lower) effects of the Teaching to give the maximum developmental help.

Programme: To keep the group operating as a channel for the successively refined impulses from the Source, and to attune the members to be able to perceive these impulses.

Characteristics: Enough serious-minded but not indoctrinated people; attitudes suitable for the transmission to act upon; an orientation suitable to accept and work with the materials provided or indicated by the Representative for the time being of the Teaching.

Modus Operandi: Meetings, reading, 'audition', performances, practices, theoretical and practical study, organisation of environment.

Deterioration: Evidenced by the acceptance of simplifications, contraction of activity, messianic and panacea thinking, hierarchical behaviour patterns believed to be sacrosanct, literal acceptance of the figurative and vice-versa, hagiography, providing social and psychological stimuli and/or reassurances, offering scope for personality-projection, assuaging desires for attention, substituting itself for diversions of a political, organisational, religious, psychological, social, academic, family and other groupings.

Contrast this with the kind of group, that of the 'man of learning' surrounded by others, of whom Al-Thauri says 'Be assured that he is an impostor and a fraud: because if he were to tell them the truth, they would hate him'.

Prerequisites for a Student of Sufism

Q: Can you give me an essential prerequisite for a student of Sufism? I think that it is to be misunderstood.

A: One essential is that the student should not attempt to impose his own conditions of study or criteria of progress.

On understanding, a student should not think that he can understand just because he wants to.

A THOUSAND WILL CALL YOU AN UNBELIEVER

On being understood, it was the great Junaid of Baghdad who said:

'Nobody attains to the degree of Truth until a thousand sincere people have pronounced him an unbeliever.'

But the sincerity he is talking about here is not real sincerity, absolute objectivity. It is the sincerity of people who imagine themselves to be sincere because they believe certain things, whether they know these things or not.

The sincere act, reflecting the real sincerity, is defined by Abu-Yaqub al-Susi, in Kalabadhi's *Taaruf*:

'The really sincere act is the one which is known by no recording angel, by no demon to afflict it, nor by the self, to become prideful of it.'

This means that human beings have to become aware of their essence, the real part of themselves, which speaks when the other elements are silent.

THE INSECT

In *Fihi ma Fihi*, Rumi says that there is a minute insect in a field, which cannot be seen at first. But as soon as it makes a sound, people are alerted and see it. People, similarly, are lost in the field of this world, their surroundings and preoccupations. The human essence within is concealed by all this disturbance.

177

THEY ALL LOOK THE SAME

A Chinese restaurant manager, asked in a London court to identify a man who was appealing against sentence for stealing chickens from a Chinese restaurant, said: 'All white men look the same to me.'*

What is seen is not always understood in its qualities which may be relevant to a given perception, as with the Chinese and the white man. The Chinese, in Rumi's terms, is 'lost' in the field of his own world. The white man, in the expectation of the court, was in his appearance instrumental: that is to say, identification of his appearance would lead to certain facts. The description, though necessary, was secondary.

The student should also regard such things as lectures as instrumental, not descriptive, remembering what Faris relates that Abu-Abdullah Shikthal answered when asked why he did not lecture:

'Existence is not real, and it is wrong to speak of what is not real. Words cannot be used to describe the Real, so why should I speak?'

The student must be prepared for experience and intakes which do not affect the ordinary consciousness where words and emotions exercise their functions.

Although 'the world' is not real, since what we perceive of it depends on our sense-perceptions which may be faulty, trained or changed: and it is hence not any kind of an absolute, the instrumental function means that it can be employed for teaching purposes. This is why an 'essential prerequisite' which you ask for is certainly that this principle should be registered in your mind. As the Sufi Gharib-Nawaz puts it:

'Every particle of dust is a cup wherein all the world can be seen.'

Some things in the world conduce towards understanding and some towards a greater involvement with the world and consequent lack of perception and false understanding.

PARABLE OF THE TREE

Sheikh Abdul-Qadir of Gilan, in his twenty-seventh address of the

Daily Telegraph (London) 25 January 1969, p. 23.

Futuh al-Ghaib invites his hearers to think of good and evil as two fruits from the same tree. 'Approach the tree itself and become its guard and attendant servant and acquire knowledge of these two branches and of the two fruits and their neighbourhoods and remain near that branch which yields sweet fruit – then it will be your food and source of strength and beware lest you should approach the other branch and eat the fruit thereof and thus its bitterness should kill you ... and when these fruits are brought before you and the sweet cannot be distinguished from the bitter and you start eating them ... you may put the bitter one in your mouth.'

In Step is out of Step

Q: Can you say something about the technical use of the term 'The Madman' for the Sufi?

A: There is a Persian saying: 'To a madman, it is enough to shout HOO!' (*Diwana-ra HOOI bas ast*). The repetition of the syllable HOO is a part of Sufi rites. Hence this saying indicates, to the intellectualist, that you merely shout this word and the well-conditioned disciple starts capering; and capering, as the uninitiated would think, without rhyme or reason. But the Sufi prides himself upon being, in the eyes of the uninstructed, 'a madman'; and so he uses the phrase himself to indicate that at a certain stage of initiation, the one syllable, once repeated, is enough to sustain him and produce in him the state which he desires.

This brings us straight away to the difficulties of a practice which is inexplicable to one set of people, yet completely LIVED by another.

The books that have been written by Sufis are partial ones; they have to be read at certain times, perhaps in conjunction with certain movements, or certain attunements, otherwise their meaning is but fragmentary like a great deal of other initiatory material which has been taken at its face value by 'outer' observers. It is as if a man were to lick the outside of an apple and pronounce it pleasant to the nose but seemingly devoid of nourishment.

Some people may say that they will not seek illumination or other-worldly truths if it involves their capering about. This is like saying that you will drive your car, providing that nobody is allowed to fill the fuel tank. Some say that they want something that they can understand before they will 'go into it'. This can be like saying that you will have to drive the train, or you will not travel in it at all.

It is this 'outer' attitude towards initiatory systems which gives rise to false cults which purport to give you 'secrets' that you can understand. Except that they do not, in fact, give you such things at all.

If you feel that you can understand a poem, providing that you are given time or peace to absorb it, and will not consider it otherwise, you can be cutting yourself off from a poem which may have been written specifically to be read or recited only under certain circumstances, which themselves may involve a negation of the conditions which you seek to impose. One example is convention, which you have created or copied from someone else. It is not enough to claim that these canons are sacrosanct. They are not, cannot be – and cannot be shown to be.

The famous phrase: *'C'est magnifique, mais ce n'est pas la guerre'* is a typical example of something that should not be, according to the Sufi belief. Indeed, it CANNOT be.

There is an interesting saying involving the use of the technical term 'madman' for 'Sufi':

'A fool can easily drop a rock into a well, but a hundred scholars may not be able to raise it out again. It may need a Sufi.'

This saying refers to the difficulty which certain intellectuals (scholars) have in dealing with fixed ideas or psychological problems (a fool).

What seems madness to some may be sanity to others: and, of course the converse. In this connection, remember the words of Sheikh Abdullah Ansari of Herat:

'The skilled artisan uses the same iron to make a horseshoe

As he does for a polished mirror for the King.'

Thirty thousand Americans die each year as a result of taking medicines prescribed by their doctors. Ten times that number need hospital treatment because of the adverse reactions produced by medicines.*

What may be good for some is certainly not at all good for others. The random application of Sufic and other processes, taken from books or transmitted by shallow imitators, is the madness: not the measured and understood application of real specifics to properly diagnosed conditions.

Daily Telegraph (London) 29 January 1976, p. 19, col. 1., quoting the Boston Collaborative Drug Surveillance Program.

'Dye your Prayer-Rug with Wine'

In one of his best-known poems, the great poet Hafiz says that you should dye your prayer-carpet with wine if your teacher tells you to do so.

This advice, alarming though it may be to the limited mind of the literalist, is extensively admired by Sufis – and not only for its poetic beauty in the Persian original.

Sufis admire this admonition because it is a classical example of multiple-meaning, where a precise developmental formula is rendered in several dimensions. Let us look at some of the ingredients separately, which, together, give the instruction and the content which can only be called a living exercise: –

1. *Shock*: 'Dye your rug with wine' is designed to shock anyone whose faith is based on the conditioning, e.g., that 'Wine can only mean something evil';

2. *Allegory*: wine stands for an inner experience, similar to 'mystical rapture' in other systems;

3. *Obedience*: the orders of the teacher are absolute;

4. *Occasion*: the teacher orders one to do something when it is indicated for one's progress. He does not say, 'Dye your rug constantly', not 'Until you dye your rug you cannot be a Sufi'. He says: 'When I tell you to dye your rug – dye it'.

5. *Analogy*: Just as the prayer-carpet is not prayer, is rather, an external thing, so, too, on that level, is wine an external thing, and therefore secondary. Similarly, obedience to the teacher, though taken by the superficial as implying a great sacrifice and high merit, is only of the crude and superficial order in the relationship between master and disciple as rug is to prayer and wine is to real mystical experience.

6. *Multiplicity of exercises*: It is not said that 'Dyeing the rug with wine is the golden key'. On the contrary, it is more than hinted that this is just one activity, one part of a measured and known activity which will lead somewhere. This is the most powerful distinguishing sign of this system. To the extent to which

the student can learn that he is working within a complex and refined system, and only to that extent, will he be able to move out of crude fanaticism and superficiality. The followers of 'systems' are always looking for – or think that they have found – the single practice, or the only one magic wand, which will give them what they want: illumination or whatever it is.

The value of this teaching cannot be over-emphasised. It will deter and annoy those who cannot profit from it. It will be utterly useless to those who want to turn the Sufi way into a mere cult. It will show up and make obvious those who are simply copyists or romantics, because they will be unable to benefit from the terms in which we have analysed it.

And all this is contained in a few lines of something which a literary observer imagines is perhaps only lyricism and the poetic outpourings of a man who approves of ecstatogenic processes.

Until the real spirit of such technical documents as this is appreciated by the student, we are not dealing with a real student at all; a consumer of poetry, perhaps, a follower, perhaps, a poseur, even, who doesn't know that he is such. But we are not dealing with someone who, in this condition, can progress beyond the exterior.

I have actually heard of people who have set themselves up as teachers and who drink wine and ask their disciples to do so, in an attempt to 'follow what Hafiz said'.

Any comment on such doubly absurd mimetic behaviour should not, I believe, be on any higher level than the joke:

'What effect did the banana diet have on your wife?'

'Well, she isn't any thinner, but you should see her climb trees!'

The Master-Dyer

Q: What kind of planning can Sufis do that people are unfamiliar with in current cultural terms?

A: Try this example:

THE KING AND THE SUFI

There was once a King who found nobody in his realm wise or great enough to succeed him. So he spent some years in enquiries and study until a possible successor, named Arif el Arifin, was located. Now the King, perplexed by the problem of how to introduce the wise man in the face of the inevitable inertia, jealousy and expectations which existed in the absence of a wise man's constant presence and recognition, asked Arif himself to make a plan.

'Who are the people most notorious in your realm for their envy and inflexibility?' Arif asked.

'The dyers of wool and cloth' said the King. 'Each one thinks that he is a master-dyer, and that his techniques and knowledge are the best. These men combine with one another very seldom, and then generally only to oppose the occasional intruder or minor dyer trying to rise in the profession.'

'Very well' said Arif; 'cause it to be announced to the dyers that the world's greatest master of their art is coming to take up his abode in your capital city.'

When the dyers heard the talk of this possibility spread throughout the city, and were shown samples of Arif the Master Dyer's work, which was magnificent, they went into transports of rage. So bitterly did they begin to hate their unknown rival that it very soon became obvious to almost everyone else that powerful emotion, not justice or fidelity to their craft, lay behind their vicious, bitter and often irrational denunciations of the interloper.

Now the people of the country in general whom the dyers had

not educated in distinguishing between a good dye – or dyer – and a bad one, heard the attacks, saw the rage, observed the frenzies. Indeed, it was next to impossible for them to avoid these things. And the main effect which the dyers could achieve, though this was of course not what they sought, was to get the name of Arif the Demon on every lip.

When Arif at last entered the town, the whole population flocked to see him. He lived quietly and with dignity among the people, who were unable to find the treachery, ignorance and evils which they had been warned against, and consequently began to conclude that they had themselves been deceived about Arif's character. Their acceptance of him, and its acceleration, were correspondingly great. Their contempt for the dyers was equally complete. People not only began to take all their dyeing to Arif, but, as in all the best tales, he inherited the kingdom as well.

Much lip-service is paid to the idea that people should not be envious of others, and many people believe that they are not jealous and that they do not oppose others. In fact the reverse is the case, and much of ordinary life uses envy as its fuel. You may recall the saying that there are three things which every individual considers to be attributable only to others: (1) lack of a sense of humour; (2) bad driving; (3) jealousy.

The planning which Sufis do, which is unfamiliar in fact if not in theory in current cultures, is contained in the saying of Dhun'nun the Egyptian, quoted by Khwaja Gharib Nawaz:

'Sufis are those who have expunged from their minds the human tendencies of envy and enmity.'

I cannot forbear from saying, though, that there are many things expressed in current cultural terms which are of the greatest importance to people who want to understand the Sufi way. Some of them may be indicated for people before they can go beyond their present contexts, as you seem to want to do. Most of the people who want 'esoteric knowledge' do not bother about the basic exoteric senses which come first. In the following tale, the first two pieces of advice could have been given to the tense 'seeker' by anyone. He did not need a Sufi:

MISTAKEN IDENTITY

A certain 'seeker after Truth' rushed into the house which had been pointed out to him as that of the Eastern sage. He grabbed the hand of the figure seated on a prayer-rug and begged for advice.

'I have three things to tell you,' said the other man. 'First, you are too excited to understand anything. Second, you are standing on my foot. Third, I am a servant – the Sage lives next door!'

Method, System and Conditioning

THERE are four factors which, when applied upon human beings, 'programme' them like machines. These are the factors which are used in indoctrination and conditioning. By their use, deliberate or otherwise, self-applied or otherwise, the human mind is made more mechanical, and will tend to think along stereotyped lines.

Innumerable experiments, recent and ancient, have fully verified the presence and effect of these factors. They are: tension alternating with relaxation, sloganisation and repetition.

Because most human beings are trained to accept these factors as part of their 'learning' process, almost everything which is presented to a human being to be learned is generally converted by him into material which he applies by these methods.

The test of a teaching system, and of its success, is whether (1) it is applied by these methods, knowingly or otherwise; (2) it develops into a system which uses these methods.

In the various groupings of people engaged in this kind of teaching whom I have contacted during the past few years, virtually none is free from this element or these factors. The result is that one set of slogans has been changed for another: and phrases like 'man is asleep', words like 'essence', certain exercises and techniques as well as literary material, have been studied so closely and so diligently that they have succeeded in the main only in indoctrination. Their instrumental effect is spent.

It is mainly for this reason that tradition repeatedly says that the formulation must change in accordance with the people, the place and the Work.

It is extremely easy to test the individuals who have developed (through no fault of their own) this ('conditioned-reflex') response to work-terms and other teaching stimuli. Such people always respond in a typical manner to approaches made to them, and in this respect they do not differ from people who have been indoctrinated into any static and linear system: political, patriotic, economic, religious, philosophical, where the extra dimension of understanding is weak or absent.

There is, however, a saving grace. This is that if we retrace our position to the point just before the learning and teaching became 'established' as a conditioning in the mind of the individuals, we can reclaim the flexibility which the work demands. The methods used to do this, however, are not ones which are familiar to most people.

You have to be able to understand before you can verify.

People ordinarily do not reach deeply enough into themselves to find out how to learn about what Sufis call Reality. They make premature assumptions about how to learn, and what attracts them must be good, and so on, which in the end defeats their putative purpose.

THE LIMBLESS FOX

In the Bostan of Saadi there is the tale of the man who once saw a limbless fox and wondered how it managed to be so well-fed. Deciding to watch it, he found that it had positioned itself where a lion brought its kill. After eating, the lion would go away, and the fox would eat its leavings. So the man decided to allow fate to serve him in the same way. Sitting down in a street and waiting, all that happened was that he became more and more weak and hungry, for nobody and nothing took any interest in him.

Eventually a voice spoke and said: 'Why should you behave like a lamed fox? Why should you not be a lion, so that others might benefit from your leavings?'

This story is itself an interesting test. One sometimes finds that it encourages people with a desire to teach to set themselves up as teachers, and enables others, who are more humble, to rearrange their ideas, so that they can learn first, no matter what they readily imagine about being able to teach and benefit others before getting their own focus right.

Everything man needs is in the world. How does he use it? Think of the Eastern proverb: 'God provides the food, men provide the cooks.'

Western Culture

Q: Why are you critical of Western culture?

A: The answer, simply, is that I am not really 'critical' of it in the way that I think you mean. You must bear three things in mind when you ask this kind of question, or risk nobody ever bothering to answer it at all : –

1. You have to have some facts to back it up, either specifics or general facts, either to support your question or to get a productive reply.

2. You have to realise that the modern world in which we at the moment live, is very widely suffused with 'Western culture', and that therefore it is almost impossible to miss it if one is critical about almost anything. It is like saying: 'Why do you kill millions of innocent beings – bacteria – everytime you breathe in?' The one may be incidental to the other.

3. This question is being asked, and answered, in a Western country, a part of Western culture, where, because of that culture, agonising self-appraisals, criticism and reproach almost *ad infinitum* have been standard behaviour for a considerable period and without which – if you only listen and read what surrounds you – life would perhaps come to a halt.

If there is any really good reason for criticising 'Western culture' as such, it is that one should deplore its failure to nurture and maintain not the criticism on which it constantly prides itself, but the clear-thinking which, say, the Greeks – supposedly Westerners – had, and which should have been passed to you, to enable you to answer this question for yourself, thus saving time and effort, and using mental capacity for something a little more advanced.

Western people, whatever their ideology, spend much time in the engineering of belief, conviction, commitment – they keep changing the name, but the process is the same. I call it not critical, but descriptive, to mention this, and to offer the remedy: in the saying: 'When you are most convinced: that is the time to use caution about your certainty.'

Western culture, like any other culture, could well take to heart this ancient Eastern saying: 'However useful a garment, it is not for eating.'

The Western Tradition

Q: Can we have tales and illustrations from the *Western* tradition which illustrate or make available the kind of knowledge which is so often quoted from the East?

A: You can certainly *have* such examples, but the problem is that the understanding of the example has, in the West, generally been trivialised – 'give a dog a bad name and hang it'. There are many jokes and stories in Western literature and folklore which may be employed in the development of wisdom. But the convention has been to write them up as short stories, or to laugh at their 'funny side'. As a result, people are inoculated against the effect which they could have in provoking insights.

Q: Why has this not happened to Eastern literature?

A: Because the concept of the 'pearl within the (banal) shell' has been constantly repeated and kept alive. Interestingly enough, the concept has been stressed sufficiently often in the Western translations and repetitions of these stories to insist on this element being maintained as a hypothetical possibility. This insistence that the oyster may contain a pearl, in place of merely selling oysters, as it were, makes it possible for the Western man to look for this content in stories which have an Eastern flavour, when he would not tolerate it in a Western story.

Q: Is there a ready example?

THE HERO HUSBAND

A: Take the tale of the woman who would not marry a man because 'he was not successful'. She said she wanted a hero for a husband. He went to Africa and became a world-famous explorer. When he came back to claim her, she said that she had married in the meantime. He demanded to know who the paragon was who had won her, so that he himself might pay homage to such a man. She confessed: 'He is only the professional at the golf club up the road'. This was made into a wry short story by a Western writer. Its depth, wisdom and sheer power is obscured by the local Western habit of looking only for 'pay-off lines', humour as humour, characterisation, plot, climax, and anti-climax, and so on.

In this process, other values of the story have been lost. But if it were put in an Eastern setting, even Western audiences might see something of great instructional value in it. And there are dozens more of this kind.

Most, but not all, of the word-artefacts formerly current in the West have thus been appropriated by shallow word-smiths or occultists. But some remain, and much more can be retrieved.

TALE OF AN EAR

The materials are often to be found in the West, in encounters, in jokes and tales, in events. But the skill in using them is not there, though it can be developed.

One of the basic Sufi needs is to enable people to see themselves as they really are, and to clear away imaginings about what they are or what they think they are doing. Here is a Western anecdote, good enough for a Sufi demonstration-tale:

A man went to the Van Gogh exhibition in New York. The place was so jammed with people that he could not get near the pictures. He went away and carved an ear from corned beef, then framed it and returned to hang it on the exhibition wall marked: 'Ear of Van Gogh'.

The crowds surrounded this object, thus allowing the true art-lover to see the paintings, and showing that they were themselves there only for sensation.

In a Sufi context, this tale would have been used both to point out the difference between aesthetics and emotion and also for the participants to see themselves as they really were.

In the West, however, such tales are usually employed only as jokes: enabling the hearer to feel amused, and perhaps relieved, that he was not there; or superior because others had been 'deceived' successfully.

It is interesting to reflect that, while the Westerner wants to know if there are traditions in his own history which will help him, the Easterner will tend to want to know whether the material will help him, wherever it comes from.

I am reminded of the old saying: The child remarks, 'That hawk is white', while the adult asks 'How sharp are its talons?'

And I hope that we do not forget, while we are on this subject, that most of the most prized traditions in the West are derived, and not without pride, from the Middle East, and especially the Eastern Mediterranean . . .

How does the Sufi Teach?

꘎꘎꘎꘎꘎꘎꘎꘎꘎꘎꘎꘎꘎꘎꘎꘎꘎꘎꘎꘎꘎꘎꘎꘎꘎꘎꘎꘎꘎꘎꘎꘎꘎꘎꘎

Q: Sufis do not teach by 'stereotypes', as you often say. How does the Sufi teach?

A: The Sufi teacher has the task of communicating his message and reality. He has to reduce, not increase, the effect of his own personality, in favour of content.

A test of the suitability of a student is to find out whether he can set aside the fixation upon a technique, person or school – and make himself open to receive a comprehensive teaching.

The Sufi teacher's mission is to be in the service of those who can learn. He does not exist to please or to displease anyone. To accord with the preconceptions of others as to appearances is irrelevant to his functions: though not necessarily, as Ibn Arabi reminds us, to his social viability.

He works in accordance with the prospects of his students and the possibility of maintaining the continuation of the community of Sufis.

He does not hand out formulas nor does he insist upon the performance of mechanical procedures. His knowledge, on the contrary, makes it possible for him to prescribe apposite studies for suitable people, at an indicated time, in the proper place.

Most people, whatever their opinions and protestations, do not want to learn. Contrary to appearances, they tend to engage in activities which they use as a substitute for learning. These activities they call 'studies'.

Sometimes this proclivity is one which has been trained into them, through books or human contact, even by well-meaning imitators. This causes it to be assumed that certain shallow experiences represent spirituality or the transcendent, or have some other significance which is in fact absent.

If you really want to learn, do not be surprised if someone tries to teach you. And do not lightly reject the method. People who do not know the real bases of a study are, of course, likely to be surprised when its methods are revealed to them.

This revelation is what is known to Sufis as heart-knowledge. Dhun'nun says:

What the eyes see is knowledge.
What the heart knows is Certainty.

False certainty is obsession, whether implanted or otherwise.

Most people nowadays are educated by means of mechanical thinking and within very limited frameworks which, in turn, enable them only to handle certain kinds of experience. This education is excellent, but only for its own purposes. Products of this training use its impoverished and restrictive principles to 'assess' such things as Sufi learning. No wonder we get bizarre results!

Rumi tells of a Sufi and a grammarian who were sitting together. The grammarian announced that 'A word must be one of three things' referring to the grammatical assessment. At once the Sufi went into a frenzy and cried out: 'I have struggled for twenty years in the hope that there was more to a word than this, and now you have removed my hope!'

In this way the Sufi tried to point out to the grammarian that his terms of study were far too narrow, and certainly could not be sustained without the preamble that 'this holds true in grammar' . . .

There is another factor in teaching and learning, portrayed in a story.

IN A LIBRARY

Three dervishes met in a library.

The first said: 'I am going to read all the books of Sufi wisdom. Then I shall ponder their meanings and see how they relate to me.'

The second said: 'I shall copy out the books in my own hand, so that their lessons may sink in. Then I shall review them in their inner and outer significance.'

The third said: 'I shall earn enough to buy all the books and I shall then read them. Then I shall question you two in order to profit from the parts of the books which your words and actions indicate you have not understood.'

'And I' said a fourth dervish, who was passing by and had stopped to listen to them, 'I shall study the third dervish in order to see if his vanity has allowed him to see what there is to see, in the books and in the products of the books.'

The Sufi may not be able to teach by direct teaching as ordinarily understood, even though people request this teaching.

It is related by Sheikh Fariduddin Attar* that the great Samnun Muhibb was once asked, on his return from a pilgrimage, to give them a lecture.

THE LECTURE

When the Sufi spoke, the people were completely unmoved.

So the Sheikh addressed himself to the candles in the mosque where they were – and it was they which rolled about and burned themselves out. The Sufi drew the parallel to his audience, and left.

---

*Tadhkirat al-Awliyya

Idiot's Wisdom

Q: Can you say something about your book *Wisdom of the Idiots*; how the tales and quotations work?

A: The great fraternity of Sufis claims these three things:

That the Sufi teaching leads to a realm of higher human enlightenment;
That whatever its changing outward forms, Sufism is timeless. It may be said to have existed always.
That the aim of Sufi teaching is to provoke experience towards higher knowledge, not simply to supply information or to deal in emotional stimuli.

Sufism has perfected, among other techniques, a characteristic teaching method which is almost unknown outside the ranks of the initiates of the Way. This method, called Diagrammatic of Impression Tales, is contained in the special use made by Sufis of oral and other literature.

Sufi stories, though they may seem on the surface to purvey a moral, or appear intended to entertain, are not literary forms as these things are commonly understood. They are literature incidentally, but teaching-materials primarily. Very many of the classical poets and writers of Persia are avowed Sufis: and their works contain such inner dimensions as those to which I am referring.

The Sufi tale, and certain Sufic quotations of other kinds, are designed, then, equally to be appreciated by the cultured, to convey information, to instruct and to provide what is called 'a framework for the reception of the illumination' in the mind of the student.

This book is designed with the intention of preserving in English not only the form but also the Sufi intention of the story.

One specific thing which can be said about the Sufi tale is that its construction is such as to permit the presentation to the mind of a design or series of relationships. When the reader's mind is familiar with this structure, he can understand concepts and experiences which have a similar structure, but which operate on a higher level of perception. It could be called the relationship of the blueprint to the finished apparatus.

This method, according to Sufi teaching, can yield enlightenment to the individual in accordance with his capacity to understand. It may also form an essential part of a student's preparation-exercises.

The process includes getting beyond the external face of a story, without inhibiting the student's capacity to understand and enjoy its humour or other outward characteristics.

In Sufi circles it is customary for students to soak themselves in stories set for their study, so that their many meanings can become available as and when they are useful for their development. This latter stage may at times require the aid of a teaching master, to indicate the time and place of such development.

It is for these reasons that, in old-fashioned terminology, Sufi tales are said to 'imprison a priceless secret', which is 'released by the power of a teaching master'.

To analyse these special tales deprives them of their instrumental value: just as taking a hammer to pieces would mean that it would cease to be a hammer. The tales have been used from immemorial antiquity as the bearers of knowledge and the instruments of understanding. But they have to be experienced aright. Here is one of the few which help in this experience, and no more can be said about the matter:

THE JOURNEY

A man was on a journey with a Sufi teacher when night fell, and both were tired and hungry. The master asked at a humble house for food and the tenant, a poor man, gave them everything he had.

In the morning, the Sufi said: 'Blessings upon you and your house,' and the two travellers started on their way.

After they had gone a few steps, the disciple said:

'We have surely not recompensed this man for his generosity. Could you not give him more than a mere blessing?'

'He has had enough. More would not be better' said the master.

But the soft-hearted disciple hung his head and with as much politeness as he could exercise, he insisted that 'all are bound to do all they can for others . . .'

'Very well,' said the Sufi, 'I shall let you see what happens.'

He went back and called their host, saying to him:

'A treasure is buried in your garden. It is under that apple tree. Dig it up and flourish.'

The two set off again, and they wandered for a year. It so happened that they were passing the same way again, hungry and tired, when they saw that the house was no longer there. It had been replaced by a palace. The formerly kindly tenant was now a great lord, and everyone around was suffering from his tyranny.

'What do you say now?' asked the teacher.

'I understand what has happened,' said his disciple. 'But if you knew that this would happen, why did you do as I asked: in fact causing this man to become an oppressor?'

The master waved his hand; and the disciple saw that they were back in the conditions of a year before. No trace of the tyrant remained: they were looking at the smiling face of the humble cottager, waving them goodbye. It was at that moment that the disciple realised that the Sufi teacher had vanished. He has not found him since; and that was many years ago.

Attacking Fires

Q: In an article in a literary journal, someone has said that you get on a hobby-horse, attacking scholars. Is this true, and if not true, what are you doing?

A: It is not only what I am doing which interests you, but what others (people in one or two literary journals) are doing. I am not an expert on them; but after someone tried to demolish me on one occasion, a well-known scholar who suffers a lot from this kind of circus sent me this, 'The Non-entity's Prayer':–

> O Lord, make me successful enough to be attacked!
> But if I cannot have this, let me remain unsuccessful enough to retain the delights of attacking others!

If you see a fireman rushing to put out a blaze, and you shout, 'Look at that man on his hobby-horse again, attacking fires!', this luckily neither stops him nor prevents other people from realising that there may be something wrong with you instead. You should also note, if you will, that in the scholarly world itself, my activities seem to be well known and well understood. You should not only look at the person who is being attacked – you should look also at the attacker and form your own opinions as best you can. Although it has taken a decade and a half, there is no lack of both advanced and respected scholars to understand and support our traditional and well-tried 'attack' method as salutary and justified. Can you say the same for the few whom you are quoting?

I have criticised unworthy and shallow scholars only. That certain academics seem to think that I mean them personally is to be interpreted by a psychologist, not by me.

If you look at the thing in isolation, of course you will get a distorted picture. Scholars delight in attacking one another; and the surest way of becoming established in certain fields is to get attacked as 'no scholar', which is a jargon word used by scholars about each other.

The real scholars have a sense of humour which the shallow ones haven't. I'll never forget the occasion when a prominent literary figure was introduced to a meeting with the words, 'I have pleasure in presenting Dr. Bloggs, who has been assailed in almost every serious periodical in his field for nearly twenty years!'

There was thunderous applause.

Rumi often points out, as do many other Sufi writers, that being an expert is not necessarily the best way to profit from something.

THE STRONG MAN IN PAIN

In a story related by Saadi (*The Orchard: On Acceptance*) a doctor visited a strong man who was writhing in pain. His opinion was that since the man had been eating vine-leaves, it would be surprising if he lasted the night. But, continues Saadi, it was the physician who died that very night. That was forty years before – and the athlete still lived!

Scholars and specialists have the problem that subjectivity can affect their thinking. Like the doctor, they may themselves suffer through their lack of knowledge: for it seems unlikely that the physician suspected that his own death was so near – in spite of being so confident about the death of another.

The Prophet Mohammed is reported to have said that the ink of the scholar is holier than the blood of the martyr. In spite of this, Sufis have for many centuries not shrunk from assailing shallow scholars and those who are really pseudo-scholars, wherever they are to be found. If to do this is to be on a hobby-horse, I am honoured to be counted as one who follows so noble an example.

But, in any case, you are a little out of date. The battle has raged away from where I sit. Some scholars attacked me, then others defended me. The first lot called the second shallow, and now they are fighting it out among themselves. I have no part in this controversy, since it is between third parties.

A Bridge and its Use

ᴉᴛ will seem improbable, yet it is no exaggeration to say that people ignore, are unaware of or even sneer at materials which could be their only hope of escaping from circular thinking.

I have learned more from people, things and ideas which are by many considered irrelevant, slight or even worthless, than from much more advertised and crudely emphasized materials.

People who cannot or will not approach these sources of knowledge may accept them when they have been put in a manner which they are prepared to accept. This indicates the serious limitation on learning imposed by so many people's refusal to look at anything which seems to them to be unsuitable, judged from its outward face.

But this is only the first part of a process. You can 'popularise' or make palatable, but at some point you must direct attention to the original thing.

If we have to act as a bridge, we must fulfil the function of a bridge, which is to conduct from one side of something to another side.

DIMENSIONS OF A FOOT

I remember the case of one person who was able to understand this, and hence to become sensitive to the existence and operation of a Sufi school imperceptible to others, by simply digesting the statement of Rumi, in *Fihi ma Fihi*:

'I am a shoemaker, with much leather. But I do the cutting and the stitching according to the dimensions of the foot.'

Deterioration of Studies

Q: How do studies deteriorate?

A: People look for new teachings, or the revelation of concealed ancient ones, when their problem rightly may be that they cannot see the presence of the teaching in the materials abundantly available to them, ancient and otherwise.

They cannot see these teachings because they have chosen to blind themselves to the intention of a teaching-technique. They have 'superficialised' their own heritage of materials. Here is an example:

Many people are impressed by the example that if they look at something for half a minute, they will find their attention wandering. Instead of looking at this as an indication of fact, complete in itself, they do two unnecessarily shallow things; they

1. Try to look at things for long periods in the hope that they will be able to develop attention capacity. They never achieve it, however, when they try in this manner, because the description of the deficiency does not of course, contain the technique;

2. Immediately assume that the person who drew their attention to their lack of attention is able to supply them with the method or system whereby they can remedy the situation. They seldom seem to imagine that, if a man says, 'This door is splintered' he does not necessarily know how to mend it.

These people have lost the versatility of thinking which was the hallmark of ancient teaching. They have 'idolatrised' ideas, by making omniscience resident in illustration. This is exactly what a totemist does. The modern man does not, however, recognise himself as a totemist, perhaps because he does not live in a tropical jungle.

THE REAL POOR

The great Sheikh Abdullah Ansar of Herat said that the really poor are those who are not independent of poverty: those who really care whether they are poor or not poor. Similarly, attachment to secondary concepts causes studies to deteriorate – for when this is the rule, the container is mistaken for the content. There has never been any lack of people who imagine that the physical absence of something is poverty, and that the ownership of material objects is riches. The question of attitude is absent.

You ask how studies deteriorate. One of the causes is the sheer weight of numbers of deluded or superficial people who demand 'deep studies' or 'spiritual knowledge'. They create a supply-and-demand situation which can cause so much imitation of teaching and learning that the imitation is taken for the real.

INDIANS PROHIBITED

In a story current in India, an Indian student in the United States heard that a countryman of his was teaching Hindu spirituality to the people of the West, and was well established there, although he still lived near Delhi for most of the year. When he went home on a vacation, the student sought out the great guru and respectfully sought to become a disciple.

'I'm sorry,' said the chief assistant guru at the Ashram: 'we don't take Indians here – only Europeans or Americans.'

The young Hindu was aghast. 'I thought that the days of colonialist discrimination were over!' he gasped. 'You mean that you won't accept me as a disciple, here in my own country?'

'My dear chap', said the great guru himself, coming to the ashram gate, 'the facts are the other way round: have you ever actually *seen* any of the terrible people who want to drink deep of Indian spirituality? I am trying to protect my countrymen from them.'

Community and Human Growth

Q: How does human growth take place in a community, and what are the dangers of operating in a randomly-collected group?

A: Take certain kinds of organisation and the beliefs about them which are commonly held. Then examine another attitude towards them, in order to learn something.

A certain society is called Freemasons. It is ritualistic, is thought to have 'secrets', and is named after a vocation. People believe that Masonry grew up because of the comradeship of masons and their desire to monopolise certain building knowledge and even to regulate the supply of labour.

Now look at apprenticeship in Europe, Africa and Asia, applied in a wide variety of crafts. Again, there are initiation and other ceremonies. There is a certain relationship, including a contract, between the master and pupil.

Now recall to your mind the special ritualism and connection contained in the institution of kingship. And the rumours and beliefs of special developments or binding force between members of families, clans and other collections of people.

What these all have in common is the belief that certain extra-ordinary perceptions can be developed by means of a certain kind of human association (call it the alchemist and his assistants, the carpet-making fraternity, one of a hundred others) whether or not the individual entering into the association is at first aware of this extra element. In other words, the verbalised form of teaching, even of introduction to higher (or inner) learning, is only one possible approach.

It is, however, not enough that there should be a collection of people with an aim of working in unison or towards an objective: even though without this, the enterprise is absurd.

Aspiration and desire are not enough: and the leadership must understand this as well.

THE MULLA AND THE DROUGHT

The conception is illustrated in this Nasrudin tale:

One day Mulla Nasrudin saw a schoolmaster leading a group of his pupils towards a mosque.

The Mulla asked:

'What is the purpose of this activity, Learned One?'

'There is a drought,' said the teacher, 'and we are hoping that the cries of the innocent will move the Heavens.'

'Cries, innocent or guilty,' said Nasrudin, 'can have no such effect without knowledge.'

'How can you prove such a dangerous statement?' spluttered the affronted pedagogue.

'Easily,' said Nasrudin, 'because if supplications were enough: intentions led by apparent necessity, there would not be a school-teacher left on earth. Children yearn for their abolition.

'So, even if the children's heartcries could have you banished, it would be the prayers of the people of knowledge alone, who understand your function, which still sustain you among us.'

In addition to the enterprise on hand, there must be a correct selection of the particular team. This selection must be effected by a teacher. But, once these conditions are fulfilled, there is no further need of one single word from any of the vocabularies of metaphysics or philosophy, esotericism as we know them.

It is for such reasons as these that spiritual teachers have traditionally followed secular jobs or been administrators or skilled in many crafts: they are teaching through a variety of methods. Only their spoken teaching, or their gymnastic or prayer teachings, however, are recognised as teaching of a higher kind by external thinkers. As a result most of what they have been doing is not recorded or regarded as extraneous or irrelevant.

Just as the random collections of people and tension, anxiety, reward and punishment and the application of dogmas and fixed techniques produce conditioned people and rigid or mechanical institutions so – in the 'organic' field of what we call evolutionary philosophy – the community with the right elements (people, time and place for example) comes into living being and grows in a special manner undreamt of by the stilted formal thinker and the wild emotionalist alike.

The foregoing explains how, if we pause to think for a moment, metaphysical teachers have operated systems which, far from being limited to the simple techniques and doctrines attributed to them, have necessarily consisted of an amazingly comprehensive design.

Only parts of this design have the tenacity to remain in ordinary transmission. Like driftwood, they are continually thrown up, or used again and again, long after their real use (as parts of their original ship) has vanished.

It therefore becomes seemingly paradoxical (though only because people approach things from a consistently naive view-point) that many of the essential parts of higher knowledge would never be recognised as such by those types who tend to regard themselves as students of metaphysics.

A 'tall, tired, tinker, totally tattered, trying to tinker a tenpenny tin teakettle' is just as likely to be a spiritual teacher as the saint with the halo drawn by some pious but unregenerate individual.

He is far more likely to have something worthwhile to communicate, certainly, than the metaphysician who regards him as a tinker alone because he is not familiar with the terminology of this ritual or that.

Unless this lesson is learnt, in one manner or another – and it has many forms – study and practice alike, formal or otherwise, are bankrupt except for the purpose of keeping people occupied: whatever they may think, or may be told, that they are doing.

It is interesting to note how traditional warnings against random groupings actually work out to be justified when one observes them. Saadi said, in a famous passage, that one dog will pollute a whole pool of rosewater. But as near as we can get to describing what happens in a randomly-collected study group is the fact that differing demands of the members from the group prevent its members – individually and collectively – from understanding and concentrating upon important and quite subtle concepts which need much attention and few distractions.

Husri, quoted by Hujwiri, says: 'The Sufi's existence is devoid of non-existence, and his non-existence lacks existence.' Such an idea needs concentration. Even a single individual finds it hard to hold it in the mind, mainly because of himself being so filled with thoughts and ideas. With a group it is even more difficult.

SPECIAL HARMONY

The group must be able to develop a perception of the meaning of the following condition, again from Hujwiri: 'The condition of mortality of the Sufi should be in abeyance, and his sensations should vanish, and his relationship with anything should cease, so that the secret of his existence may emerge, and his separate parts be unified with his essence, his real self, and that he should persist in being.'

In practice, let alone in theory, groups of people are not usually interested in arriving at such states, even though they may imagine themselves to be mystics or esotericists.

There are many people going around, nowadays they can easily be found, who have tried to live in randomly-collected groups, and have failed. They then look for other groups, or try to further their spiritual or psychological development in some other way.

It is, however, easy to see why they have failed: they have not been *prepared to prepare* for such an experience. They either felt that they were ready for the experience; or else that membership of such a group would give them what they needed.

Such an attitude is quite understandable, and exists in any situation where there is a shortfall of information, however much goodwill there may be. They have perhaps forgotten the second line of the proverb:

Put your dough into the oven when it is hot:
After making sure that it is in fact dough.

The Value of Question and
Answer Sessions

Q: Can you say something about the special needs of 'Time, Place and People', and the value of question-and-answer sessions and their limitations?

A: If you place great reliance upon the technique of group-meetings with question-and-answer periods, you may make progress, but at a certain point it will stop.

This is because any teaching which does not use all kinds of procedures (exercises, study-tasks, theory and practice and so on) *in due proportion* will inevitably arrive at a point where some people have obtained as much as they can from each procedure and thereafter will go 'downhill' as far as their development is concerned.

Neither can this question of *due proportion* be understood by people (teachers or pupils) who are not on a stabilized higher level of consciousness. There is no intuition, no delegation of authority, no painstaking research, no seniority in years, no other factor, which can substitute for the knowledge of what procedure to apply, with whom, in what manner, unless that special attunement is there.

To carry on in defiance of this fact produces social or imitative-academic groupings. They can call themselves what they like: they will not progress except socially.

The same is true of bodies of people stabilised upon the performance of ritual, commemorative procedures or stereotyped phraseology, however hallowed by tradition.

The existence of so many bodies of teaching, in so many cultures and epochs, with so many different outward forms is a manifestation of original groups which were tailored for the community of that place, that time, that teacher.

Of all human activities the one involving studies beyond ordinary perceptions must above all be projected in accordance with time, place and people: the last includes the direction of the effort, as is well illustrated by this story:

IF YOUR HANDS ARE FULL

Terribly afraid one dark night, Mulla Nasrudin travelled with a sword in one hand and a dagger in the other. He had been told that these were a sure means of protection.

On the way he was met by a robber, who took his donkey and saddlebags full of valuable books.

The next day, as he was bemoaning his fate in the teahouse, someone asked:

'But why did you let him get away with your possessions, Mulla? Did you not have the means to deter him?'

'IF my hands had not been full' said the Mulla, 'it would have been a different story.'

The use of the story, of course, is to indicate that people may have a transmitted formula ('weapons are a defence') without the ability to understand how to employ it.

Like Nasrudin, they go through the motions, merely carrying the instruments ...

The unusual tenacity of replication of mere form which is to be observed in religious transmission is evidence of human determination, not of effective content.

The ancient Chinese, Babylonian and Egyptian civilisations, as social examples, for instance, endured for thousands of years not because they were especially good and true and necessary: but because they were promoted and maintained by determined men and women, and because there was in addition a quota of inertia in them which prevented laudable change. They did not develop beyond a certain stage.

People appreciate and value form, and therefore do not at first appreciate the reality of Sufis, though they may think they do, mistaking certain outward form for Sufi reality. It is for this reason that the great ancient among the Sufis, Sahl son of Abdullah of Tustar, said: 'You may not appreciate Sufism at first, but once you do you will appreciate it until the end of your days.'

Form can even include expectation, since people all over the world, and of all types, tend to prize the experience of expectation and especially the desire for reward. Form implies the acceptance of automatic or conditioned expectations, and Sufis therefore in their teaching circumstances defy this. As Yahya son of Maaz of Balkh said, over a thousand years ago, in this connexion: 'Ascetics renounce this world, but Sufis renounce expectations of the next one as well. Ascetics seek the pleasures of Paradise, but the Sufi is a stranger even to Paradise.'

His contemporary Sari al-Saqati (who died in 867 of the Christian Era) underlines how the attachment to form and to one's self are intertwined, and says: 'True wisdom is non-attachment to the self and devotion to Truth.' And Sufism is traditionally termed 'Truth without form.'

Talking of the limitations of question-and-answer sessions, the onus of limiting these to useful content and length is upon the teacher.

In his *Table-Talk**, the great master Jalaluddin Rumi said:

The Night passed and our talk did not end:
What sin was the night's? It was our speech
which was too long.

And do not forget the occasional enlightenment of what lurks within some supposedly spiritual people, which can slip out in question-and-answer circumstances. Traditionally, in India, couched in the form of a joke, there is an argument that false gurus can learn to be real ones by suddenly seeing their own inadequacies. This is the story:

'Guruji, why don't you enroll your boy into the Teaching?'

'Because it is against my principles to teach the sons of the rich for nothing!'

*Fihi ma Fihi, edited by Professor Faruzanfar in Tehran, 1952.

Dedication, Service, Sincerity

Q: Is there any real sincerity behind the feeling of the sincerity that is open to doubt?

A: One of the most embarrassing pieces of knowledge to have is to know when someone is doing something for his own entertainment, but is convinced that he is doing something for someone else.

It makes one feel ashamed for such a person, and it makes me shocked by the cultural defect which has trained this wretched individual to imagine that he is serving someone or something, when he is instead obtaining personal gratification.

At this time, and probably for some time to come, there is no hope that most of these people can ever be shown what they are doing: doing to themselves and to others.

Not least sad is the fact that, while someone is pursuing self-gratification believing it to be something else, he neither gets any deep gratification, nor does he ever do anything for anyone else, for a cause, for his real self.

Instead of looking at this problem, man prefers to preen himself and crow: 'Look what I have achieved since I came down out of the trees'.

Isn't that more sad than still being in the trees?

This is a most important technical problem. It can be solved, certainly in the case of some people. But first it must be observed. No culture of today provides any generally applicable theoretical or practical method of drawing attention to it, let alone doing anything about it. And yet it remains one of the major stumbling-blocks to human progress.

Instead of showing that disguised gratification-seeking is a masquerade, and just as inhibiting as any other make-believe (you can't do anything else while you are engaged in pretence) many human cultures sanctify and employ this flaw. Instead of saying: 'You are amusing yourself by engaging in this or that national, cultural, religious, spiritual game,' they may say: 'This is not a game: it is serious. In fact, it is the way to heaven.' For lack of a high enough level of understanding, leaders of thought operate too shallowly.

This is because, at some time in the past, a shortage of technicians who know what really is happening caused a majority of the ignorant to take the place of most of the wise.

Giving people tasks, or letting them choose them, will often either make them inured to such tasks, or else may cause them to derive sadistic or masochistic pleasure from such activities which entail service, dedication, suffering and so on: without an additional dimension of insight.

The only hope is for there to be someone present to prescribe, from time to time, what a person should do and what he should not do, to strengthen his real efforts, to prevent himself becoming a parrot or machine, or to stop sanctimoniousness getting the upper hand.

It is unpopular to say that someone might know better than the individual himself as to the course which he should pursue.

Unpopular, yes. But one cannot hope that everything right will always be popular. The people who go raving about that they 'must sacrifice' are the last people who, for their own sake, should be allowed to make sacrifices. But what happens? Every organisation known to you is on the lookout for just these people, in order to fuel itself from their sacrifice.

Understanding this is what we call seeing oneself and seeing others.

One can help by giving you undertakings to involve yourself in which neither flatter you nor exploit you. But you have to do something towards it, too, you know. This something is not becoming an acceptor, rejector or being uncertain.

It is for you to study this theory and watch it in practice, and keep yourself open to work and study, act and live without forming a part of an unnecessarily over-simplified pattern, which is the way in which the majority of people operate.

THE TREASURE CAVE

Q: People say that premature insight, beyond ordinary understanding, is worse than none: because one cannot use it or be used by it. They also say that someone may lose through greed and yet benefit others. What does all this mean? Can it be put in a more comprehensible form?

A: Greed is the cause of loss and of the inability to profit from apparent gain. This is as true in metaphysics as in ordinary life. But one individual's greed may benefit others – though this effect does not concern him, and does not give him anything.

An ancient tale, still current, puts all this into a more memorable form:

TALE OF THE VILLAGER

There was once a brave villager who had not overcome his attachment to non-essentials. One day he was riding his donkey past a magical cave at the precise moment when it made one of its periodical appearances to humanity. Boldly entering, he found piles of treasure, which he took outside and stuffed into his saddlebags. When the donkey was fully loaded, the man remembered that he had left his stick behind, and he ran back into the cave to retrieve it. But the time for the cave to vanish again had arrived. No sooner was he within than it disappeared, with him inside.

The man was never seen again, and his donkey wandered back to the village. After waiting for him to return, the people sold the donkey and its burden and enriched themselves...

Sufis and Scholars

Q: What is the traditional Sufi objection to certain types of scholars, academic pedants as you have called them, based upon?

A: These scholars may often be regarded as decorative and useful people. Their decorative and utilitarian aspects, however, should be clearly perceived, in accordance with the principle that misunderstandings and distortions always occur when something is not defined which could be defined.

They frequently desire attention, and do all they can to get it. They do not seek to propagate their ideas so much as to require that people think that they are being scholars. I am constantly approached by eminent ones begging me to cite their works, because citations mean importance. This activity is part of their desire to be seen, the self-display aspect. Again, some of them are jealous of special clothes and other appurtenances, and rituals of all kinds, which contribute towards their visibility. This characteristic is observed also in other human groups, in certain animals and birds and is not in itself to be considered undesirable, even if only because we gain some pleasure from such displays.

Like containers, and permutation, accumulation and analysis agents of various kinds, they are able for the most part, to hold, to preserve, even to pass on – but not to effect any real change in – the materials with which they are concerned. A limited scholar who translates a book, for instance, may be giving its contents to someone who can absorb it, like a jug which contains water which will ultimately be drunk by others.

Scholars of the lesser sort, however, being human and not animal or inanimate, sometimes tend to confuse their own desires with their real effect and possible functions. This is only because they may have an image of themselves which has been fostered without being investigated. As one of them said in this very room to some of us the other day, 'We just can't help it!'

Investigated it may not be, but it is observed. It is from Oxford, not the Sufis, that the joke comes: 'I am the Master of Balliol College: and what I don't know can't be knowledge!'

Scholars cannot readily be studied by other scholars, who are by virtue of their involvement unlikely to be able to attain sufficient objectivity.

Scholars, however, can be studied by Sufis. There are innumerable Sufis who have once been scholars: but there is no single Sufi known to us, perhaps to all history, who has subsequently become a scholar. Scholarship, therefore, may be regarded as a stage after which one *may* become a Sufi.

Sufis never have followed scholars, though they have frequently equalled or excelled scholars in scholarship.

Sufis can do this because they do not regard scholarship as an end but as something useful: with the advantages and limitations corresponding to this function. Scholars, quite often, do not show signs of understanding that there is anything beyond scholarship, and therefore they are incapacitated – while they remain at this stage – from being able to have a higher objective. One must always have an aspiration higher than one's actual status in order to rise, even in an existing field.

Such scholars, because they cannot move beyond their conception of scholarship, are driven to believe and to practise two things:

1. They tend to make themselves believe that scholarship is of the highest nature among things and that scholars are a high, even special, product with some kind of property-interest in truth or even a peculiar, perhaps unique, capacity to perceive it. The historical records of scholars in this respect, not to mention their individual experiences in being refuted by events, do not daunt them.

2. Because they know inwardly that this posture of theirs is not true, those of them in the appropriate field are compelled to resort to the study of the work of their opponents (the Sufis). This is why scholars study the works of Sufis, but Sufis do not have to study the works of scholars, as one Sufi has cogently remarked.

This tendency of the lower attempting to emulate the higher in spite of disabling limitations is evidenced in the behaviour of children, animals and other less-developed or insecure individuals. Small boys pretend that they are adults, or else study what they imagine adults to be doing or saying. In the process they quite naturally refrain from allowing themselves to register the adults' assertion that boys are still only boys.

It is appropriate to stress here that, whereas a child may grow up, a man does not become an immature boy again. The scholar is too naive (in knowledge, if not in contentiousness) for any Sufi to become one of the type we are describing. This stage the Sufi has already passed, if he needed to pass through it.

When a child does not properly grow up, he will either be an unformed, infantile man, or else he may die. The alternatives to progress are these two. What he imagines about himself, or what he manages to convince others about himself, do not affect the reality of the situation, though they may affect opinions as to the nature of the reality. Few people will disagree that there is a difference between the reality, the observed fact, and the supposed facts created by opinion and maintained by constant repetition.

Any careful study of academic work will show how surprisingly often there is an unawareness, for instance, of the difference between polemic and informational communication.

The Sufi's opposition to the scholar is not any opposition to scholarship. It is an opposition to regarding scholarship as something which it is not. If, for instance, one were to believe that bread and milk were the only true and valuable forms of food, it could mean that those who ate bread and milk might imagine that they had perceived and were operating at the apogee of nutrition. On the other hand, where there are other nutritions available, and when these are superior in some or many respects to those which are only supposed to be the solitary or best ones, a critical situation exists.

The other objection which the Sufi traditionally makes is in the best interests of the scholar and his followers. It is widely known that an erroneous belief about oneself, particularly a fantasy that one is more important than one really is, can have an unpleasant and destructive effect upon an individual and on those who may rely upon him. To ignore such scholastic imaginings when in a position to comment upon them in a salutary manner is tantamount to allowing a person to damage himself and others – whether this damage arises through ignorance or malice. All social requirements of virtually all communities are unanimous in disallowing such a situation as this to pass unremarked, once it has been observed.

If the means to deter people from this course of irresponsibility do not exist (or cannot be made use of) the role of the Sufi is to make available the information upon the basis of which others may be able to preserve themselves from the spread of the disability. Or he might otherwise contribute towards redressing the imbalance.

Protection and guidance is a function of the Sufi which takes precedence over any psychotherapeutic role. Yet it is easier for the Sufi to do his own job than it is for the afflicted to see his own situation, because the victim can sustain and maintain his disease only by dogmatic activity and constant effort, propaganda and so on. He continues to fuel his own morbid condition because he has lost touch with the fact that the ailment is not really a part of himself at all. He therefore fears to lose it, since he now imagines that such a loss would mean a loss of himself or a part of what he takes to be himself.

When the malaise is further linked with the desire to maintain social or other prestige, or to secure his bread and butter, the inadequate academic's position is tragic indeed.

This is the condition described by ancient authors in their own language, when they tell of people who are infested by demons and imagine that the demons are themselves.

The opposition of Sufis and scholars, like that of literalists and experientialists throughout the human community at all times, also has another face, one which is extremely interesting.

Many – perhaps the majority – of the scholars who initially opposed our books on traditional psychology, have become warm supporters of the concept of extra dimensions in learning, and I count many of them among my personal friends. In the past ten years there have been several books and numerous monographs in which scholars have shown this change of heart. How does this come about?

You should note that it is a matter of sociological evidence that the people who make the best friends are not those who are attracted to one another, or to each others' ideas, at first. On the contrary, it has been shown that the person who opposes you is likely to become a firmer friend than one who becomes your friend immediately. This may seem odd: it is certainly something which has been known for centuries to thinkers and experientialists, as I shall illustrate in a moment.

On the perceptual, as distinct from the superficial, level, there is a communication which leads to harmony between nominally opposed people or attitudes. Were this not so, we would never get agreement following disagreement. But there is a stronger indication than that.

The first illustration we can use, in order to offer this phenomenon in terms somewhat familiar to our present audience, is the saying of Jalaluddin Rumi to the effect that 'things which are apparently opposed may in reality be working together'. The reason why people do not ordinarily link this with the essential harmony of opposites is that they are using only the secondary self to assess the saying. Since they do not perceive this co-operation of opposites when it starts, they think that the opposition which they feel is the central factor.

Secondly, if you cast your mind back to the New Testament, where Jesus is credited with saying that you should 'love your enemy', you will see that, from this point of view, you might as well harmonise with someone who opposes you, because this opposition is quite possibly the beginning of friendship, however it may appear on the surface. 'Love your enemy', therefore, is not to be regarded as a noble sentiment which makes you a better person, especially: but as an injunction which actually describes the deeper dimensions already existing in the relationship.

Although hard to illustrate for those who have not experienced it, this parallelism between paradoxical homilies and essential fact is encountered in conditions of deeper understanding. Difficult to illustrate in personal terms, especially where individual disputes are concerned, it can be determined as existing in social contexts, where the superficial self is not operating. Reconciliation, familiar to all of us in personal and community terms, is not so much the unification of opposites as the uncovering of the basic truth of the situation, masked by subjectivities.

Sufis and scholars seem to oppose one another. But when they know one another's approaches and knowledge, this 'opposition' disappears.

THE SHARPSHOOTING SCHOLARS

Scholars themselves know a great deal about the besetting sin of their profession, that of over-specialisation and blinkered dogmatism. Here is a story about the whole matter, told me by a scholar who himself admitted, unlike many others, that he knew that he was like one of the characters in the tale: but that there was nothing, he believed, that he could do about it:

A number of academics, it appears, were enrolled in time of war into the infantry. After training they all proved to be crack shots, capable of hitting the bullseye far more often than any other recruits.

The time came for them to be sent into battle. As the enemy advanced, the order was given to fire. Nobody moved. 'For goodness' sake', shouted the commanding officer, 'why don't you shoot?'

'How can we, you fool?' roared back one of the scholars, 'When we haven't been trained to fire at *people*?'

An Enterprise is measured by Intention, not by Appearance

⊃⊂

Q: Can you comment on the statement: 'The Success of an Enterprise is measured by its intention, not its appearance'?

A: This statement is simpler than it looks, although it conceals some of the misunderstandings of the past.

If someone is trying to dig a hole, the intention is to dig a hole. The success of the digging of the hole will be whether the hole is actually dug. But, in appearance, the man may be trying to find gold. If the observer thinks that the intention is to find gold, he will call the hole 'a failure'.

It is the same with teachings, institutions, theories and so on. Many have been successful which appeared to be failures. Many failures have appeared to be successes, because the intention behind them was not widely known.

The danger in this situation is twofold:—

1. That self-appointed observers may completely misunderstand intentions.
2. That people, originally intending success in one range, may yield to the temptation to produce what can easily be called 'a success' in some other range.

The psychological mechanism exists whereby an individual can convince himself that he was really trying to do something other than he really was, so that he can harvest the 'success'; and this is equally true of societies.

Human progress is slowed down or halted when people aim for evident success (success measured by what people can easily describe as success) and lose impetus for success of intention.

Example: 'False Success':–
When Mulla Nasrudin, falling off his donkey and laughed at as a result by schoolboys, says: 'I meant to fall off, anyway'.

Example: 'True success':–
When a team of doctors succeeded in inoculating a whole population against some endemic organism, whether or not the inhabitants think they are performing a magical ritual.

Example: 'Possible ingredient of success, not essential to it':–
When some, or even all, of the inoculated people learn the background and purpose of the inoculation.

Sufi Organisations

Q: Can you say anything about Sufi organisations, today and yesterday?

A: Sufi organisations come into being from time to time. Among their purposes is the attraction, concentration and transmission of certain perceptions.

These organisations may or may not have what is ordinarily taken in conventional societies to be an outwardly spiritual or 'esoteric' shape.

This surface aspect is not necessarily important.

A major objective of Sufi activity is sometimes expressed as aiding the human transformation process.

This process can take place only if the organisation, visible, identifiable or otherwise, is adequately attuned to the human being.

This attunement itself may impose 'unlikely' externals upon an organisation.

All such entities are temporary forms. When they have completed their effective lifespan, others take their place.

The outward form or husk may, however, persist and contrive to perform social or other comparatively less significant functions. The inheritors of these forms seldom, if ever, realise that the entity is 'organically dead'.

This is why almost the last place in which to seek the continuation of a transmission such as the one being discussed is in apparently well-established traditionalistic bodies. These are more efficiently described as archaeological relics, easily recognisable as such by those who know their original extent, purpose and vitality.

They develop a sort of quasi-adaptability, or else a rigidity – or a combination of these. The consequence of these characteristics is to cause them either to seek support from new formulations or else to try to fight them. They always, however, lack real adaptability consistent with contemporary needs.

This peculiarity arises when there is a pre-occupation with preservation of archaic, anachronistic forms. Effective higher teaching, in contrast, always seeks to employ any form within which it can complete its mission.

THE CAUSE AND THE EFFECT

Understanding Sufi organisations involves knowing what lies behind appearances. As Rumi says in his *Fihi ma Fihi*, 'In it what is in It':

If a sleeve moves, the hand has moved it. But if the hand moves, the sleeve does not need to move, necessarily. So, if you look at the caused and do not know the cause, you imagine that 'sleeve' is something with a life of its own!

Not even a King is immune from the rule that people jump to conclusions based on superficialities. This can happen with technology in the scientifically-based West:

The English King Edward VII saw a hissing vehicle lurching towards him. 'What the devil is that?' he exclaimed, then gasped: 'Good God! It is the Devil!'
But it was a motor-car . . .*

*J. W. Day, *King's Lynn and Sandringham Through the Ages*. Ipswich, 1977.

8

Sufi Studies

Coming Together

Q: What is the harmonisation of a community through what is called the 'Coming-Together' method?

A: The Kernel of the visible aspect called 'Sufism' is the basic human unit: the members who meet together and carry on the studies prescribed for them by a contemporary teacher.

This is necessary to the realisation which comes from being a Sufi. It may be called community, communion, meeting. It is unimportant what it is called, what is important is to see how every form of human search which later becomes a system, a 'religion', or an enterprise of any kind, originally depends upon this coming-together. It is often called the *Jam* – coming together; pronounced as if to rhyme with 'hum'.

Meeting for worship, teamwork of all kinds, learning in groups, all are derivations and usually diluted ones, of this basic factor.

It is the Sufis, the real Sufis, who preserve the original means of operating in this *Jam*. As time passes, in ordinary communities without special safeguards, the working of this coming-together becomes less and less effective, more and more formalised or generalised, until the *Jam* no longer exists. What takes its place is social 'togetherness', or emotional enthusiasm, or conditioned response to being in a collection of people.

No higher attainment is possible to man unless the circumstances of the coming-together are correct; unless it is a communion including the right people, at the right time, in the right place. Impatience, ignorance, sentimentality, intellectualism tend to cause people to convert the true '*Jam*' situation until it becomes something else.

This essential knowledge has always existed amongst humanity, and continues to exist. But superficial and in general popularised thinking have obscured the real working of this coming-together, until people can only see innumerable forms of deteriorated '*Jam*' – which they accept or reject according to whether they seem attractive, plausible or 'true'.

It may often be impossible to re-form a degenerated coming-together community. It will then be possible to regenerate it only by breaking old habit-patterns and regrouping people who can really be harmonised. This may cause a very different – and perhaps unacceptable – appearance of the whole effort to those who have become accustomed to a false situation. The selection of participants on the basis of their capacity and not their assumed importance always causes discontent in those who have lost the power to adapt. This kind of lack of flexibility is, in turn, an inevitable characteristic of people and groups which have been running on automatistic patterns and which need revivifying.

It is an evident fact that true communities and organisations 'run down' and develop peculiarities other than were present in their origins. They may do this because of the ascendancy of undesirable characteristics in the participants, or because there is a widespread tendency for people and groups to attempt to stabilise themselves by using the nearest available organisation, irrespective of whether this kind of stabilisation loses more than it gains.

This is the major perennial reason for the cyclic emergence of living teachers. It is they alone who can restore harmony and balance in circles and individuals which have sacrificed these things in the search for continuity and reassurance in the hope of stabilisation.

Were it possible to attain the object in a systematised way, the means to do so would have been enunciated and recorded many thousands of years ago: just as the laws of ordinary material stability and performance are recorded and employed in physics or in applied arts.

The reactions of an audience to the efforts of a real teacher to redress the balance of an organisation are always predictable. They will include despair, confusion, desire for stimulus, fear that something might be taken away, rejection, and a desire to accept in order to profit by the 'new phase'.

Mulla Nasrudin objected to the captain of a ship making fast the sails aloft, when as he said: 'Can't you see that the trouble is at sea-level!'

The teacher, however much he may regret it, can never escape the necessity of saying that it is *he* who has the technical knowledge: who decides whether the sails or the hull have to be attended to.

If he calms the 'Mulla' by passing ropes around the hull, the ship may never reach port: though the 'Mulla's' death in the storm may take place in the circumstances of the utmost tranquility, sure in the knowledge that his desires have been fulfilled.

There are two kinds of community: one, the community produced and maintained by what is today called indoctrination; the other, the one accumulated and harmonised by starting with the right materials and the right knowledge.

The situation with regard to the understanding of the subtler potential of the group and its finer tuning has its analogy in Rumi's explanation of the difference between the different levels of perception of religion. As he says in *Fihi ma Fihi:*

> Some are but children on the Path, they drink the milk of the Koran, its literal sense. And those who have reached maturity have a separate perception and another understanding, that of the inward significance of the Koran.

Concealment of Shortcomings

Q: I have seen in an English translation of *AWARIF EL MAARIF*, a Sufi textbook, a statement to the effect that a disciple should conceal his teacher's shortcomings. How can a man be a teacher if he has shortcomings?

A: One might almost put it the other way round – how can a teacher be a man *unless* he has shortcomings? But your question is more properly and probably usefully answered by pointing out that the fact that someone is a disciple means that he is likely to regard some actions of a teacher, which he does not understand, as shortcomings. It is a matter of understanding.

If the student imagines that something said or done by his teacher is a shortcoming when it is not, and this student maintains publicly that his teacher has deficiencies, the results will be undesirable for everyone.

Mark Twain is reported to have said that as a youth he thought his father ignorant. When he grew up he was surprised how much the old man had learnt in so few years. Supposing, then, that in the years between his first and second assessments of his father, he has published the 'fact' that his father was ignorant, what would the consequences have been?

But the statement is, above all, a reminder of the need for understanding being paramount.

Furthermore, you should know that the Sufis have always maintained that whatever comes into this 'abode of decay' – the world – must partake of its imperfections.

Ghazzali, one of the greatest Sufis, said in the 12th century that: 'The learner should know that he gains more from mistakes of his teacher, even if that teacher makes mistakes, than he gains from his own rightness, even if he is himself right.' Everyone interested in Sufism should ponder this statement carefully.

Saints and Heroes

Q: You talk about 'Heroes' and 'Saints'. How are these terms being used?

A: A hero is a person who exerts himself at whatever cost, for the sake of values which are recognised by his community as vital. These are always regarded as vital because some form of assessment has arrived at them, and some form of acceptance has 'established' them in the mental set of the people. They are, in short, not necessarily truths, but certainly are agreed principles.

A saint, on the other hand, is someone who exerts himself for the sake of what must be done, not what is assumed must be done. His source of knowledge about this necessity is factual (real knowledge, not assumption).

Those religious people who sacrifice themselves because they are emotionally conditioned to a doctrine are heroes perhaps, but not saints. Those heroes who sacrifice themselves because of real knowledge, though this may appear to be logical or intellectual knowledge, are in reality saints, as Sufis use the word.

People tend to follow the 'heroic' trait in heroes and those whom they adopt as saints alike merely because, being prone to conditioning and emotional arousal, the public can recognise 'social sacrifice' which belongs to the domain of heroism, but not, in general, 'essential sacrifice', appertaining to the realm of sainthood. The latter word, in Sufi usage, denotes objective knowledge, not simply miracles or the odour of sanctity.

Put it like this: If a man dies because by doing this he will save others, and the situation is obvious (an enemy is at the gates) he will be considered a hero, even a saint, or both. But if he dies, or does not die, and makes a sacrifice which is not always understood by his fellows, for a cause which they themselves are not heedful enough to perceive, he may be a saint. They may or may not canonise him, depending not upon their perception of his santliness, but upon their opinion of his saintliness or heroism, which is a very different thing.

Our Mulla Nasrudin shows quite clearly in one of his adventures how people try things 'heroically', and still do not learn – but, on the other hand rationalise their situation so as to satisfy their own desire to prevail. The result is ludicrous to a detached observer, while it may still remain 'logical' to whoever subscribes to the assumptions which prompted the act.

Invited to a grandee's court, Nasrudin was offered a horse to ride.

TRICKS AND HORSES

As soon as it was brought to him, he placed his right foot in the left stirrup, sprang up, and landed on its back, facing the animal's tail.

'Perhaps you are not accustomed to the mount of gentlemen' sniffed the aristocrat.

'Perhaps not,' said Nasrudin. 'On the other hand, I prefer to believe that I can see through the tricks of people who try to palm off back-to-front horses on me.'

The Levels of Service

Q: I have heard the 'Three Levels of the Service Situation'. What does this mean? How does this accord with Wisdom and how does repentance accord with both?

A:
1. *Structural Level*: A man works, obtains money, his employer benefits by selling the product at a profit.

2. *Psychological Level*: Man 'A' serves, service makes him happy. Man 'B' and/or an organisation benefits through material or emotional gain from 'A's service.

3. *Higher Level*: 'A' serves, acquires merit, avoids consuming it in the form of self-satisfaction or attention-demand. 'B' (or an organisation) benefits because of 'A's progress, and feeds back this benefit into its teaching.

Q: But how can a person acquire the balance to derive just so much self-satisfaction from the Stage of Service, and no more, so that he will have 'savings' of constructive service to be of future avail to him?

A: There are five requirements which make it possible:
1. The man (or woman) must be able to allow that the foregoing analysis may be correct.

2. He must familiarise himself with the argument, remembering that shallower contentions about analysis of situations and the nature of service are already rooted in his brain.

3. He must realise that merely supposing that he understands the foregoing is often simply a prelude to forgetting it.

4. He has to undergo specialised exercises which help to make it possible for his brain to work consistently in another manner as well as in the conventional one which is now customary to it.

5. He has to examine himself to see whether he is expecting too much from his studies or from life in the immediate reward sense,

and hence being forced to devour valuable experiential nutrition as emotional stimulus to assuage the tensions caused by his random expectations.

As to the matter of wisdom and repentance, it is important to note that theologized thinking has assumed that religious people repent in order to gain Divine wisdom or acceptance.

But if you realise that numerous authoritative Sufis make a point of the perenniality of Sufism, you will see that there is a stage apart from the current religious frame. In other words, the Sufis claim that before religion must come sense and understanding. Anything else is mechanical or emotional with a likelihood of insufficient depth of understanding.

There are a large number of texts in which this point is made, so we can merely adduce one significant instance here. Abu-Nasr Sarraj in his important *Kitab al-Luma*, explains, after saying that Sufism stems from an era preceding the present Islamic one, that wisdom comes from repentance, partly. Repentance, for the Elect, the mystic, is repentance for forgetting God. But for disciples, learners, wisdom is through repenting one's own short-comings. Before the religious life and understanding comes, the mass of psychological blocks which cause shortcomings must be dealt with. The service situation, about which you have asked, involves activities which cut through these blocks, many of which are concerned with a fixation upon oneself.

The matter of balancing the amount of personal stimulus which is permissible is dealt with in Book Six of Saadi's *Bostan* in a memorable passage which enables one to keep the matter in mind. There was once an enlightened man who was given a silken scarf by the King of Khotan. He expanded like a blossom from pleasure, but kissed his hand and said: 'How good the honour of the Shah of Khotan – but how much better one's own [Sufi] mantle!'

I find this an interesting illustration, because it accords one the right to a necessary degree of emotional stimulus while maintaining the relative importance of the rest of life. This principle is seldom noted in theologized literature, where all things of the world are condemned very often without regard for the necessity for a certain degree of environmental stimulus.

Ritual and Practice

Q: I have been told that you have said that it is not always worthwhile to discuss with questioners the status and value of rituals and practices of cults. Why is this?

A: It is only worthwhile discussing these with people who have the necessary basic information about cult-behaviour and human groups. This is, of course, already available in popular editions of sociological and psychological texts.

Time is wasted if one has to explain elementary ideas to people who have come for advanced ones.

It is possible to communicate useful materials only to people who have taken the trouble to inform themselves about what is already known about, say, the social character of cult-groupings.

So many people who have in fact taken this trouble exist and want more advanced information and discussions, that it is unfair to them to try to perform at their expense the elementary educational task which is just as well done by mass-circulation books.

It is lazy and unworthy of people to come for such information to people who are trying to do more advanced things. It is preposterously ignorant of people who are trying to teach to imagine and to lead others to believe that they can teach everyone.

If the applicants have not learnt the first steps, which they can do so easily from readily available materials on cult-formation describing pitfalls and imaginings about cults, what reason has anyone to suppose that they will be able – or willing – to learn the second steps? Such attitudes do not work in any other field; there is no evidence known to me which indicates that they work in our area.

People who are willing to learn for themselves what they can on a lower level are thereby giving us evidence that they are ready to learn more. If we are given the reverse evidence, would we not be fools to try to teach them?

PRICE OF THE FIRST LESSON

It is worth remembering the tale of Nasrudin when he wanted to learn how to play a musical instrument. The fee was five silver pieces for the first lesson, and three for the second and subsequent ones. 'Very well,' said the Mulla, 'I'll start with the second lesson.'

People talk and think endlessly about what rituals and other practices do for them or do not do for them. But what are their qualifications for assessing such things?

Rumi gives us an arresting passage in *Fihi ma Fihi* when he recalls that someone may embrace a pillar in the dark, mistaking it for a loved one. He thinks, for that moment, that this is an experience of love. But what is it really?

A person, he continues, may have a whole range of vivid experiences in a dream, which cause him great sorrow. When he wakes up he finds that it was a dream and he loses all his regrets in an instant, even though seconds before they were very real to him. Now he may have an exactly similar dream again, with all the former sorrow recurring. In his sleeping state he does not remember that it was a dream: this, then, becomes for the time being, 'reality' for him.

To be Present

IF you believe that mechanical regularity in studies, or physical presence, are basic to higher knowledge, you are mistaking them for something else. This other thing is either a reversion to school repetition-learning days, or an unthinking assumption based upon your experience of imitators.

Either realise this, and satisfy your attention-demanding and comfort-seeking appetites separately from your studies; or realise it and accept whatever the Teaching can offer you.

In the latter case, you will have to follow a course dictated in its conditions and forming by effectiveness and not sentiment.

It is the true discrimination between diversion and genuine aspiration which generally precedes the emergence of the capacity to learn.

Physical presence is not always real presence.

Mechanical performance of actions and reliance on totemistic objects and slogans, which is in fact what many people do and imagine that they are following a teaching, are forms of attachment to what are or amount to objects. Of course, genuine aspiration is hard to maintain, and it is the falling by the wayside of the people ('the birds') in Fariduddin Attar's classic *Mantiq al-Tair*, the 'Conference of the Birds', which is caused by their craving this attachment.

Even the intellect, as he reminds us in that book, cannot help – only what is called by the Sufis Love; and yet this itself is love of something to which one cannot attach as to a person or even to a familiar concept. Many Sufi practices, carried out in accordance with the right directions, aim at defeating this mechanical tendency and awakening the capacity for attachment to the Real.

Being physically present, seeking system and a certain kind of familiar regularity in studies, is something which comes from automatistic thinking. To demand it because one has a predilection for it is hardly constructive.

Q: But [someone said] in all forms of study known to me there is regularity and organisation, a system, which is adhered to. Surely it is no wonder that people look for system, and not surprising that if they do not find it, they cease to be interested.

A: Let me ask you a question, to help me to get things clearer, then I will answer you. The question is: 'If there is a formula for approaching a study, written down, say, seven hundred years ago, and found in books published continuously since then, and practised by millions of people, would you yourself be negligent if you did not know about it and asked questions about how to find this formula, or would the people involved in this study be responsible, rather than you?' [The questioner answered]: If the answer to the question which I have just asked were available in English at this time, in a generally circulated book on this subject (since I think I have read all of them) then I would be negligent, and not you or others like you.

A: [Continues]. Very well. Now, have you read Professor Arberry's 1961 translation of Professor Faruzanfar's 1952 edition of Rumi's thirteenth-century *Fihi ma Fihi*, published in England?

[Questioner]: Yes.

A: [Continues]. Let us now look at that book. On page sixty Rumi likens the stages of a journey by sea to one on land, and also makes clear the differences between the two, does he not? He tell us that, whereas the landmarks are visible – which I will call the familiar system – when going by land, the equivalent stages, if you are travelling by sea, are not visible in the same way, not marked. They are known to the Captain. The ship's captain knows them, but they are not told to landsmen, since they are not able to understand. Can you therefore say that the system is not there, and that it is not being carried out? Certainly not. Do you now see that you are asking for the recipe for making jam by the method for growing wheat?

[Questioner]: I do, indeed. I can only say that I am not accustomed to thinking in that way, to approaching things by such a method ... Obviously, I need to take a more flexible view of these written materials.

The Way to Sufism

Q: Could we have any remarks on the present character of receptivity of man to Sufic ideas, as seen from the Sufi viewpoint?

A: Metaphysicians, no less than market researchers, monitor the condition and receptivity of the minds with which they are trying to communicate.

The main difference between the activities of, say, the sociologists and those of the spiritual workers is that the results of the latter are not widely published, publicised, employed in academic treatises. They are used in supplying verification material for trainees who would otherwise find it impossible to credit the facts about humanity.

Which facts? Here are instances:

You may have something to teach, and yet be unable to teach it because the people who 'want to learn it' effectively prevent themselves from learning; at the same time protesting that they 'want to learn', or 'cannot understand'. Such people reason unconsciously, that if they protest you will keep your attention upon them. In this way they gain your attention (or hope to do so). In any other way, they might lose it.

Of course, if you try to point this out, you will find that the answer – again preventing progress – will be 'this man is excusing himself', or 'he is mistaken'.

It is for this reason that it is traditional to confine one's teachings to a small rather than a large group: those who really are prepared to learn.

If you speak, or write, in the above vein, a certain proportion of the would-be elect will protest that you are insensitive, or even that you are not teaching metaphysics at all. This is because they have been accustomed to a belief that real teaching is something which they will themselves instantly recognise.

Now it is a matter of almost daily verification in real esoteric classes that it is easy to become established as a 'true meta-physician' in the eyes of the self-styled students of higher thought. What do you have to do? Nothing more or less than make them feel emotionally aroused. All you have to do is to make sure that you use what they regard as 'spiritual' terminology.

But say the above words, or publish them, and you will, in all likelihood, immediately be accused of being superficial, unaware of the 'real values', and so on.

It is little wonder that many sensible people will have nothing at all to do with the people known as 'spiritual'.

Few organised communities and doctrinally-aligned movements realise, and it has never been widely known, that they inhabit a ghetto. There is a rigid exclusionism in ideas which too often characterises a 'systematic' approach to higher human development and makes it impossible to help raise man higher. Methods have been devised and operated for thousands of years to circumvent this. These methods are externally so dissimilar from the familiar atmosphere, phraseology, ritual and form of 'meta-physics' that not one self-styled Seeker After Truth in twenty will recognise them.

But say this, or write it, or try to transmit it, and you will often be derided, accused of heightening mystery, or of taking 'essential mystery' away – of anything that comes into the mind of a frustrated person.

If you try to set the record straight by describing the barriers, pitfalls, misunderstandings and limiting factors, you will widely be considered to be someone who is complaining, at the very least.

These are some of the characteristics of the present-day situation which mean that progress is extremely difficult.

The fault lies partly in the cultural infrastructure. There is a widespread lack of real higher experience, as distinct from imagined experience. There is a serious lack of suitable information about areas of higher study which are not generally known nor reproduced in books. As a consequence of this, any teacher will in the contemporary world find that he is like the university professor ushered into a lecture-hall to speak of nuclear physics, and finds that his students have not yet learned simple equations.

Mention this, and you will most surely be accused of giving

yourself airs and graces.

Try to live down this reputation, and you will have a hard time of it.

You may have to associate people with yourself literally for years before the fact penetrates into their minds that you are not a monster, not a mahatma, but a man trying first of all to teach them the basic tools of their own possible learning process, which should have been in their possession years before. It is these tools that should have been conveyed by the secondary type of teacher who passes on traditional learning.

Take another instance. Primitive thought depends strongly upon regularity, upon rhythm, upon reassurance. This is per-petuated in our time in the atavism whereby people have been encouraged to believe that they must be taught at a certain time (preferably the same time each day or week) in the same surround-ings, in the same manner. Tell them that this belongs to children and they may take it in one way, but they will tend to become confused and refuse, in effect, to take it in another.

But do the reverse: give them authority figures, canonical books, hierarchies of authority, symbols, chants and costumes, and they will worship you and believe that you are on the 'right lines', whether they are or not; whether or not you have made up the cult the day before.

This, too, real teachers have been compelled to demonstrate in actual instances before people would credit it.

If you cannot rationalise their previous learning with your teaching, you will have a hard time of it. You will be like a man telling a bedtime story to a child who refuses to agree that the wolf did not really eat up Red Riding Hood's grandmother after all.

You will break the primitive totems at your peril. The irony here is that, if you allow yourself to be discredited in the eyes of the learner, you will harm him as well: for he has no other recourse, more often than not, than to adhere to some other system: one which will reassure him while inhibiting his progress.

Now there is another category of people. Those are the ones, who listen to, or read, entire expositions like the foregoing, and feel that they are exactly right. This feeling leads them to suppose that they must surely be first-class material. The real fact is that people who can attain a higher knowledge are those who can feel it in the right way: not just the people who decide that they are the 'right people'.

In contemporary civilisations there is hardly a real thought about the possibility that people who feel a thing strongly may be feeling it in an erroneous and unconstructive manner except in delusion situations; let alone a word or words to describe the various states in which one can feel the conditioned conscience.

The bitter truth is that, if a real metaphysical path is to be opened and maintained, it has to be mainly recruited from and staffed by people who have perhaps never heard of 'higher consciousness' or 'self realisation' in their lives. This is because the associative mechanism which does so much harm to man has long ago taken over the major part of the mentation of the would-be illuminated. Those who can save them are those whom they tend to discount, even to despise. They are people who are often younger, less experienced.

Esoteric studies today, as viewed by someone from outside, are an oldster's world, redolent of all the bitternesses and stupidities of the unregenerate old. A bitter thought in itself? Only if you are yourself bitter. If you can see a little more objectively, these remarks are statements of fact, and therefore of constructive potential.

What is so amazing is that people will so readily throw away the promise of a lifetime for what Rumi called the 'nuts and raisins and games' of shallower satisfactions.

No wonder riper minds, hearing of esoteric studies, laugh and shrug them off.

Are *you* innocent of confabulation, rationalisation, of accepting lower satisfactions, of calling self-indulgence 'higher activity', of oppressing others in the name of an assumed seniority, a little brief authority, of suppressing your own inklings and of masquerade?

At the risk of adopting unfashionable terminology, I have to say that for all these and many other ways of thinking, feeling and acting, payment has some time to be made.

The question of the present-day receptivity of people to Sufi ideas has not changed since the times when, 1,000 years ago, Hujwiri in his *Revelation of the Veiled* gave a little story which pointed out that you cannot receive if your mind is blocked with crude aspirations.

FAVOURS AND SLAVES

A dervish and a king met. The king, following the custom in the East when a ruler meets a subject, said: 'Ask me a favour.'

The dervish said: 'I will not request a favour from one of my own slaves.'

The king asked him how he could see him as a slave.

The dervish answered: 'I have two slaves who are your own masters: greed and expectation.'

The receptivity of man to Sufi ideas, which you ask about, is sometimes clouded by the demand for 'being given' something. I say clouded, because there are really three conditions which have to be looked at. First, there is the potential of the human being – the endowment which he already has; second there is the intervention of the teaching function; lastly there is the effort which the individual makes in accepting the teaching and preserving the endowment.

The last item is one about which people seem to have the least idea. Human potentiality is an endowment: and one which can be preserved, enriched and also spent.

So, in addition to getting something, how about some attention to the matter of not losing something? Although I admit that this is a matter more easily understood by perception of how people are wasting their assets in this direction, at least the question can be stated in so many words.

THOUGHTLESSNESS

There is a parable about this, attributed to Jesus, but which does not appear in the approved gospels: though this does not make the analogy itself any less true. It is found in the putative Gospel of Thomas, which was found in Egypt in 1945.

In this story, reference is made to a woman carrying a container of meal and walking a long distance. Unknown to her, the meal flows out behind her 'and she did not know how to work'. When she arrived at her house, she put down the container and found it to be empty. This parable refers to the 'Kingdom of the Father', and its applicability to our contention about the imperceptible loss of potentiality, through a form of thoughtlessness (called by the Sufis 'heedlessness') is very apposite to this subject.

SELLING HALF THE HOUSE

About giving and getting, Nasrudin visited a house-agent one day: 'I want to sell one half of the house I live in' he said.

'But Mulla, I know your house – you only own one-half of it.'

'That is exactly the point. I want to sell my half to buy the other half with the money I raise from the deal.'

The Giving of Charity

Q: Have you any remarks to make on the giving of Charity among Sufis?

A: One commanding principle of all Sufis, binding upon them, is secret charity. Charity takes many forms. As to monetary charity:

If money is given with a sense of joy, that joy is 'payment' for the charity, and the good which comes to the giver is restricted to that emotion. Although this kind of giving is familiar to most people, it nevertheless remains the minor form of charity. The second part of the minor form of charity is to give in order that the person may help himself. Thus a person might buy a tool for a carpenter, so that he could earn his living. This may not be emotional, but could still be 'calculated' charity. Its limitations make it less than true charity.

Money or valuables are given by Sufis, or those who desire to be counted among them, in accordance with the principle: 'Let your left hand not know what your right hand does.'

A Sufi will:

Give before being asked;
Give whatever he has, without counting it;
Give when asked;
Give no emotional or calculated charity unless he can give true charity.

It is meritorious to give money to a Sufi for him to distribute it. He will give it out, in large or small amounts, to those who are deserving; not necessarily in accordance with their outward need. A beggar or a poor man may get a thousand gold pieces, not just a copper coin.

Charity does not always involve money, as you know. Charity is not only given, as you call it. It is lived and performed, which means 'being and doing.'

As Saadi, the great dervish, says in his *Gulistan:*

'You who are unmoved by others' suffering are not entitled to the name of man'. Charity has been made into a great virtue only because of the low level of human decency.

If you still think that charity is not a necessity but a high virtue, you do not even know what your contemporaries, in your own civilisation, have discovered, and which has been published in mass-circulation newspapers on the subject. Here is an example of the charity of animals:

CHARITY OF THE RATS

Dr. J. T. Greene, of Georgia University* took ten white rats and trained them to obtain food pellets by pressing one of two levers in their cage. One lever produced fewer pellets and was hard to depress, and the rats soon found this out and ignored it, concentrating on the other. Now the experimenter wired the levers so that when the one which yielded food was pressed, a rat in the next cage received an electric shock.

What did the food-seeking rats do? First, they recognised that their actions were giving their neighbour pain; then no less than eight out of ten of them went over to the other lever, even though it was hard to work, and concentrated on it, saving their fellow from further harm.

*Sunday Express (London) 7 September, 1969, p. 21.

The Number of Readings of a Book

Q: I understand that the study of books is very important. Can you say something about how Sufis feel about reading, and the number of times a book is read?

A: A Sufi book will have to be read in the ordinary way several times. If the mind of the reader is not correctly prepared, he will reject the book, read it selectively, or else indoctrinate himself with the contents. All these results are undesirable.

The above facts, however, account for the effects of literature upon the minds of various people. The human mind is an organism in which what it absorbs will be to one man meat, another poison. This effect is inherent in the mind of the reader much more than in the book.

And yet people persist in considering books, in their possible effect upon people, as always the same. This stupidity is one of the less attractive legacies of mechanical scholasticism, which, indeed, usually *requires* a standardised mind to approach each and every book.

Many people are proud of how many times they have read a book. They point to well-thumbed copies as evidence of their diligence. In some circles, indeed, 'a tattered bible' is still taken as an evidence of piety.

And yet hardly anyone knows that the condition of the book, the treatment which it has received at the hands of the reader, will leave traces upon it, which will have an effect, just as will the typeset content, long after the impressions upon the book have been made. Borrowed books carry an imprint. Books which one has used too many times carry this imprint, this 'smell of infidelity' as it is called in Persian, from one reading to another.

It is for this reason that people are often asked to read many times several copies of the same book, even if it means buying new copies after each second reading. This is something which may not be well-known, but it is effective nevertheless. Today's refined barbarian could find in such a procedure only the suspicion that it is a device to sell him more copies of a book!

It will be noticed from the foregoing material that our study methods are just as much concerned with matters of little-known fact as they are with psychological factors which people know but do not apply. This is why the curriculum of a School requires all-round attention to the needs of the teaching, the material taught, the students and the teacher.

Rumi teaches of the use of books in a book (*The Diwan of Shams-i-Tabriz*) where he denounces books as a source of wisdom. They are, as in the case of the one which he is writing at that moment, instrumental:

The Man of God is a wise one by means of Truth:
The Man of God is no lawyer from a book ...

Literary passages, teaching instruments, may need much time and various experiences before they exercise their true potential effect upon the human being. In his *Ruh al-Quds* (Spirit of the Holy), Ibn Arabi tells how he was taught through a quotation from the Koran given him by Abu-Abdullah of Ronda, in Spain. This great Sufi, who had many extrasensory abilities, chose a passage and asked Ibn Arabi what it meant. The latter did not answer him, but when the meaning came to him he found Abu-Abdullah again and told him the answer. This was four years later. In conventional temporal terms, therefore, this one lesson had occupied four years. Since we have started publishing books of Sufi tales and encounters this kind of reaction has become more and more frequent from readers of the books: those, that is, who are not so impatient that they abandon the study as soon as it yields no immediate results of the kind which they demand of it.

And, as Kalabadhi says in his *Taaruf*:

Patience is to be patient with patience.

Q: Should we not familiarise ourselves with all Rumi's work, especially as so much of it is now translated into English and other Western languages?

A: You should note that Rumi is talking to a specific audience. How do you know which part of what he says refers to YOU? In the case of the extracts from the Koran which he uses so extensively, you can see that he is using them as a 'given', as you would use, say, mathematical formulae. That is to say, he is talking to a community which accepts these extracts as literally and figuratively true. This enables him to stress certain points and to drive home others. Dealing with a contemporary audience which either rejects these passages, or challenges them, or wants to analyse them, we cannot use them as our 'givens'. We have, instead, to refer to psychological data accepted by our constituency, and this is what we do. Doing otherwise would vitiate the value of Rumi's work as a whole. He, in turn, did exactly the same thing with the materials which he built into his writings.

Decline in Religious Influence

Q: Reading Sufi writings by the classical authors seems to show that there is a clear distinction drawn between religion and obsession. Is failure to observe this distinction the cause of current religious decline?

A: The decline in the influence of religion has been due, in the main, not to religion itself, but to the very shallowness of many practitioners. People who are indoctrinated and mistake implanted obsession for faith, are themselves destroyers of the very thing which they imagine themselves called upon to try to protect.

In fact, of course, they have no such call: and their capacity to protect something which is other than their imaginings makes for a comical situation.

What many people call religion (which is heavily admixed with self-deception, until it discovers the difference between inculcated belief and something else which might be called real faith) remains at a primitive stage of existence, and cannot really expect any serious consideration from people who are accustomed to thinking in the terms of thought outside it: terms which have long ago purged themselves of the grosser elements. Remember, sophisticated arguments and the ability to play with words do not add up to an advanced form of thought, only a cunning one.

Dedicated religionists such as we commonly meet are, of course, no more religious than an atheist. They are crude emotionalists who happen to have adopted religion as the field of their operations. Religion is their medium of action and expression: not the basis of their behaviour.

In this respect they resemble more than anything else the political, economic or other cult-enthusiasts who are a psychological and social phenomenon, not a religious one.

Anyone who knows more and discusses 'religion' with such people would be like an astronomer discussing astrology with a star-worshipper.

For this reason the regeneration of religion would come from people whom we would not always readily associate with 'religion' as we know it.

This principle is well known in other fields: where, for instance, great inventions come from the untechnical; since the main-line scientist and technologist has become obsessed with his field and its dogmas. Yesterday's dogmas are tomorrow's impossibilities.

In traditional terms, this is the condition of looking at the chrysalis when one should look at the butterfly: and also at the whole range of development, from egg to grub to chrysalis to butterfly.

I fancy – I certainly hope – that when people say, as so many do, that 'Christianity has not failed: it just has not ever been tried out' they mean that only the obsessionality or scholasticism have been tried. And if it has not been tried, might I enquire: When do we start?

Remember, the first Persian book on Sufism – Hujwiri's, says:

'The worst man is the one who is imagined to be serving God, but in reality is not: the noblest is the one imagined not to be a devotee of God, who really is such.'

The cause of religious decline is that so few people have the opportunity of the alternative to implanted obsession – a frail thing – represented by the faith which comes through experience. The Sufi Muhammad ibn Khafif said: 'Faith is believing in the heart in the knowledge which comes from the Unseen'. He did not say that it was believing in something said to one, or drilled into one, or admitted at moments of excitement and consequently becoming part of a fixation.

WHY HE IS STILL NORMAL

There is a wry joke in the East, aimed at stressing how the decline in religion is due to the ineptitude and sometimes worse of the practitioner, especially at the supposedly higher level of the activity. Like a cartoon, it is deliberately over-emphasised, to make the point:

A spiritual teacher is saying:

'My first disciple was so weak that the exercises killed him. My

251

second drove himself mad by doing his meditations too concentratedly. My third pupil became dulled by contemplation. But the fourth is still completely normal.'

Someone asked: 'Why is that?'

'It could be', said the guru, 'because he refuses to do the exercises . . .'

Why can't we have a
British Karakul Lamb?

Karakul, sometimes known as Persian lamb, is the fur of a sheep which has for ages flourished in Central Asia, notably in Afghanistan. More recently, attempts have been made to rear the Karakul sheep in South-West Africa, and their skins are marketed as 'South-West African Karakul'.

Because of nutritional and environmental factors, there is a difference.

Experts and others can tell the difference between the two kinds of skin.

There are many reasons why we cannot grow a Karakul sheepskin in Britain, in spite of the fact that there is a demand for them.

But the fact that they are brought into this country from outside does not decrease the demand. On the contrary, it probably increases it. It certainly increases the price.

If anyone were to say: 'Why can we not have a *British* Karakul skin?' the foregoing remarks would probably be what he would be told by an expert.

Suppose we use this example to illustrate, however partially, my remarks that something which belongs to one culture should not – in the metaphysical sphere – be imported into another? Am I not *importing* something from another culture, or even series of cultures?

It must immediately be noted that the relevant factor here is whether the import belongs uniquely to the culture from which it was imported, or whether it does not.

If I import a *habit*, like wearing sandals, from Greece, where it is hot to Greenland where it is cold, I am doing the wrong sort of importing. If, on the other hand, I import something of use, like wool, from a place where it grows to a place where it can be used, I am probably doing something useful.

It is a sad commentary on the primitive state of thinking upon this matter that people try to safeguard their existing ways by excluding things which are of use and including things which are useless.

The difficulty on the part of the ordinary man to know what is useful and what is merely secondary, cultural material, is in part due to his impatience and greed – he wants anything that *might* be useful, (or *is* attractive) in part due to the fact that nobody has told him the elementary fact that certain things are not only useful but essential imports, and partly due to the fear that something brought into his life or thinking from another source might not suit him.

From this point of view, in metaphysics, you will see that he is at a very low level of accomplishment, which would not be able to persist for very long in the technological sphere of a simple society after it had once been impinged upon by a more developed one.

Of course, there are time-honoured ways of introducing into a society something which it needs but does not want to accept. Many of them are still being used. King Abdul-Aziz ibn Saud, in order to 'prove' that the radio was not an evil thing, had to broadcast verses from the Koran so that clerics could testify that it must be a good thing, since it was assumed that the devil could not quote the Koran.

There was the case of St. Francis who in a famous story told the Pope that his ideas and organisation were really ancient ones belonging to the Church, which had been neglected and concurrently developed elsewhere and were now finding their real place.

In parts of the world it is still customary for someone who has taken a pill given to him under modern medical doctrine to take it to the local magician to have it made 'really potent' by means of a spell.

More in our own locality of operation, you may observe the almost magical 'rationalising' effect of an explanation which enables the hearer to reorganise his prejudices in a seemingly orderly way. You can say to him: 'I am telling you the same thing which was preached by so-and-so, and here is the correspondence of the ideas.' He will feel much better. He does not primarily want truth, he wants reassurance, system, safety.

Or you can do it in another way. You can say – and it works – 'This does not appear to be the same but it works wonders'. This can stimulate his greed, enable him to overcome prejudices in the 'higher interest' of something extra possible for himself.

Why am I describing these mechanisms, and why do I disapprove of them?

For no other reason than that they are the easy, superficial way. You may say: 'What I am telling you is the same as what you learned from so-and-so' and you may be telling the truth. This truth may be important, and its proper realisation can have a very important effect. But, once you say this truth, you may expect the hearer to *use* this important truth for purposes of rationalisation. Instead of letting the basic truth have access to his consciousness, he exhausts its energy for him by using it to make acceptable, to superficial thinking, things about which he has had doubts.

This primitive and futile use of important fact is, metaphysically speaking, the sign of an immature man or woman.

This is an important point at which we part company with the more conventional psychologist. The latter, far from complaining about this 'mechanism of rationalisation', tends to regard it as useful (for integrative purposes, for example) except where it produces a state of mind at variance with social norms, particularly his own.

But the psychologist as familiar to us today is generally dealing with what *we* call the false personality of man: the superficial (though necessary) intellectual-emotional system with which he works. We are attempting to contact and inform the deeper individuality of the human being.

How does this tie in with our Karakul Lamb? Quite simply. The people who think that we are importing something, even though we prefer to say we are re-introducing it, if they are 'satisfied' by our explanations and thus rationalise them through greed or for some other motive, are as inaccessible to what we are really saying and doing as those who disregard everything we say or do.

Indeed, in a more elaborate form, their reaction is the same as the ground-plan of this Mulla Nasrudin anecdote:

'That is a very dangerous lake, Mulla' said a local fisherman; 'and people who swim in it are always being found dead at the bottom'

'That's all right, friend', said Nasrudin, 'I'll keep well away from the bottom...'

Indeed, when this teaching is projected, as it in fact is, in another convention than the metaphysical one, the people who *reject* what we are saying in the metaphysical idiom often show a marked potentiality for understanding. Bear in mind here that it is only the superficial thinker who assumes that our teaching, if it is a genuine one, is not bound by the limitations of so-called 'metaphysical' vocabulary. It can be taught in any manner. But it can be taught to so-called metaphysicians only in the jargon, or some equivalence of it, which is conditioned into them already.

These remarks should be absorbed because of the unacceptably narrow view unfortunately acquired by many people who try to understand psychological, religious, philosophical and metaphysical ideas.

Abdulkarim Jili, the author of the important Sufi work *Insan-i-Kamil*, 'Perfected Human Being' who died in the fifteenth century of the Christian Era emphasises that *Being* is thought, and the external aspect of Being is the world. Through the multiplicity of perceived ideas and objects, of course, Sufi doctrine holds that real being may be perceived. This is the doctrine of 'The phenomenal is the Bridge to the Real', but it is instrumental in function. This means that the things of the world which conduce to higher perception have little meaning but much potential use. People look for meaning and are ignorant of use. So they value secondary worldly ideas instead of choosing them as instruments.

Teaching Methods and Prerequisites

ᖃᑌᑐᑕᑌᑐᑕᑌᑐᑕᑌᑐᑕᑌᑐᑕᑌᑐᑕᑌᑐᑕᑌᑐᑕᑌᑐᑕᑌᑐᑕᑌᑐᑕᑌᑐᑕᑌᑐᑕᑌᑐᑕᑌᑐᑕᑌᑐᑕᑌᑐᑕᑌᑐᑕ

Q: According to the Sufis, is there any knowledge of the difference between teaching and conditioning; and do people know what they want when they set out to learn?

A: People are conditioned not only by deliberate indoctrination, but also by systems whose proponents themselves are ignorant of the need for safeguards to prevent conditioning. People are also conditioned by a constellation of experiences. In most human societies, unanimity of thought has been arrived at by an unrecognised conditioning process in which virtually all the society's institutions may be branches of the conditioning process.

This information is neither new nor necessarily exciting. But it is essential. What is new about it is that it has been concisely and effectively revealed in studies made in the West, notably since the end of the Korean war. If you do not know or believe the foregoing, you will either have to accept it as a working hypothesis, or else leave all attempts at studying other matters aside until you have caught up with this information in the generally available sources on the subject. In such a case your basic information is incomplete, and your prospects of progress are as limited in a higher sense as if you were trying to become an academic but were not yet literate.

Certain traditional teaching-systems have continuously maintained the knowledge of this 'conditioning by environment' factor. The essence of their systems has been twofold: (1) to stress the fact of conditioning, in order to redress the imbalance produced by it; and (2) to provide study-formats and human groupings in which the conditioning cannot easily operate.

No such systems deny the value of conditioning for certain purposes: but they themselves do not use it. They are not trying to destroy the conditioning mechanism, upon which, indeed, so much of life depends.

This is the first lesson: People who are shown for the first time how their views are the product of conditioning tend to assume, in the crudest possible manner, that whoever told them this is himself opposed to conditioning, or proposes to do something about it. What any legitimate system will do, however, is to point out that conditioning is a part of the social scene and is confused with 'higher' things only at the point when a teaching has become deteriorated and has to 'train' its members.

The second lesson is that the majority of any group of people can be conditioned, if the group is in effect a random one: non-contitioning-prone groups can only be developed by selecting people who harmonise in such a manner as to help defeat this tendency.

People who hear this may tend automatically to assume that this is a doctrine of the elite. But this assumption is only accepted by them because they are ignorant of the process and the bases. The primary object is to associate people together who can avoid conditioning, so that a development can take place among these people which in turn can be passed on to larger numbers. It can never be applied to large numbers of people directly.

Many people who hear for the first time that conditioning is a powerful, unrecognised and spiritually ineffective development react in another manner which is equally useless. They assume that since conditioning is present in all the institutions known to them (including any which they themselves esteem highly) that it must always be essential. This is only due to the fact that they are not willing to face the fact that any institution may become invaded by a tendency which is dangerous to it. This is not the same as saying that the institution is based upon it.

When people are collected together to be exposed to materials which will defy or avoid conditioning, they will always tend to become uncomfortable. This discomfort is due to the fact that they are not receiving from these materials the stimuli to which they have become accustomed as conditioned people. But, since they generally lack the full perception of what *is* in the materials, (and since it is a characteristic of conditioning materials that they may masquerade as independently arrived-at facts), such people do not know what to do. The solution to this problem which they will tend to adopt is some kind of rationalisation. If they receive no accustomed stimulus of an emotional sort, they will regard the new or carefully selected materials as 'insipid'.

This is a further lesson. Everyone should realise that the vicious circle must be broken somewhere and somehow. To substitute one conditioning for another is sometimes ridiculous. To provide people with a stimulus of a kind to which they have become accustomed may be a public or social service: it is not teaching activity of a higher sort.

Unfortunately people have been so trained as to imagine that something which is hard to understand or hard to do, in a crude sense, is a true exercise. Hence, people are often willing to sacrifice money, physical effort, time, comfort. But if they are asked (say) not to meet, or to sacrifice the attention of a teacher, this they find nearly impossible to bear, simply because their training is such that they are behaving as addicts. They may want sacrifice or effort, but only the kind which they have been trained to believe is sacrifice or effort. 'Stylised effort', though, is no effort at all.

Most unfortunately, they do not know that the system to which they have been trained has always (if they have developed such a taste for it as we have just described) fulfilled its optimum possible developmental function at a point long before we are likely to have encountered them. It has now become a vice, ritual or habit which they are unable to recognise as such.

The prerequisite of an advanced form of teaching is that the participants shall be prepared to expose themselves to it, and not only to some travesty which gives them a lower nutrition to which they have become accustomed.

This is in itself a higher stage than any repetition or drilling or rehashing of words or exercises or theories. And, in its way, it is a challenge. Can the participants, or can they not, really enter an area where their effectively cruder desires and automatic responses are not pandered to?

If they cannot, they have excluded themselves from the Teaching.

In order to become eligible, it is the would-be students who have to 'sort themselves out'. They have to examine themselves and see whether they have merely been using their studies to fulfill social desires, or personal psychological aims, or to condition themselves. They should also be told the simple fact that, for instance, if you shout 'I must wake up!' often enough, it will put you to sleep. If their sense of power, for instance, is being fed by means of the suggestion that they are studying something that others do not know, they will get no further. If they are deriving any personal pleasure or other benefit from 'teaching' others, they will not learn any more. If they depend upon their study-community alone or mainly for friends or somewhere to go once or twice a week or month, they will get no further.

There has been a confusion between teaching and the social or human function. To help or to entertain someone else is a social, not an esoteric, duty. As a human being you always have the social and humanitarian duty. But you do not necessarily have the therapeutic duty; indeed, you may be much less well qualified for it than almost any conventional professional therapist.

It is impossible to spend time with virtually any religious, philosophical and esotericist group, or even to read its literature, without seeing that a large number of the people involved, perhaps through no fault of their own, and because of ignorance of the problems, are using these formats for sociological or psychological purposes of a narrow kind. It is not that their spiritual life is right in these groups. It is that their social life is inadequate.

'As above, so below'. Just as in ordinary worldly considerations there can be inefficiency or confusion as to aims, so there may be in approaching higher knowledge. You may be able, initially, to pursue higher aims through lower mechanisms and theories, but you cannot pursue them by indulging short-term personal interests.

You must follow your personality interests somewhere else. In an advanced society there are more institutions catering for such outlets than anyone could possibly need. Make sure that your professional, commercial, social, psychological and family needs are fulfilled in the society to which you belong. The rest of you is the part which can be communicated with by means of the specialised techniques available to those who have a comprehensive and legitimate traditional learning: and who have the means of safeguarding it.

This is what you have to study first of all. Most people are trying to effect something else, no matter what they imagine that they are doing. Fortunately, it is not hard to recognise this if enough sincere effort is expended.

In ordinary life, if you think that your family is largely a commercial proposition, people will point out that you are misguided. If you thought that your profession was mainly for social purposes, people would soon put you right. It is time that you were correctly informed in this field as well. You must know, or find out, the difference between meeting to learn and experience something, and meeting in order to be emotionally stimulated or intellectually tested or socially reassured.

There is no harm at all in a social ingredient in a human relationship: far from it. But when this gets out of balance, and a human contact becomes an excuse for a social contact, you are not going to learn, no matter what materials you are working with. 'Due proportion' is a secret skill of the teacher.

The repeated upsurge of apparently different schools of higher study in various epochs and cultures is due in large part to the need to rescue genuine traditional teachings from the automatism and social-psychological-entertainment functions which regularly and deeply invade and, for the most part, eventually possess them.

Certain physical and mental exercises, as an example, are of extremely significant importance for the furthering of higher human functions. If these are practised by people who use things for emotional, social or callisthenic purposes, they will not operate on a higher level with such people. They become merely a means of getting rid of surplus energy, or of assuaging a sense of frustration. The practitioners, however, regularly and almost invariably mistake their subjective experiences of them for 'something higher'.

It is for this reason that legitimate traditional higher teachings are parsimonious with their materials and exercises. Nobody with a task to perform can possibly (if he knows about his task) do so in a manner which is not benefiting people on the level required.

The foregoing information should be read and studied and understood as widely as possible. Without it there is little possibility of serving any group of people, anywhere, otherwise than socially or with shallow psychology, no matter what theories, systems or exercises are employed.

Where there is ideology, conditioning and indoctrination, a mechanical element is introduced which drives out the factor of extradimensional reality perception which connects the higher functions of the mind with the higher reality.

Sufi experiences are designed to maintain a harmony with and nearness to this Reality, while mechanical systems effectively distance people from it.

WHO GUARDS THE COAT

Attar, in his *Recitals of the Saints*, tells a story of the great Sufi Habib Ajami, when he went to a river to wash, leaving his coat lying on the ground. Hasan of Basra was passing and saw it. Thinking that someone should look after this property, he stood guard over it until Habib returned.

Hasan then asked Habib whom he had left looking after the coat.

'In the care' said Habib, 'of him who gave you the task of looking after it!'

This anecdote, intended to indicate the way in which affairs work out for Sufis, is often taken by raw imitators as something to copy, so that they test 'destiny' by abandoning things and neglecting duties: with results which correspond with their stage of ignorance.

Sorrow in 'Spiritual Enterprises'

Q: How is it that involving themselves in spiritual enterprises can cause so much sorrow and trouble to some people? Some become deranged, and worse characters than they ever were before ...

A: First, remember that this tendency has been observed and commented upon by all religious and other systems. People are always being driven off their heads by something or other, however respectable the creed, and nobody has yet found any method of preventing this. People sorrow and go mad everywhere, and in everything.

Secondly, attempts are always made by those who are really aware of this psychological problem to cut down on the harmful effects, not of the processes, but of the state of mind of the sufferer upon whom the processes are grafted or applied.

It is for this reason that Sufi teachers have tried to ensure that certain of their disciples do not undertake various exercises. Some of them even insist that such people do not – for instance – perform the pilgrimage to Mecca, which is an obligation for all Moslems. For this reason the Sufis have been blamed for 'opposing that which is permitted or enjoined', by people who are too stupid to understand that, in Islam, the sick are not supposed to do things, even when enjoined, which might increase their infirmity.

The 'sorrow and trouble' to which you refer are due to an inner sickness. This sickness is one which is made worse by anything – even spiritual things – which approach it, because when a spritual element approaches certain forms of sickness, the ailment itself distorts the approaching element and misuses it. You can verify this for yourself, by noting how a perfectly salutary thing, employed in the wrong manner or at the wrong place, or with the wrong people, can cause damage.

STEPPING OFF THE FOURTEENTH FLOOR

There were two news items in the British newspapers not long ago. In one of them, a man stepped off the fourteenth floor of a building because of his 'religious' faith, confident that 'God would save him'. He died. In the other case, it was assumed by spiritually-minded people that a man was possessed by devils. An attempt was made to 'exorcise' these demons, by a ritual taught by the Church. The attempted casting-out of the devils by a Priest of the Church of England was followed by the man murdering his own wife, within hours of the ceremony, by tearing out her eyes and tongue.

Such things can happen when people mistake for a spiritual matter a medical one. This, in turn, happens when people imagine that their doctrine, not their experience, enables them to identify 'spiritual' matters. Dogma has these limitations: the newspapers are frequently to be seen featuring such tragedies as lead to 'sorrow in spiritual enterprises', generally because of this reason.

It has often been observed by Sufis that people who try to follow spiritual paths without the primary training of disengaging their pride frequently encounter sorrow and worse.

'People who try to mould the world's evil ways' says Hasan of Basra* – which to the Sufi includes one's own personality without doing it in correct sequence – 'are ruined.'

People become deranged by following what they assume to be spiritual ways, by trying to do what is not only impossible but absurd.

I would list the harping on the fear of death rather than equally upon its importance as a transition-phenomenon, and also the misguided search for 'security' of implanted obsession (often believed to be faith but in reality only dogmatism) as the two most frequent causes of the sorrow and trouble to which you refer.

There are two quatrains in Persian by the eminent Ustad Khalilullah Khalili, a great contemporary Sufi, on this. Just compare his emphases with the contextless ones which so many people imagine to be spirituality.

*Cited in Attar's *Tadhkirat al-Awliyya*.

DEATH AND MOUNTAINS

In the first* he says:

'I fear not death, for it is my helper ...
It took my forefathers to their destination:
This elegant and easy-paced conveyance of mine!

In the other, he speaks of conditioning, crystallised into stupefying but useless rigidity, as a mountain, and the flexibility of the
understanding Seeker as a bird: in an observation of the bird to
the mountain:

O Mountain! High and mighty, reaching into the skies.
How you seem absorbed in self-regarding.
Although only a small bird, yet I am free
To dance on a flowerhead, while your feet are in chains...**

*Quatrains (Persian) Baghdad: Al-Maarif Press, 1975, 70/71.
***Ibid.*, 32/33.

Shock-Teaching

Q: Could you tell us a Sufi shock-teaching technique?

A: Sufi teaching techniques strongly feature the challenging statement, made in order to cause a multiple effect upon the hearer.

Mansur Hallaj, notoriously, said: 'I am God!' for precisely this reason.

If someone in the West says, in slightly more contemporary language: 'Hitler was a great man!' the shock of this will cause the hearer to react, instantly.* In some people it will make them realise for the first time what it is like to hear such a statement, what the people who used to say this were like. It will also cause some to realise that, perhaps, the question as to Hitler's greatness or otherwise is irrelevant to their own situation. It will make some realise that they are obsessed by this 'greatness' or otherwise, revealing how their opinions can be triggered by the use of a phrase. In some it will show how almost any sequence of words can be used to 'programme' people and to cause 'belief' or 'opposition'.

This is the technique sometimes used by Omar Khayyam and his school.

Unless this is understood, of course, Khayyam cannot be understood, because some academics take his words at their face value. When he says: 'Every violet is a beauty-mole from some former beloved', they must imagine that this is reincarnation or poetic imagery, when it is in fact 'shock'. The theory of reincarnation was a heresy in his culture.

The Sufi literature is full of this kind of experiential teaching-

*Although Hitler died in 1945, almost universally regarded as a monster, the shock-effect of calling him 'great' had, for many people, worn off in a generation. A German teacher found that many young compatriots knew little about their former leader by 1977. Many of them, too, thought that he had in fact been a great man. *Time* (New York) 18 April, 1977, p. 13.

material. Its presence effectively filters out the superficial and the shallow.

People are conditioned to like certain remarks and to dislike others. This is almost always useful, until one gets to the point where hypocrisy takes advantage of the prevailing postures and enables people to manipulate situations and evade reality. Again, there are examples available in every culture in which people are not permitted by convention to say certain things which are true, because if they do they are regarded as immodest, boastful or hostile to others. This sort of preservation of the *status quo* may be good or it may be bad. Sometimes it produces 'tunnel vision'.

In order to act upon such situations, or to point out the limitations of coercive custom, some of the greatest Sufis have not shrunk from risking the most extreme opprobrium. I do not think that their contribution in this respect has yet been equalled.

SILENCE AND SPEECH

One good example is found in Hujwiri's *Revelation of the Veiled* (Nicholson's translation, 1911):

'I have read in the Anecdotes that one day when Abu-Bakr Shibli [one of the most eminent of the ancient Sufis] was walking in the Karkh quarter of Baghdad he heard an impostor saying: "Silence is better than speech".

'Shibli replied: "Thy silence is better than thy speech, but my speech is better than my silence, because thy speech is vanity and thy silence is an idle jest, whereas my silence is modesty and my speech is silence." '

Anyone who imagines that Shibli was acting in this way because he had a bad temper, or that he was impatient or straying beyond modesty is in need of such Sufi shock-teaching, since such an individual would not yet have learnt that there is a possibility that someone whom he regards (through conditioning) as out of order may in reality be uttering what is in fact an exact description of prevailing circumstances.

The main objection to supposedly immodest words is that they have a bad effect upon the person who speaks them, or teach observers to be 'immodest' and not humble. In the case of such a person as Shibli, his status was (and is) such that the former is not possible, and the latter interpretation could not occur: since Shibli was known to be wholly veracious.

This attitude may seem odd to people not accustomed to it. 'Oddness of appearance is not contradiction of fact' as the saying goes.

It is conditioning, as much as ignorance, which perpetuates the ignorance of humanity stressed by Khalili* when he speaks of the world and humanity's place in it:

Performers and spectators of the arena are we
Bewildered at our work and at the world's
We, little playthings in the hand of Time:
Made to dance each time its tune is played!

---

*Khalilullah Khalili: (Persian) *Quatrains*, Baghdad: Al-Maarif Press, 1975, 47/48.

Emotional Expectations

Q: Why does a Sufi group go on, sometimes for years, reading books, meeting and apparently not getting anything done, without any measurement of its progress, and without a sense of how things are going?

A: Such a group has to 'wear out' emotional expectations. It also has to provide circumstances in which the irrelevant and customary associations, characteristics brought in from other systems may be displayed and observed, so that everyone can see what is central and what is not. If the members of the group are not seeing these things, it is not a Sufic group at all. Much of its visible work is that of a 'preparatory group'. This does not mean that it might not be extremely important: for where else are you going to obtain this opportunity of living through and observing your reactions and those of others, outside of social groupings where the lessons are either obscured or twisted to provide superficial, tribal-type, conclusions?

If you refer again to the published narratives which illustrate the coming-together of people, the effect of interchanges to show up unworthy or irrelevant behaviour or the uselessness of facile interpretation, you will find the material against which you can check the behaviour of people in such a group, if you are in one.

The main characteristic displayed by the questioner is that of a person who wants something ('progress', or 'a sense of how things are going') without carrying on an active observation and digesting of experience happening in and to the group. In traditional terminology familiar to people of all cultures (used in this instance not as a reproach but as a technique) we have here too much greed ahead of capacity, too much dissatisfaction due to greed and false premises, too much laziness which gives rise to a person being a potential victim of an exploiter who might appear and promise automatic progress without effort or right alignment.

Anyone who seeks to escape from his inherited culture's moral demands need not think that they may have no *function* as exercises. He has to re-learn the other possible functions in traditional principles, and he can do this through more study of narrative and illustrative materials and in participation in very preliminary group work, through more of such activity, not less.

Finally, individual and sub-group progress is not always visible to all participants on demand.

OBSESSED WITH THE WORLD

Contrast this approach with that of the mechanical religionists, who merely cultivate obsession. Fariduddin Attar gives a tale of the great woman Sufi Rabia, when she was ill. A certain scholar came to see her and, as he sat beside her bed, he repeated again and again arguments about the evils of the world.

But Rabia could see through this and told him that he obviously loved the world very much. People speak again and again of things which they love, whether they do so in pleasant or unpleasant terms. To be attached to something, favourably or otherwise, is the basic condition. 'If you had no truck with the world,' Rabia reminded the man, 'you would say nothing about it, favourable or otherwise.'

Jumping to Conclusions

ASSUMPTIONS can stand between the student and what he might learn, if these preconceptions are not correct or if they are not functional.

The assumptions that spiritual paths should take this or that form, should be followed by this or that type of person, should belong to certain kinds of recognisable institution, etc., these ideas not only block learning – they often transform it into a search for the expected diversion, and therefore, in reality if not in appearance, towards becoming a part of the entertainment industry.

To connect with people at the outside edge, so to speak, Eastern sages have grown beards and worn turbans; to point up the jumping-to-conclusions syndrome, others have behaved like lunatics; to alert those who are most teachable, yet others have not compromised with expectation to any real extent. And frauds and adventurers, to exploit the only-too-obvious assumptions, have never been slow to accord with them – to tell people what they want to hear.

If you cannot question your assumptions, you must stand up to be counted among the people of whom some may be right: but who include a large number of people, conditioned to bigotry, who *must* be wrong.

Perhaps worth thinking about is the illustrative test which was recently applied to over two hundred people who had been attracted to a certain spiritual teaching. They were given a number of statements and literary extracts and asked which of them were genuine and which not. Over eighty-five per cent of these people got the answers wrong: they identified the spurious documents and statements as genuine.

This indicated at least two things: (1) that these people, for the most part, had not been attracted to the teaching through any ability to discern its legitimacy; and (2) that since most of them had rejected the real materials, the likelihood was that they would eventually reject the teaching materials and procedures of the genuine school, since they displayed an overwhelming appreciation of the spurious as 'authentic'.

One of the commonest assumptions among people who only imagine what a real teaching might be, is connected with 'initiation'.

All over the world you will find people willing and anxious to initiate others into spritual schools.

But, as the procedure is still preserved among the Sufis, initiation – the pledge of fealty to a teacher, only takes place 'several years after his admission to the Order of Dervishes'. This is because, until the student knows enough, and until he has learnt something, he cannot truly commit himself to the deep studies. To get him to engage himself to follow a path while he is still not capable of it is a real mark of ignorance or imposture.

THE CHRISTIAN IN MECCA

On the other hand, someone may be ready to learn and to understand when he is regarded by externalist tests as being quite unsuitable. The great Shibli one day made this very clear, in a story which contains several interesting features.

Shibli announced one day, in Baghdad, that he wanted a thousand dirhams, for shoes for the poor, for the Pilgrimage to Mecca. A certain Christian offered the money, providing that he would be allowed to accompany the caravan.

Shibli told him that only Moslems could make the journey. So the Christian offered to come as a pack-animal: from whom no affirmation of faith was required. So they set off, with the Christian in harness. At each stage he cleared the ground for the pilgrims.

When they arrived at the Great Mosque, Shibli told the Christian that he was not permitted to enter the precincts of the Kaaba. The Christian prayed that he might be allowed to enter. Then a voice was heard, inviting the Christian in . . .

Jumping to conclusions is one of the greatest barriers to learning, though not to actions which make people imagine that they have verified something or made discoveries.

Mulla Nasrudin went one day to a shipyard. Seeing a fire, which he had not expected to be associated with the sea, he asked a workman what it was for.

'We make tar' said the other man, 'and cover the cracks in the underside of the boat. That makes the vessel go faster.'

The Mulla went straight home and made a bonfire. Then he tied up his donkey and melted some tar in a pan. As soon as he brought the smoking tar near the animal, it broke loose and ran like the wind.

'It works all right' said Mulla Nasrudin.

The Rosary and the Robe

Q: What is the origin of the belief that the 'holy man' is, for example, constantly practising austerities, should be dressed in rags, avoids contamination, and so on?

A: This is the easiest of all questions to answer. You could probably have seen that yourself if you had phrased it differently. For the benefit of those who cannot answer it:

The origin is in the observation of the initial austerities, etc., visibly practised by the devout. Because they have no information as to the purpose, stage of development or nature of procedure of such an individual, outward observers imagine that this must automatically represent the essential and invariable behaviour of the 'illuminate' (and his random spectators who are in a mimetic mood).

It is as if an unthinking person were to see the arm-waving of a railway signalman in training and extrapolate from that the belief that

*All railwaymen must at all times, or to become experts, wave their arms;

and

*If the man at this level does this, the top man must do it, and perhaps if he does, twice as auspiciously.

Malobservation, facile assumptions, mechanical reproduction of activities based on incomplete data, in any area of human activity or learning spells failure, not success. If you doubt this, test it. Plenty of organisations bear these marks.

So, in order to correct basic mistakes we must be able to conceive that there might be mistakes. When this is done, further mistakes and useless procedures may be avoided.

In place of becoming a consumer of emotional stimuli, while concurrently imagining that one is experiencing spirituality, the student must be prepared to attempt those things which are prescribed for him. Both practice and test in the Sufi way are *real* ones. Those which centre upon appearance and fads are false ones. One such test, for those who have developed a taste for absurdities, is to adopt and maintain a normal life.

GOD WAS DEAD

Among the Sufis there is a story, related by Attar, of a dervish who applied to enter a monastery wearing black. When he was asked – by Ibn Khafif, who died about 1,000 years ago – why he was in mourning, he answered that his 'God was dead'. The people there expelled him forty times before they absorbed the fact that his 'god' – that which he had worshipped – had been his secondary self, the conditioned personality.

Husain ibn Mansur, asked by someone 'Who is a Sufi?' answered: 'The one whose Essence is single'.

Random Exercises

Q: Some groups of Sufis and others carry out frequent and regular exercises, 'dances', and all sorts of activities in which everyone takes part. Why do you say that one should not do the things which have brought others into high spiritual states?

A: First, please note that there are always plenty of people who carry out automatic processes, and they are always glad to get others to join them. If you know of any, and you want to join them, you will be likely to do so. If you do, you can make your own test of whether this is the best way of going about things. In other words, why are you here if you can get these things elsewhere?

Secondly, assuming that you are here because you want first to compare what we say with what other people say, I can only repeat that what suits one person at one time does *not* inevitably suit another.

LANGUAGE OF BIRDS

There is a story which preserves this by analogy. A worthy man once prayed that he might know the language of the birds. One day when he was sitting quietly under a certain tree with a birds' nest in it, he realised that he could follow the meaning of their chirruping. One bird was telling another that the king's son was ill, and that human beings were so stupid that nobody knew that by giving him lemon-water he would be saved. The man immediately went to the royal Court, where he found that the young prince was indeed ill, and his life was despaired of. He prescribed lemon-water, and the prince recovered. The king ordered that the 'doctor' be rewarded with as much gold as he wanted.

Now this worthy man had a friend who was very unworthy indeed, and he confided to him the way in which he had become rich. So the unworthy man prayed that he might be able to understand the language of the birds, as he wanted to become rich like his friend. The faculty developed in him. Sitting under a tree, he heard the birds talking. They said: 'Under this tree is sitting an unworthy man, who wants our secrets. We shall let him have one of them. It is that at this very moment a ravenous tiger, whom we have called from the jungle to eat him up, is advancing upon him.'

As he stood up to run, the unworthy man was seized by the tiger and devoured.

Why should one not do the things which have brought others into high spiritual states, the questioner asks. If one were a machine, and if all people and situations were alike, if people were pieces of wood to be shaped: of course one should neglect all the manifold attendant circumstances and apply exercises randomly . . .

This question implies that everything is always the same. Reflection might well have told our questioner otherwise, if he had but turned the question around, so as to use his own thinking capacities. By turning the matter over in one's mind, the question might become:

'Under what circumstances would it be true that random exercises should not be carried out, or mechanical imitation should be shunned?'

One very good reason not to 'steal' exercises and apply them randomly (which means without insight and knowledge) is that this can have the same sort of effect, in its own sphere, as other, more familiar, forms of 'theft.' Sometimes this – as in the example I am now going to give you – carries its own penalty.

Here is the parallel, and, humorous though it may be from one point of view (you should laugh at it and look for the additional dimension of instruction) it is a good equivalence of what can happen to people who adopt metaphysical things and then wonder what has happened to them: or why nothing has happened:

WHAT HE STOLE

A newspaper [The London *Daily Telegraph*, 27 October 1976, p. 17, column 4] reports that a housebreaker stole a local councillor's cheque book and identification pass and used them in shops.

His intention was to get money and goods. What did he get?

His defence lawyer explained in Court. In every single one of the nine shops which he visited, identifying himself as the councillor, he was assailed by complaints about the public services. 'At one stage, to get out of a shop, he even left his telephone number for a lady shop assistant to contact him about the transfer of a house.'

He was found guilty of forgery and housebreaking: but the disparity between his expectation and the reality was due to the fact that he made assumptions about what would be likely to happen if he did certain things: and his ignorance was his undoing.

If people know about the effects of these exercises, they do not need to ask such questions as we have here. If they do not, it cannot be explained to them better than through an allegory such as this, taken from real life.

I like the headline to the account. It is: 'The thief who stole another man's burden.'

IF IN DOUBT, HAVE THEM OUT

Random exercises are more likely than not to have the effect which taking Mulla Nasrudin's advice would have had, in this example of his wisdom:

'Nasrudin, you are a man of experience,' said a philosopher; 'Have you heard of a cure for aching eyes? I read a lot, and mine are giving me trouble.'

'All I can say is,' replied the Mulla, 'that I once had pain in two teeth. It did not stop until I had them both out.'

On the Lines of a School

Q: When is a student in a school, and when is he only 'working on the lines of a school'?

A: When you are in a school, and not working along the lines of a school, you are not effectively in a school at all, are you? If you are in a workshop and you are fast asleep, it is, effectively, a bedroom, is it not?

When you are 'working on the lines of a school', you are in a school. The only kind of 'working' that I can think of in which it could be said that you are '*only* working along lines' is if you are being imitative. For instance, I would call 'working on lines', as near as I can interpret the phrase, as 'pretending to do something'; as when one might be amusing oneself while imagining that one is doing something more useful or important. But I would not use your turn of phrase to describe this condition, since I assign a technical-term value to the word 'working'.

'Working' means to me 'doing what a school does and not pretending to do it or inventing reasons or interpretations for it.' In this kind of working, it is the relationship between the people and the activity which constitutes 'The Work', and this work cannot but be along the right lines.

If I wanted to look at this question so as to obtain some sort of study advantage from it, I would have to rephrase, and to make a general kind of statement, like:

'People want to learn. What tends to prevent most of them, consequently at best providing considerable delays in learning, at worst a distorted kind of activity for personal and group amusement, is the maintenance of disabling tendencies, manifested by greed to learn, lack of self-observation, desire for social esteem beyond a reasonable amount, reluctance to learn creating a desire to fantasise instead, personal over-valuation or impatience resulting in attempting to achieve irrelevant or premature target . . .'

Sufi study must be real, not imitation. 'Working on lines' is imitation.

To be engaged in the work of a school, the student must be able to approach this definition, given by Abu'l-Hasan Nuri, that the aim is to achieve 'freedom and generosity and abandoning [unnecessary] burdens, weakness of mind and liberality with the world.'

As Hujwiri explains, this means that to attain to real Sufi status, freedom includes the leaving off of the influence of attachments – what we would call the effects of conditioning and meanness – and giving those things which belong to mundane estimation 'generously', as it would appear, to those who prize them.

This is the 'reality without a name' in Abu'l-Hasan Fushanji's memorable cry, over a thousand years ago: 'Being a Sufi today is a name without a reality: and formerly it was a reality without a name.'

People constantly insist that, since information and knowledge about Sufi principles and practices are so widespread, all that is needed is to put them into practice.

And yet one sees almost every day how the really sad thing about supposedly serious people is that they actually disdain to learn from things which they regard as trivial: but which have important lessons for them if they would only see. The fact is that they do not see, and that is why there has to be a real school, to make sure that all appropriate actions and teachings are observed.

The tale of the Emperor's New Clothes, of course, teaches that one should be able to learn from any source and not reject it when it is not interesting enough to you, or if it lacks a million dollars, or a PhD, or mighty arms, or a spiritual reputation ...

It is characteristic of humanity (which includes people trying to 'work on the lines of a school') that, while all necessary knowledge or information may be present, people either take no notice of it, or only adopt such parts as they please.

This current example [*The Times*, London, 18 November 1976, p. 8, col 2/4] puts it in a nutshell. Just because it is about eating and not about other intakes, however, how many people will spot the parallel?

The German Society for Nutrition checked 50,000 households to see how people ate. In spite of widespread public information about wrong diet and overeating, it was found that the damage done to health through wrong eating habits stands annually as DM 17,000 million (£4,250 million or $7,225 million). The damage done by smoking and drinking is only DM 3,000 million a year, in contrast. One West German in two is overweight. All categories of people get the wrong balance and quantities of calories and proteins. Only 10% of the populace are their correct weight. Almost everyone gets too few vitamins.

Like all the other parallels which one notes, this is not intended to single out a specific community – in this case Germans – for we may find similar, equivalent, data everywhere.

Conduct-Teaching

Q: We read about people spending time with Sufi teachers, and we know that Sufis may remain in contact with those who want to learn for periods of years. Many accounts of the lives and actions of Sufi teachers and their interactions with disciples and also members of the ordinary public have been constantly published, originally in the East, and more recently widely in the West. What is the purpose of the 'conduct teaching' of the Sufis, as distinct from the purpose of spiritual exercises or explanations and admonitions?

A: Interaction-teaching between a teacher and a learner has many aspects. One which is perhaps the most readily grasped but very neglected in understanding by students is that the impacts, stimuli and activities devised by the Sufi are intended to illustrate behaviour and expose subjective reactions. Great Sufis 'shocked' people, for instance, to let them experience the narrowness of their own cast of mind. Sufis continue to shock narrow-minded people, though there is of course no guarantee that such people will benefit from this experience. Sometimes mere onlookers benefit instead. Remember that the definition of a learner is one who learns, not one who thinks that he is a student.

How the Sufi goes about this programme, what he says and does, what he does not say or do, will depend upon local conditions, as you can see in the traditional literature. 'Sufism', as has been said by one of the ancient Sheikhs, 'was formerly imparted by signs alone'. This requires a learner who can read signs. Similarly, with the introduction of literature, experiences of one kind and another can be imparted, illustrated – and so on – by literature, or partially through the written and spoken word, as well as through conduct. Benefiting from this will depend upon whether the student is in alignment with the material. He generally is not, being too greedy for 'truth' and 'progress' to develop the basic calm and relative humility towards the materials to do more than 'consume' them, as emotional stimuli; which he could have done with anything.

Sheikh Ibrahim Gazur-Ilahi, among the Sufi directors, has emphasised that when the Teacher has finished his own journey, he repeats it again and again, each time with one learner. This is referred to as the analogy of the seed being in the plant, and the plant in the seed.

The 'conduct teaching' of the Sufis has to be adapted to the students, and cannot be a mechanical thing, applied to all people in exactly the same way.

Q: But, since this information is so generally available, and is contained in the works of the great Sufi teachers, why do more people not seek it?

A: This has always been a fact. It is answered today as always, by the observation:

'The wise know because they have paid for their wisdom. You do not accept their counsel because it is offered for so much less than they have paid for it'.

Conduct-teaching has many other dimensions, after the stage of showing people to themselves. One might quote it as equivalent to the situation referred to by Blackett, when he said: 'A first-class laboratory is one in which mediocre scientists can produce outstanding work.' The conduct-situation enables people who have some potentiality to excel themselves. In this kind of situation, too, people are encouraged to learn in the manner in which they can do so, not in the manner which they try to impose on the subject. In the scientific parallel again, Mackay* says: 'We shall have to learn to refrain from doing things merely because we know how to do them.'

Conduct-teaching is often reported in real and devised anecdotes. Mulla Nasrudin stories often show this characteristic: reflecting both the conduct of the wise and that of the stupid, in addition to their other and more internal dimensions.

One such story, designed to be used as a paradigm in life situations, is this:

*Alan L. Mackay, *The Harvest of a Quiet Eye*, a Selection of Scientific Quotations, London Institute of Physics, 1977.

THE MAN-VINE

Some men were planting vines, and Nasrudin asked them what they were doing.

'Digging these in so that they will produce fruit.'

'That is exactly what I would like,' said the Mulla 'so please plant me and I will bear fruit.'

After as many objections as they could think of, the men were prevailed upon to do as Nasrudin asked.

Not long afterwards they saw him walking about. One of them said:

'We told you that you can't grow fruit by being planted like that.'

'You haven't proved it yet', said Nasrudin, 'for I only uprooted myself for a bit because I was cold – not because I'm not going to produce fruit.'

The Curriculum of a School

Q: Could you give us a view of the curriculum of a School, from 'inside the School' so to speak?

A: In our teaching, we must group correctly these elements: the pupils, the teacher and the circumstances of study. Only at the right time and place, with the teacher suitable to these, and with the right body of students, can our studies be said to be capable of coherent development.

Does this sound difficult or unreasonable? Let us compare these requirements with an analogy of our needs: the ordinary educational institution.

If we are learning, say, physics, we must have a man skilled in physics; students who want to learn and who have capacity and some background for the study; and adequate laboratories and other facilities for the studies to take place.

A physics teacher could not make any real progress with a class of idiots, or people who primarily wanted power or fame or gain through physics. These factors would be getting in the way of the teaching. A class of brilliant students, faced with a man who knew no physics, or who only had a smattering, would make little progress. A good teacher, with a suitable student body, could do little unless the instruments and equipment, the building and so on, were available as and when needed.

If anything is strictly demanded by the teachers of the perpetual Higher Teaching, it is these requirements.

Yet this principle, so well established in conventional studies of all kinds, is largely passed over and has fallen into disuse, among esotericists. Why? Because they have a primitive and unenlightened attitude towards teaching. Like an oaf who has just heard of physics or only seen some of its manifestations, the would-be student wants it all *now*. He does not care about the necessary presence of other students. He wants to skip the curriculum and he sees no connection between the building and the subject of physics. So he does not want a laboratory.

Just observe what happens when people try to carry on learning or teaching without the correct grouping of the three essentials:

Would-be students always try to operate their studies with only one, or at the most two, of the three factors. Teachers try to teach those who are unsuitable, because of the difficulties of finding enough people to form a class. Students who have no teacher try to teach themselves. Transpose this into a group of people trying to learn physics, and you will see some of their problems. Others group themselves around the literature and methodology of older schools, trying to make the scrap material of someone else's physics laboratory work. They formalise rituals, become obsessed by principles and slogans, assign disproportionate importance to the elements which are only tools, but which they regard as a more significant heritage.

Anyone can think of several schools, cults, religions, systems of psychology or philosophy which fall into the above classifications.

We must categorically affirm that it is impossible to increase human knowledge in the higher field by these methods. The statistical possibility of useful gains within a reasonable time is so remote as to be excluded from one's calculations.

Why, then, do people persist in raking over the embers and looking for truth when they have so little chance of finding it? Simply because they are using their conditioning propensity, not their capacity for higher perception, to try to follow the path. There is intellectual stimulus and emotional attraction in the mere effort to plumb the unknown. When the ordinary human mind encounters evidences of a higher state of being, or even when it conceives the possibility of them, it will invariably conclude that there is some possibility of progress for that mind without the application of the factors of teaching-teacher-students-time-and-place which are essentials.

Man has few alternatives in his search for truth. He may rely

upon his unaided intellect, and gamble that he is capable of perceiving truth or even the way to truth. This is a poor, but an
attractive, gamble. Or he can gamble upon the claims of an individual or institution which claims to have such a way. This
gamble, too, is a poor one. Aside from a very few, men in general
lack a sufficiently developed perception to tell them:

1. Not to trust their own unaided mentation;
2. Whom or what to trust.

There are, in consequence, two main schools of thought in this
matter. Some say 'Follow your own promptings'; the other says:
'Trust this or that institution'. Each is really useless to the ordinary man. Each will help him to use up his time.

The bitter truth is that before man can know his own inade-
quacy, or the competence of another man or institution, he must
first learn something which will enable him to perceive both.
Note well that his perception itself is the product of right study;
not of instinct or emotional attraction to an individual, nor yet of
desiring to 'go it alone'. This is 'learning how to learn'.

All this means, of course, that we are postulating here the need
for preparatory study before school work takes place. We deny
that a man can study and properly benefit from school work until
he is equipped for it: any more than a person can study space-
navigation unless he has a grasp of mathematics.

This is not to say that a man (or a woman) cannot have a
sensation of truth. But the unorganised and fragmented mind
which is most people's heritage tends to distort the quality and
quantity of this sensation, leading to almost completely false conclusions about what can or should be done.

This is not to say, either, that man cannot take part in studies
and activities which impinge upon that portion of him which is
connected with a higher life and cognition. But the mere application of special techniques will not transform that man's consciousness. It will only feed into, and disturb, more or less permanently,
centres of thought and feeling where it does not belong. Thus it is
that something which should be a blessing becomes a curse. Sugar,
shall we say, for a normal person is nutritionally useful. To a

diabetic it can be poison.

Therefore, before the techniques of study and development are made available to the student, he must be enabled to profit by them in the direction in which they are supposed to lead, not in a short-term indulgence.

Thus our curriculum takes two parts: the first is the providing of materials of a preparatory nature, in order to equip the individual to become a student. The second is the development itself.

If we, or anyone else, supply such study or preparatory material prematurely, it will only operate on a lower level than it could. The result will be harmless at best. At worst it will condition, train, the mind of the individual to think and behave in patterns which are nothing less than automatic. In this latter way one can make what seem to be converts, unwittingly play upon emotions, on lesser desires and the conditioning propensity; train people to loyalty to individuals, found and maintain institutions which seem more or less serious or constructive. But no real progress towards knowledge of the human being and the other dimension in which he partly lives will in fact be made.

The preparation of the student is as important as anything else which he does. The Sufi poet Hafiz says:

'The Seeker must not be unaware of the way and method of the stages.' This awareness comes through following the teaching course, which is taking part in the activities of a school, plus abiding by the directions of your teacher.

In learning how to learn from a Sufi school, the intending student should take note of this admonition, which indicates his difficulties:

'If you are too soft, you will be crushed; if you are too dry, you will be broken; if you are too hard, you will cause hurt; if you are too sharp, you will inflict wounds.'

The curriculum of a School is one which may work with secondary things, but which employs them instrumentally, and certainly not imagining that they are primary things.

In the words of Sheikh Al-Intaki, quoted over a thousand years ago by Hujwiri in his *Revelation of the Veiled:*

the honour of the ordinary [person] is to accept secondary

[things as real] causes, while the honour of the dervish is to reject secondary [supposed] causes, insisting on The Cause.

The School works with what is primary. The (to some) apparently purposeful activity of those who use correct materials but apply only the ordinary, limited senses, is portrayed in the actions of Nasrudin with his seedlings:

RIGHT IDEA, WRONG MATERIALS

The Mulla once spent a whole day transplanting some seedlings in his garden.

When he stood back to admire his work, a sudden thought struck him.

Dusk was falling as he started to pluck the plants from the ground, wrapping them in sackcloth by the light of a lantern.

Going home along the fields some cronies called to him. 'Whatever are you doing, Nasrudin?'

'Acting in accordance with careful consideration. I realised – late in the day, but not too late as you see – that it is better to keep one's property in the house, under proper supervision.'

The secondary ('commanding') self in everyone is the false self which everyone takes to be the real one. It stands in relation to the real being of the person as the face does to the person: virtually a persona. Everyone, says Rumi, in *Fihi ma Fihi*, likes a mirror, and is enamoured of the reflection in the mirror of his attributes and attainments: though he does not know the real nature of his face.

The veil which he sees on the looking-glass he imagines to be his face. 'Take the covering from your face, so that you may see me as the mirror of your real face: so that you will realise that I am a mirror.'

The curriculum of a School, from 'inside the School' as you put it, is based on the teacher being able to be that mirror. He is therefore able to assess the peculiarities and needs of the student. His miming is often of the student, so that the latter may see himself mirrored and react accordingly.

Knowing all about Someone

Q: Is it enough to associate with a man of knowledge to acquire some of it? Does the Teacher not need the Student?

A: You must remember instances, at least, when you have not said anything and everything in your mind.

Have you ever thought about the people whom you may know who do not discuss with you things which they know, even though such things might be of abiding interest to you?

You may 'know a man well', even meet him every day of your life, 'share his opinions', exchange ideas. At the same time, you may have no conception of his possession of certain knowledge and even of his capacity to pass it on if the conditions are correct.

He may not seem an enigma to you; but he may be as deeply concealed as anything on earth.

The conception that one knows all about a person because of shared experiences and the exchange of confidences is not a true one. It is based upon the misconception that people cannot avoid communicating whatever they are discussing with one another.

Knowledge does not automatically 'brush off', any more than it can be transmitted by words alone; neither is it to be conveyed by training of any ordinary kind.

You cannot, therefore, learn real knowledge merely by associating with someone who has it – especially if you do not even know that it is there, and if you are not focussed correctly to learn.

Someone or something has first to impart to you how to perceive the presence of knowledge. Without preparation there can be no teaching.

As to the need of the Teacher, the great teacher Jami in his *Lawaih* says (Essay XXI) 'The Absolute does not stand in need of the relative, except for its manifestation, but the relative needs the Absolute for its very existence.' Similarly, the teacher is to be regarded as more important than the student in the situation of learning.

That is to say, the Teacher is so to be regarded by the learner. The Teacher himself may regard the learner as more important, but that is a matter for the Teacher, and there is no point discussing his attitudes when the conversation is about learning and not teaching.

Remarks upon the Matter of the Dervish Path

≈≈

Q: Can you give us a number of outstanding points which should be studied by those interested in the Dervish, the Sufi, Path? How do the miracles attributed to Sufis come about?

A:

I. The human environment produces certain subtle changes in the individual which penetrate his whole being. Instead of undergoing only these changes, man has a chance to gain access to a form of self which is, by comparison, infinitely superior. To use the technical term: he is at present 'only half awake'.

II. This change, although it increases man's awareness of his destiny, does not interfere with his ordinary human relationships. On the contrary, it enriches them.

III. In order to take part in this process, there has to be the coincidence of a teacher with the doctrine, the application of the doctrine in a way suited to the pupils; and the right environmental circumstances. Nothing less than all these factors will do.

IV. One way of rendering the message given here is that there is a deeper truth, and a wider dimension, in which man already partly lives, though he is ordinarily indifferent to it. There is the hope that he can become as aware of it as he is of the familiar world.

V. The self-realisation of this dimension enables a man or woman to attain heights of achievement in the easily-perceptible world and in other areas; and prevents him from becoming the tool of a mere conditional existence, with all its anxieties and ultimate meaninglessness. Man tends to be unhappy not because of what he knows, but because of what he does not know.

VI. It is only through the attunement of a group of people, each with the possibility of this attainment, correctly harmonised into a true community (whether physically in contact or otherwise) that true understanding and the next step in human progress can come.

VII. The unity and integration of this group are essential to individual as well as collective success. In fact almost the only opportunity for man to realise his individual importance is through the support of a group of suitable people.

VIII. This doctrine and the manner of its application have been known and propagated from time immemorial. They are, in fact, the property and destiny of man. They link with a past in which this development was much more widely known, through a present where it has fallen into disuse except for a few, to a future in which The Great Work will be the entire legitimate goal of mankind.

IX. 'The New Man', 'The Real Man', 'The Perfected Man' are all terms used in different formulations, throughout the ages, for this activity, which has been called 'secret', 'hidden' or 'initiatory' for reasons other than people realise.

People are interested in miracles, when they would do better to be interested in Truth. Miracles are by-products or else part of the special extradimensional activity in which certain people are involved. This involvement is because they acquire added functions with every addition of knowledge or capacity, just as in ordinary education but in this case in its own realm.

An example, among many thousands, of the activity which is carried on by extra-sensory perception in Sufi service shows how 'miracles' are linked with duty. Ibn Arabi in his *Ruh al-Quds*, tells how one evening he felt an urge to go to see Abu-Abdullah al-Khayyat ('The Tailor') of Seville, and made his way a fair distance to see him. Al-Khayyat said: 'Why were you so long? You have something with you which I need'. Ibn Arabi took the five dirhams which he had in his pocket and gave them to him. The other Sufi told him that he had need of the money for a certain poor man called Ali al-Salawi.

Meetings, Groups, Classes

Q: There is great interest in meetings, groups and classes. Are these forms the aims of Sufi teaching?

A: People who do not understand how higher teachings operate, or who have been trained to think in a shallow manner about them, are naturally confused when they meet written and spoken materials which do not fit into their preconceived patterns.

Nowhere is this more strikingly evidenced than in the matter of communication and relationships.

After hearing a few hundred people explain how they feel, after reading a few dozen letters from 'seekers', even a machine would surely see the pattern of shallow assumption upon which even the most ardent of this type allow themselves to work.

People who live in approximately the same area think that they should be grouped together, willy-nilly. People who are not of a mind to read books agitate for 'personal contact'. People who live in distant places crave travels, visits, materials to devour. People with whom you have been out of formal contact become distressed, bitter, interested in sources of readier gratification. People jealously (if unconsciously) cherish the 'cult of the Centre', whose distinguishing mark is the belief that 'If I could only go to such-and-such a place all would be well.'

Virtually none of these people has any true concept of how a real community comes into being, how it develops, how its local manifestations are working, what its future might be – how they could benefit from what is being done.

If you circularise people with details of how a local class or group is run, they all want to be in a local class or group. It is just like mentioning a lollipop to a child: it may have been thinking about something else, but this key-word can possess its thinking mechanism to the exclusion of everything else.

For a moment, as an exercise, transpose this situation into some other field, and you will see that such behaviour is so primitive, so crude, so unfortunately wasteful of energy, or understanding, of everything, that it is obvious that something has to be done for such people. Anyone prone to such behaviour-patterns is in no position to benefit from any higher knowledge at that point. He is, however, a suitable prey for one or other of the people or bodies which offer instant assuagement of tensions by going along with the individual's infantile behaviour.

The real higher community to which you could belong is organised and has its being and communication in its own manner. It needs, and operates by means of, both local and other groupings. Its members study, attract, retain and give out currents of knowledge irrespective of the form in which their studies are couched. For some people at some times it is important that they be 'isolated' from others. Such 'isolation' which is regarded as a curse by people who live in remote places is generally an inestimable advantage which has been allotted to them, not anything else. As and when a time for closer contact in the conventional sense arrives, so do the means for its attainment. But if the individual simply wants to be a member of a herd: Sufis are prevented from pandering to this desire.

In respect to higher teaching, the individual has to learn the difference between 'wants' and 'needs'. He can learn this only after basic teaching. When a child says that it needs something, it often means, until it understands the difference, that it 'wants' that thing. 'I need a lollipop' does not describe the situation at all. Only experience can show the difference between wants and needs.

There is an inbuilt demand for 'togetherness' in human beings. Whoever learns this and panders to it may quite easily become rich, famous, respected and so forth.

To play upon this tendency is not only wrong in ordinary principle, it is unproductive in our work, because it would mean that we were doing one thing while pretending to do another.

Remember, that because this work and this community operate in a manner essentially unique, they have no need for organising in a primitive manner or catering for neurotic or infantile demands disguised as 'needs'.

Furthermore, as soon as we have made this plain, and as soon as individuals and groups have realised that they need not indulge in their social masquerades, the community and the work invariably make it possible for the activity, the contact, the study and the learning necessary to take place.

In short, this community is neither a troop of baboons nor a military force, dependent upon desire and fear, upon reward and punishment, for the continuance of its action.

This community operates in accordance with a sensitive pattern. This pattern is its protection and its strength. If you try to organise yourself or others in a lesser pattern, you are out of touch with this work. You have, in short, disengaged yourself from higher development, and chosen to stabilise your life upon simply living out your life by diversions, just like someone putting off time in a waiting room.

Work in the manner and with the materials indicated by the teaching. Plan, by all means, if you really know the plan.

The Sufi authority Abu-Nasr al-Sarraj illustrates the need for plan and priorities in study in his *Kitab al-Luma*. He quotes the words of one of the most eminent Sufis, Bayazid, who taught Abu Ali of Sind the formal rituals of Islam, while Abu Ali taught him, in his turn, the experiential doctrine of Sufism.

And one of Bayazid's disciples reported that he heard not a word from his master for thirteen years, the time he spent with him . . .

The misunderstanding of the need or otherwise of constant association with a master as a kind of magic key is due – at least in part – to the deterioration in behaviour of those very numerous groupings which were originally Sufis, but which have over the centuries become mere cults.

Many ancient Sufis insisted on solitude and anonymity, refusing to associate with people.

Muinuddin Chishti, who introduced Chishtism into India and is buried at Ajmer, was a notable example. While some of his precedents have been adopted by later followers, who imagine that they follow his teaching, his proclivity for solitude has been ignored.

'He would not allow, generally,' says Dr. Sharib 'more than one Dervish to accompany him on his travels. He would stay in desolate and deserted places. Sometimes he would stay in a graveyard. The moment he came to be known he would stay there no longer. He hated publicity.'

The great peril in study-groupings is, of course, that they become miniature tribes or families, cults and frames for finding social satisfactions, not learning, let alone understanding.

This pattern asserts itself, and often quite obviously, in most imaginedly religious communities and activities. For this reason Sheikh Abdullah Ansari has called prayer 'only abstaining from food', formal prayer 'the work of old men and women', pilgrimage 'a pleasure of the world'.

People can learn from groups and meetings only to the extent to which they have overcome the four traps which Ansari stresses:

Ingratitude in good fortune
Impatience in ill fortune
Discontent with their lot
Hesitation in serving their fellows.

Internal Dimensions

THERE are internal dimensions of meaning in all the materials used in our work. In these materials I include those written, spoken, seen and handled, as well as the ones which are performed and experienced.

The unlocking of the inner dimensions, as in all valid traditions, is something which has to take place as and when it *can* be effective. It is not a matter of detective-work, puzzle-solving or disguised recreation. On the contrary, these elements must be kept in their places, which are very minor ones.

The inner dimensions are present in order to convey a certain experience at the moment of their revelation. This experience supplies an element which the student needs in order to carry him further in his development.

Unlocking inner dimensions just for the sake of so doing is not only superficial: it robs the operation of its development value.

Take a rough example as an illustration.

I say: 'This is our work.' This word comes to be associated with certain significances in the mind. 'Work' means action. But if, subsequently, I reveal to you that 'Work' in fact also stands for, say, 'World Organisation for Research into Knowledge' and is composed of the initials of that phrase, you see another range of possibilities in this. But merely to do this is banal when no constructive purposes are present.

This is why the 'revealing of secrets' is a stage after familiarisation with the materials and concepts. The 'revealing' must – and does – take place on a level and under circumstances appropriate to the goal: the development of human kind.

Impatience with this process will simply turn you into a trivial person, playing with words, objects and concepts. If you play with something complex, treating it as if it were simple, it will not operate to its real capacity. An electronic device, for instance, which may be extremely delicate, efficient and costly, may simply look like an object used in a children's game. If you use it for playing games, you are playing: so do not deceive yourself that it is acting on a more effective part of you just because it is not a disc of wood, and because the game delights or depresses you.

There is hardly a derivative book on metaphysics in currency in which the author has succeeded in avoiding this tendency: and fewer still which are not distorted in meaning by their readers.

There is small wonder that more conventional people laugh at metaphysicians, and that most of the latter succeed mainly in teaching themselves and others to play diversionary games with what can be, in fact, vital materials.

There is a need to repeat this in different forms because of the fact that people are surrounded, all the time, by 'game' tendencies, within and without themselves, which can be counteracted only by an appropriate quantity and quality of the other type of material and descriptions of its uses.

Remember, the mere study and absorption of such admonitions as this give you a guard and a means of maintaining a sense of truth far greater than you would imagine.

Internal dimensions, properly conveyed, are the most useful of the materials which we have. Incorrectly and shallowly used, they are the least useful.

BURNING THE KAABA

It is to draw attention to the essential that Sufis appear to attack the derivative or secondary. Attar tells how Shibli carried a flaming coal through the streets, saying that he was going to set fire to Kaaba, the holiest place of Islam, so that people would concern themselves not with it but with the Lord of the Kaaba.

Explanation

Q: From your remarks and writings, I have observed people's behaviour relating to 'higher knowledge', and found it to be as you describe. People imagine that just because others have spoken of it, they are themselves candidates for this knowledge without really listening to the people who tell them how to approach it. They also study selectively, expecting that the bits and pieces which appeal to them will give them what they want, not regarding the whole learning as necessary. They vie with each other for 'experiences', emotional stimuli and even for personal credit and minor, social advantages, while at the same time claiming that they seek 'higher things'. What is your explanation, if you have one, for this absurd behaviour?

A: You don't need 'my explanation', because you only have to ask yourself what this kind of behaviour means to normal people, and where it is to be found.

You only have to ask an anthropologist or an historian of education or science for him to tell you that this is behaviour characteristic of less advanced people, disadvantaged or barbaric ones, in the face of the introduction of something 'new' to them.

This analysis is impossible only to those who have not looked at the structure and who are misled by the superficialities, such as what the cult calls itself.

If the people you describe were seeking, say, scientific knowledge or money, you would yourself be able to say at once that they are either savages or neurotics at worst; at best people who have virtually no basic information or training enabling them to approach what they imagine they need so much. It is an important task to make this basic information available, so that people can get their feet on the starting-line, as it were, rather than sprawling all over the place.

Western culture prides itself on being able to tell one thing from another. This is an opportunity for its people to display this wholly desirable talent, training and ability. When they do so in sufficient quantity and quality, real study can begin and cannot be stopped.

In the East, of course, there is a convention whereby a teacher points out characteristic human behaviour by adopting it himself, and this shocks or reminds others so that they learn without the defensiveness of their being tackled head-on being produced.

This behaviour keeps alive the sense that learners should not flatter themselves that they are important because they are engaged on a spiritual task – rather that they need due humility.

When I was a small boy and went into my father's study one day and left the door open, he did not tell me to close it. Instead he said:

'Oh, I seem to have left the door open. Would you kindly close it?'

That memory has stayed with me for over forty years.

HIRI AND THE ASHES

Abu Osman al-Hiri did much the same thing when someone tipped a quantity of ashes over him from a window. The people with him wanted to reproach the person who did it. But al-Hiri only said: 'We should be a thousand times grateful that only ashes fell on one who deserves hot coals!'

Q: Why do you not speak more of God in your public utterances?

A: The more usual complaint (which shows that you cannot please everyone) is that I dwell too much on matters of religion. But the reason that I speak less than others do about God is to be answered very much as Ibn Arabi is reported to have done. He said: 'It is not worthy to deal with cleanliness when one is clearing up rubbish; cleanliness is the result of necessary preliminaries.' I admit, of course, that Arabi was brought before an inquisition for his 'love poetry' now recognised as great mystical literature ...

It is also reported that Rabia said: 'To accuse someone who is preparing an apple from being concerned with its peel is sheer ignorance, though it may seem to describe the situation.'

A Sufi teacher of my acquaintance said in my hearing when someone asked him to talk about God: 'It would be an insult to God to speak of him to you; and it would be valuing *me* too highly to assume that I dared to talk of God.'

Most people's 'God' is their vanity, their own self-conceit, their epithet, used for emotional and intellectual purposes. It is important to speak of a thing, let alone God, with reserve unless it be warranted.

The using of the word 'God' must depend upon the state of understanding of the person who uses the term and the person or people hearing or reading it. As Shabistari said in his Sufi manual *The Secret Garden*, in the fourteenth century:

'If the Moslem knew what an idol was, he would know that there is religion in idolatry. If the idolater knew what religion was, he would know where he has gone astray. He sees in the idol nothing but the obvious creature. That is why, according to Islam, he is a heathen.'

'Man' says Rumi, in *Fihi ma Fihi* ('In it what is in it') has three spiritual states. In the first he pays no heed to God at all, but worships and pays service to everything, woman and man, wealth and children, stones and clods. God he does not worship. When he acquires a little knowledge and awareness, then he serves nothing but God. Again, when he progresses farther in this state he becomes silent; he does not say, "I do not serve God," neither does he say, "I serve God," for he has transcended these two degrees.'*

*Rumi, *Fihi ma Fihi*, Professor Firuzanfar's edition, translated by A. J. Arberry (as *Discourses of Rumi*) London: John Murray, 1961, pp 205–6.

KING PENGUIN

☐ *Selected Poems* Tony Harrison   £3.95

Poetry Book Society Recommendation. 'One of the few modern poets who actually has the gift of composing poetry' – James Fenton in the *Sunday Times*

☐ *The Book of Laughter and Forgetting*
Milan Kundera   £3.95

'A whirling dance of a book . . . a masterpiece full of angels, terror, ostriches and love . . . No question about it. The most important novel published in Britain this year' – Salman Rushdie in the *Sunday Times*

☐ *The Sea of Fertility* Yukio Mishima   £9.95

Containing *Spring Snow, Runaway Horses, The Temple of Dawn* and *The Decay of the Angel*: 'These four remarkable novels are the most complete vision we have of Japan in the twentieth century' – Paul Theroux

☐ *The Hawthorne Goddess* Glyn Hughes   £2.95

Set in eighteenth century Yorkshire where 'the heroine, Anne Wylde, represents the doom of nature and the land . . . Hughes has an arresting style, both rich and abrupt' – *The Times*

☐ *A Confederacy of Dunces* John Kennedy Toole   £3.95

In this Pulitzer Prize-winning novel, in the bulky figure of Ignatius J. Reilly an immortal comic character is born. 'I succumbed, stunned and seduced . . . it is a masterwork of comedy' – *The New York Times*

☐ *The Last of the Just* André Schwartz-Bart   £3.50

The story of Ernie Levy, the last of the just, who was killed at Auschwitz in 1943: 'An outstanding achievement, of an altogether different order from even the best of earlier novels which have attempted this theme' – John Gross in the *Sunday Telegraph*

KING PENGUIN

☐ *The Pork Butcher* **David Hughes** £2.50

War crimes, secrecy, and a brief, voluptuous love affair are all preying on Ernst Kestner's mind as he drives back to the French village where he spent the summer of 1944. 'An unforgettable experience' – *Observer*. 'A true and illuminating work of art' – *Scotsman*. Winner of the W. H. Smith Literary Award

☐ *1982, Janine* **Alistair Gray** £3.95

'This work offers more hope for the future of fiction, considered as art and vision, than the vast majority of novels published since the second world war' – *Literary Review*. 'Bawdy and exuberant . . . he is in love with the power of language to encompass life' – Robert Nye in the *Guardian*

These books should be available at all good bookshops or news-agents, but if you live in the UK or the Republic of Ireland and have difficulty in getting to a bookshop, they can be ordered by post. Please indicate the titles required and fill in the form below.

NAME _____ BLOCK CAPITALS

ADDRESS _____

_____

_____

Enclose a cheque or postal order payable to The Penguin Bookshop to cover the total price of books ordered, plus 50p for postage. Readers in the Republic of Ireland should send £1 R equivalent to the sterling prices, plus 67p for postage. Send to: The Penguin Bookshop, 54/56 Bridlesmith Gate, Nottingham, NG1 2GP.

You can also order by phoning (0602) 599295, and quoting your Barclaycard or Access number.

Every effort is made to ensure the accuracy of the price and availability of books at the time of going to press, but it is sometimes necessary to increase prices and in these circumstances retail prices may be shown on the covers of books which may differ from the prices shown in this list or elsewhere. This list is not an offer to supply any book.

This order service is only available to residents in the UK and the Republic of Ireland.

PENGUIN BOOKS OF POETRY

THE PENGUIN POETRY LIBRARY